WINDOWS

TO THE

EAST

EASTERN CHRISTIANS
IN A DIALOGUE OF CHARITY

WINDOWS

TO THE

EAST

EASTERN CHRISTIANS
IN A DIALOGUE OF CHARITY

EDITED BY JAROSLAV Z. SKIRA
& MYROSLAW I. TATARYN

© 2001 Novalis, Saint Paul University, Ottawa, Canada

Cover design: Suzanne Latourelle, Maria d.c. Zamora
Cover artwork: Marianna Savaryn
Design and layout: Caroline Gagnon

Business Office:
Novalis
49 Front Street East, 2nd Floor
Toronto, Ontario, Canada
M5E 1B3

Phone: 1-800-387-7164 or (416) 363-3303
Fax: 1-800-204-4140 or (416) 363-9409
E-mail: novalis@interlog.com

National Library of Canada Cataloguing in Publication Data

Main entry under title:

Windows to the East : eastern Christians in a dialogue of charity

Includes bibliographical references and index.

ISBN 2-89507-167-5

1. Orthodox Eastern Church—Congresses. I. Tataryn, M. (Myroslaw), 1956– II. Skira, Jaroslav Z.

BX320.3.W56 2001   281.9   C2001-903368-0

Printed in Canada.

We acknowledge the financial support of the Government of Canada through the Book Publishing Industry Development Program (BPIDP) for our publishing activities.

CONTENTS

To those brave Christians
who are opening windows
and inviting their sisters and brothers
to a renewed *koinonia*.

Acknowledgments

Christian faith is fundamentally a religion of reception and giftedness. Christians are inheritors of a tradition formed and nurtured over two millennia, respondents to having been wonderfully gifted by the trinitarian God, whose love is so overflowing and creative that all that we see and do not see is a gracious and loving gift. So too, this volume is an act of reception and a recognition of giftedness. The editors and readers are the fortunate recipients of the prayerful work and insight of many individuals. We have been gifted with the harvest of those who have tilled the soil on our behalf. Words of thanks are in order.

Recognition and thanks must be expressed to Mrs. Lesya Nahachewsky. She was the first to dream of the possibility of annual grassroots meetings of Eastern Christians in Saskatoon, Saskatchewan for the purpose of exploring their common tradition. Appreciation is given to those who responded to her call: the members of the Windows to the East Committee, representing the parishes of All Saints (Ukrainian Orthodox Church), Holy Covenant (Evangelical Orthodox Church), Holy Dormition (Greek Orthodox Archdiocese), Holy Resurrection (Orthodox Church in America), St. Vincent Lérins (Antiochean Orthodox Church), and the three Ukrainian Catholic parishes of Holy Dormition, St. George, and Sts. Peter and Paul. Many individuals from these communities have contributed much of their time and energy over the years and we hope that this volume is in some way a symbol of the Church's thanks for their devotion and effort. But a special word of thanks also belongs to two remarkable individuals whose particular commitment to Windows kept the journey going over the years and helped immensely to bring this volume to fruition: Mr. Martin Zip, chair of the Windows to the East Committee and Dr. John Thompson, President of St. Thomas More College (1990–2000).

Thanks to Gladys Neufeld and Maria Truchan-Tataryn. Their contribution in the process of transcription of the lectures and editing of the text has made the production of this volume possible. Finally, a thank you to St. Thomas More College, whose institutional support for the lecture series and financial assistance for this volume demonstrate an unswerving institutional dedication to witnessing the Word of God intelligently, reasonably, and charitably both in the academy and on main street.

I. Introduction

Seeking the Way Together in Changing Times: Eastern Christians in Conversation

JOHN THOMPSON

On the evening before his passion and death, Jesus gathered his followers to celebrate the Passover supper. As Jesus shared the bread and wine with them, he said simply: "Do this in remembrance of me" (Luke 22:19). Since the time of Jesus' first followers after Pentecost nearly two millennia ago until today, Christians have gathered in communities, small and large, in fidelity to Jesus' words to celebrate the Eucharist, to give thanks for God's gift of salvation in Jesus, and to care for each other. In remembering, Christians are joined together, "re-membered" as the Body of Christ whose body we share and are. Our "remembering" is not simply about a past, historic event. Our "remembering" is the continuing presence of the Lord among us. Early Christians spoke of their shared faith in the risen Lord simply as "the Way" (Acts 9:2). After centuries of division between Christians East and West as well as among Eastern Christians themselves, members of Eastern Christian parishes in Saskatoon are seeking "the Way" together in a grassroots ecumenical effort. In a series of yearly conferences, they have met for the past seven years to hear speakers, to discuss concerns, to converse, and to pray together. Without denying their differences, they have sought to discover what they hold in common as followers of the Lord. This effort represents a pivot point – an emotional, social, intellectual and religious turning and sorting. Divided for too many years by other memories, they now seek to retrieve, sort, and heal those memories against the "remembering" of the Divine Liturgy and the Lord's Prayer for unity that his followers ". . . may all be one. As you, Father, are in me and I am in you" (John 17:21; 1 John 1:3). They are seeking "the Way" together.

These contributions are one of the fruits of this local ecumenical initiative among Eastern Christians in Saskatoon. In the early 1990s, Mrs. Lesya Nahachewsky, completing an M.A. in Eastern Christian spirituality, sought to elicit and encourage discussion about common concerns and a shared heritage among Eastern Christians. In 1993, she brought together parish representatives of the Antiochean Orthodox Church, the Evangelical Orthodox Church, the Greek Orthodox Church, the Orthodox Church in America, the Ukrainian Orthodox and the Ukrainian Catholic Churches in Saskatoon. She proposed that they sponsor a conference inviting two speakers within the Eastern Christian Tradition, one Orthodox and one Catholic, to explore their Eastern Christian heritage. The conference was to be called "Windows to the East." Mr. Martin Zip, a local print shop owner, designed and printed a logo. Since Mrs. Nahachewsky was teaching a course on icons at St. Thomas More College (STM), she proposed that the conference be held at STM. In planning meetings held in homes, the group took the first tentative and uncertain steps toward a conference. As might be expected, for persons of different Eastern Christian Churches who had not worked together as a group, these meetings went forward in fits and starts of cooperation and suspicion. Funding for the conference came from Eastern Christian parishes and groups, from businesses, and from individuals. No fees were charged for admission, although a request was made for donations. The first conference was scheduled for February 1994. At 6:40 p.m. on Wednesday, February 2, a typically cold Saskatoon winter evening, only the members of the organizing committee, filled with fears that no one else would come, occupied the auditorium. By 7:00 p.m. and for two successive evenings, nearly two hundred persons gathered. The Very Reverend Robert Barringer, C.S.B., Ph.D., and Daniel Sahas, Ph.D., two Eastern Christian scholars, spoke on "Exploring the Heart of Eastern Christianity." They answered questions each night. Two groups of panellists responded with their observations and concerns.

Those attending, many of whom had not been in the same room before, shared refreshments afterwards. Some were still conversing well past 11 p.m., and it was not just the attraction of the wine and cheese provided by the College that kept them. On Saturday evening, participants gathered for Vespers at Holy Resurrection Church.

The first "Windows to the East" brought surprise and joy for a number of the participants. Several of the panellists articulated their delight at being together with others who called themselves Eastern Christian but with whom, though living in the same city, they had not been present before. One panellist remarked simply, "This is amazing." This first conference represented a lessening of suspicions and a promising, though tentative, first step of "the Way." In the image used by Father Barringer, they were "strangers on the same pilgrimage," beginning to regret their social distance, beginning to recognize each other and beginning to consider the possibility of journeying together. It seemed to me a somewhat uneasy joyfulness, as I wondered whether the conferences would conti-nue, whether the suddenly felt solidarity would last.

The next year brought some confirmation. More than two hundred attended each of the two evenings. The presence of two bishops, their authoritative teaching on the Eucharist and Church, their shared understanding of the Christian faith, and their obvious affection for each other had an encouraging and unifying effect on many present. The contrasting personalities, styles and speech of Bishop Seraphim and Bishop Samra could not hide their unanimity in faith. In reply to several questions, after one bishop had answered, the other simply said, "Amen." More conversation and the hospitality of wine and cheese closed each evening. By the end of the second "Windows to the East," a number of those present had begun to walk forward, however tentatively, with a changing perspective of looking for what they held in common, rather than for differences, in their Christian faith and practice. A growing recognition of each other as fellow pilgrims on the same journey was developing. Perhaps now they were becoming better acquaintances in Christ.

In order to situate "Windows to the East" in its social setting of Saskatoon, in Saskatchewan, one of three Prairie provinces in Canada, I provide a brief demographic summary on Eastern

Christians based on the 1991 Statistics Canada census. Though somewhat dated and limited in cross tabulations for religion, this census remains the most recent national, provincial and metropolitan area census data available on religion in Canada.[1]

At the time of the 1991 national census, 387,395 persons identified themselves as Eastern Orthodox and 128,390 as Ukrainian Catholic for a total of 515,785 Eastern Christians in an overall Canadian population of 26,994,045. Eastern Christians made up 1.9% of the Canadian population. One out of fifty Canadians identified with an Eastern Christian faith tradition, either Eastern Orthodox or Ukrainian Catholic.

Eastern Christian Canadians are, on average, more than four years older than Canadians as a whole. The average age of Eastern Christians in the 1981 census was 36.5, 39.1 in the 1991 census. The average age of the Canadian population in 1981 was 32.3, 34.5 in 1991. Among Canadians as a whole, in the 25–44 age group, 21.3% had university degrees. Among Eastern Christian Canadians, 21.5% had university degrees.

In the Canadian Prairie provinces, 162,700 identified themselves as Eastern Christians, about one person in thirty.

	Eastern Orthodox	Ukrainian Catholic	Total	Population of Province	% Province
Manitoba	20,799	33,400	54,100	1,079,400	5.0%
Saskatchewan	19,500	20,200	39,700	976,000	4.1%
Alberta	42,700	26,200	68,900	2,519,200	2.7%
Total	82,999	79,800	162,700	4,574,600	3.6%

In Canada as a whole, the ratio of Eastern Orthodox to Ukrainian Catholic is three to one. In Manitoba the ratio is five to eight; in Saskatchewan it is one to one, and in Alberta it is eight to five.

Saskatchewan has two metropolitan areas: the capital city of Regina and Saskatoon. In the 1991 census these two metropolitan

areas accounted for 40.7% of the province's population and
39.4% of Eastern Christians.

	Eastern Orthodox	Ukrainian Catholic	Total	Met. area	% Met. area
Regina	3,530	2,935	6,465	189,440	3.4%
Saskatoon	4,090	5,075	9,165	207,825	4.4%
Total	7,620	8,110	15,630	397,265	3.9%

Among the 19,500 in Saskatchewan who identifed
themselves as Eastern Orthodox in eight specific Orthodox
Churches, Greek Orthodox (11,775) and Ukrainian Orthodox
(5,675) accounted for 89.5% of all Orthodox.

Among the nearly 40,000 Eastern Christians in Saskatchewan, 40.3% indicated Ukrainian as their mother tongue and
51.5% reported English as their mother tongue. In Saskatchewan
as a whole, in the 25–44 age group, 16.3% reported having a
university degree. Among Eastern Christians in Saskatchewan,
14.1% reported a university degree. Many Eastern Christians
who immigrated to the Canadian prairies in the first decades of
the twentieth century were of Ukrainian origin. Many came from
peasant backgrounds, without formal education. They eked out a
farming existence under most adverse conditions of poverty,
unbroken land, harsh climate and widespread prejudice. Their
achievements are all the more remarkable. Dr. Stephen Worobetz,
an outstanding surgeon, was named the first Ukrainian Lieutenant-Governor of Saskatchewan in 1970. Dr. Sylvia Fedoruk, an
outstanding scientist, was the first woman Lieutenant-Governor
of Saskatchewan in 1988. Mr. Roy Romanow became the first
Ukrainian Premier of Saskatchewan in 1991. The Canadian
Institute of Ukrainian Studies at the University of Alberta and the
newly established Prairie Centre for the Study of Ukrainian
Heritage at St. Thomas More College at the University of Saskatchewan are engaged in documenting this history and the many
significant contributions of people of Ukrainian ancestry in the
Canadian prairies. Like others in Saskatchewan, Eastern
Christians are increasingly urban, living in pluralistic settings of

neighbourhood, work and occupations, schools, and recreation where daily activities and contact with persons of ethnic and religious backgrounds different from their own are commonplace.

Eastern Christians in Saskatchewan and in Saskatoon, including those attending "Windows to the East," do not appear, from the limited Statistics Canada census cross-tabulations for religion, to be demographically different from others in Saskatchewan. For many of these Eastern Christians, their ethnicity and faith tradition have represented a distinguishing aspect of their identities as Canadians. "Windows to the East" suggests that, in the context of increasing pluralism, these persons are being brought into dialogue, so as to clarify and deepen their faith identity while also seeking common ground. What has happened at Windows has been specific to Saskatoon. Yet this brief overview suggests a parallel and a potential applicability for Eastern Christians and others beyond this immediate setting. Speakers view this grassroots effort as part of a large movement, its manifestation and agency.

This volume is evidence that "Windows to the East," a grassroots ecumenical initiative among Saskatoon Eastern Christians, with some Protestants and Roman Catholics also participating, coalesced around the courage and risk of Mrs. Lesya Nahachewsky and others. It was a pilgrimage in progress waiting to be noticed. This volume contains the major contributions presented during the past seven years. Though it represents the partial and most tangible record of these conferences, it cannot capture much of their social, conversational and prayerful context. The continuation of "Windows to the East" speaks to an emerging ecumenical leadership and a growing recognition of each other among Eastern Christians of different churches. Despite major differences of history, culture and politics, "Windows to the East" represents an important step along the road to the unity among his followers for which our Lord prayed to his Father. Initial enthusiasm and felt good will, however, do not eliminate the need for the difficult and painstaking work of healing long-standing animosities and divisions, and of developing closer relationships among Eastern Christians of different churches.

I have been privileged to be witness to this grassroots initiative. As president of St. Thomas More College (STM), my role has been facilitative, allowing this emerging impulse toward unity among Eastern Christians in Saskatoon to have a space in which to express its hopes and concerns. As a Catholic college, federated with the University of Saskatchewan, STM has been able to offer an academic setting for "Windows to the East," one in which both faith and intellectual life are taken seriously. Although the College appeared to be neutral ground – neither Orthodox nor Eastern Catholic – I worried that in offering our facilities we might be perceived to be up to Roman Catholic tactics of co-optation, since we have historically been viewed as part of the problem. So far, the College has proved a hospitable setting for "Windows to the East."

I am a Roman Catholic and a sociologist. I might best characterize my own involvement in "Windows to the East" as a participant-observer. I have been empathetically present. As someone who is not an Eastern Christian but who served on the organizing committee, I have been an outsider inside. As a Christian listening to this extended conversation among Eastern Christians, I have been an insider outside. Like some others on the outside who were also present, I was seeking to be enriched and renewed in my faith by a tradition as old and as new as Christianity itself, but one from which my Western Roman Catholic Tradition and my faith experience have been cut off for centuries. In speaking of the heritage of the Eastern Christian Tradition, Pope John Paul II has said that Roman Catholics need both lungs to breathe.[2] Until "Windows to the East," I did not know that I was only breathing by half. I have been blessed in these presentations and in my relationships with Eastern Christians. Some of these persons I knew in other settings before "Windows to the East." Now I know them and others I have met at Windows as fellow Christians who are on the same pilgrimage. I am beginning to breathe a little more fully and somewhat easier.

The original organizers chose to call the conference "Windows to the East." They had hoped that, as an ecumenical venture, "Windows to the East" would allow Eastern Christians to see each other, despite differences which had long obscured their view of how much they shared. They had also hoped the conference would allow others to look in, to see the riches of the Eastern Christian Tradition, a tradition present in the Canadian prairies, though too little known and even misunderstood by other Christians. A year after the first "Windows to the East" began, with much hype Microsoft introduced a new and improved computer operating system: Windows 95 with "icons." Despite Microsoft's use of the name Windows, there has been little danger of confusion. Our Windows, as a grassroots effort, has fittingly not had much fanfare. Despite promising publicity, Windows 95 was still prone to crashing. "Windows to the East" has continued to struggle forward out of the desires and efforts of participants to overcome past ruptures and present obstacles, seeking unity.

As a metaphor, "Windows to the East" also points to the need for changing perspectives – conversion – to move beyond past grievances, to retrieve the riches of the Eastern Christian Tradition and to engage that tradition with and for changing times. A faith tradition is not a thing or an object, but a living and lived reality. It is a window on the transcendent. However, unless the tradition is constantly revisited, reconsidered and renewed, it will become opaque, a curiosity piece that ends up obscuring the divine. The contributors to this volume have revisited the Eastern Christian Tradition most effectively – retrieved it in dialogue with our times. Readers will discover that some of the contributors found the metaphor of windows appealing and useful. How we relate to God, to ourselves and to each other depends upon the images, the conceptions by which we "see" the tradition. In the initial conference of "Windows to the East," Daniel Sahas employs the metaphor of windows to urge participants to learn about their historical formation, to enter into dialogue among Orthodox and non-Orthodox, to engage in contemplation and to make their tradition better known in the West. In the final contribution, "Windows of Life," Maria Truchan-Tataryn presents icons as windows in their capacity to reveal the reality of the divine beyond and the divine present in us and in creation. Most significantly, she argues that we ourselves become icons – "windows that reveal the transforming power of Christ to the world." That's a long way from a computer symbol on a phosphorescent screen!

The contributions are diverse in content, as might be expected from themes and presentations spanning seven years and attempting to address emergent needs in an ecumenical setting. The contributors, chosen by the organizing committee, are diverse in background, education and occupation. Most have formal theological education with graduate degrees. They are bishops, priests, scholars, artists, educators, pastoral workers, spouses and parents. Three are women and eleven are men. They are addressing a varied audience comprised largely of Eastern Christian lay persons from local parishes drawn to this ecumenical effort over seven years. While committed to their faith, active in their churches, and interested in Church and personal renewal, few in the audience have formal theological education. The contributions are also diverse in form, reflecting the faith needs of Eastern Christians and the expertise and experience of speakers. They carry the orality of the conferences and the dual concerns of comforting and challenging. Some contributions are scholarly in tone, with argumentation and documentation, intent on providing theological, scriptural and historical frameworks for key issues as well as providing critiques of society and culture. Other contributions are pastoral in tone and in content, intent on evoking appropriate understandings of, attitudes toward, and practices of the faith and relations with others. Several are devotional in approach, exhortatory, inspiring attitudes of reverence, respect and awareness in worship and prayer. Rooted in a shared Eastern Christian Tradition, based on Scripture and the Divine Liturgy, these contributions seek to deepen participants' faith commitments in community within the tensions of modern living. In providing an overview of each contribution below, I have tried to identify the questions addressed by each speaker.

In general terms, I have described the audience attending the "Windows to the East" conferences: Eastern Christian women and men, from parishes in Saskatoon which sponsored "Windows," and other Eastern Christians, some from as far away as Manitoba. Other Christians also attended, among whom were Lutherans, Anglicans, Mennonites and Roman Catholics. Some faculty of St. Thomas More College, the University of Saskatchewan, and the Saskatoon Theological Union attended. This volume will be of interest to these conference participants and other members of Eastern Christian parishes, some of whom have asked that the talks be published.

Beyond the immediate vicinity of Saskatoon and the Canadian prairies, others will find this volume both useful and encouraging. North American Eastern Christians, both clerical and lay, will find encouragement, insight and prayerful reflection in the questions and themes of the speakers and in this ecumenical, grassroots initiative of Windows. Christian teachers will discover here a rich tradition that will give them and their students a fuller understanding of, and appreciation for, the Christian faith as unity in diversity. Pastors will find here the desire of "ordinary Christians" for substantive and prayerful preaching and a longing for unity, which moves beyond identity defined as "against" rather than "with." Theologians and students of theology will encounter informed theological scholarship and insight related to pastoral and personal concerns of daily Christian living, the Divine Liturgy and personal prayer. The strong emphasis on the relational foundation of faith communities in the Trinity and their grounding in the incarnation is offered here as an antidote to destructive elements of popular culture and as an imperative to service in and to our society. Informed general readers will discover not only a critique of contemporary culture, but a response to that culture embodying a positive and intelligent Christian vision of the human person in the divine likeness as it has been recovered from elements fundamental to the Eastern Christian Tradition.

There is another audience for this volume. The music of international artists Arvo Pärt and John Tavener and Canadian artist Imant Raminsh has been growing in popularity. Their music represents a different "Window to the East" – a clerestory facing East. As a window on an outside wall of a room that rises above an adjoining roof, such a clerestory ajar allows the morning sunlight and music outside to waft into the room of Western popular culture without its source being directly visible or recognized. While many Eastern Christians treasure the music of these artists as integral to worship, many other persons know their music only as part of popular culture. Some, attracted by the New Age movement with its expressive individualism, eclectic and even ephemeral spirituality, find more than relaxation and reduction of stress in the music of these artists; they find beauty, depth and mystery. Many who hear their music, however, are unaware that it arises out of these artists' Eastern Orthodox faith – words that struggle for understanding in the heart, sounds that encourage those who listen to hear, rhythms that attend to silence. These artists bring Orthodox fidelity and contemporary cultural sensibilities into a renewed search to express the Ineffable for persons in our times. This volume offers such persons insight into the spiritual depths and dynamics of

Eastern Christianity, heard in the "sounding icons" of Pärt, Tavener and Raminsh.

This volume represents an invitation to dialogue between East and West that hallows common ground while creating room and respect for greater diversity within the Body of Christ. All readers will find in the icons in the book a prayerful presentation of the mysteries of our faith and an invitation to awareness of the divine presence among us.

Overview: "Windows to the East" Conferences, Speakers and Talks

1994 – Exploring the Heart of Eastern Christianity

The first meeting of "Windows to the East" in February 1994 raises the fundamental question of identity. As Western citizens who call themselves Eastern Christians but are not well known in the West, who are they, what distinguishes them? How are they to understand themselves religiously, ethnically and culturally? What is their historical background and how has it shaped their present realities? Despite obvious differences, what do they have in common as Eastern Christians? What distinguishes the Eastern Christian Tradition as a way of life? What is its relationship to Western Christianity? Robert Barringer, C.S.B., Ph.D. and Daniel Sahas, Ph.D., two scholars who have been engaged in the North American Orthodox-Catholic Dialogue, friends and co-authors of *Rome and Constantinople: Essays in the Dialogue of Love,* address these questions in two complementary ways.

Father Barringer provides a welcoming talk in a conversational tone to establish an orientation and overview in asking who participants are and how they got there. He provides the image and theme of "strangers on the same pilgrimage" for characterizing, as well as challenging, how Eastern Christians see each other and Western Christians. He offers an historical and geographical overview, accounting for the differences and separation within the Christian East. Father Barringer suggests that overcoming estrangement and division will only take place through grassroots dialogue as "strangers" understand the historical and political factors of their divisions, understand that they are on the same pilgrimage and, like the two disciples on the road to Emmaus, recognize the same Christ among them and develop empathy for each other. He asks for an appreciation of diversity in dialogue.

Professor Sahas' scholarly contribution identifies the features which distinguish an ethos or interior way of life of Byzantine Christian spirituality, as well as the factors and conditions out of which and against which the ethos has been defined and taken shape. He marks out this ethos in its transcendent reality of religious experience as no longer tied to or dependent upon societal and historical conditions of its formation. He identifies key features that, held in tension, have defined and distinguished Orthodoxy and established within its tradition a dynamic balance. He sees this ethos, though too little known in the West, as a genuine and solid spirituality able to counteract the eroding rationalism, individualism and materialism of contemporary culture. Professor Sahas' analysis concludes with the centrality of prayerful silence before the mystery of God.

1995 – Centrality of the Lord's Table: Eucharistic Perspectives

Two bishops address the second "Windows to the East" on Eastern Christian understanding of union with and the presence of Christ in the Eucharist. Although the styles and backgrounds of these two bishops are strikingly different, their talks are pastoral and devout in tone, paralleling sermons in structure, and in strong agreement about the centrality of the mystery of the Eucharist for the life of the community and for the personal divinization of Christians.

Bishop Seraphim asks how the Eucharist both symbolizes and affects the whole and centre of the Orthodox Tradition in its beliefs and practices as a living faith and community. To show the centrality of the Eucharist to the life of the Church as union with Christ, he draws on the Fathers, on theology arising from experiences of God, and on scriptures.

Bishop Nicholas Samra asks how the divine presence is manifested today and what the role of the Eucharist is in that presence. He too focuses on the centrality of the Eucharist to the life of the Church, with an emphasis on "giving thanks," community, and unity in the Body of Christ. Proper understanding of the Eucharist and Christians as the Body of Christ counteracts the dangers of contemporary individualism. Bishop Samra draws on Acts 2:42-47 to elaborate his vision of the Church as a community which is the living and present Body of Christ.

1996 – Prayer in the Modern World: An Eastern Christian Perspective

The third "Windows to the East" moves in a devotional and personal direction to explore both the theological understanding of and the daily practice of prayer. This session brings together two priests who are also scholars. Both are engaged in theological education of persons studying for ministry in the Church.

Father Thomas Hopko asks two related questions. What is prayer as found in the Scripture, the Church Fathers, the saints, and Tradition? How do persons pray always, or, how do they "become prayer"? Father Hopko shows that the Orthodox Tradition is at odds with much of modern culture. A scriptural understanding of prayer highlights this opposition to a self without relationship to God and others. Prayer anchors our relationship to the Trinity and represents a conversation with God within us. Prayer represents the paradox of becoming more who we are by entering more fully into union with God, giving praise and thanksgiving. Prayer is about being in touch with reality, about fidelity to truth.

Father Andriy Chirovsky addresses two questions about prayer today. How do we pray in light of the deep divisions within the Body of Christ? What is prayer in relationship to our bodies? Father Chirovsky examines prayer through the lens of long-standing and deep-rooted religious divisions. Focusing on the painful divisions he finds among Eastern Christians, he sees intractable disunity as the very subject of our prayer to God, who desires unity and who can effect that unity. While he attends directly to the deep divisions and contrasting claims, he argues that what unites far outweighs that which divides and that new ways of seeing each other are needed. Prayer for unity can have transformative power: we are to be, with God, co-authors of Christian unity. Pointing to the close connection between aesthetics and spirituality, Father Chirovsky explores the importance of bodily positions and of practices utilizing the senses.

1997 – Holy Trinity:
Exemplary Paradigm of Community,
Evangelism and Ecumenical Relations

The fourth "Windows to the East" focuses on the central mystery of the Trinity, asking how faith in a Triune God is fundamental to Christian living, what difference it makes in daily life. Two priests, theologians who are scholars and teachers, address this topic. They point to the relevance of the Trinity in two ways: Father Stylianopoulos indicates its foundational character for Christians; Father Tataryn examines its social implications for agency in the world.

Father Theodore Stylianopoulos addresses the question of how central, integral and coherent the belief in the Trinity is to the New Testament, the Fathers, the language of worship and prayer, and the sacramental life of the early Church. He asks this question against the backdrop of philosophical arguments maintaining that all gods, despite different names, are the same and that the Trinity has been read back from later periods into the New Testament and the early life of the Church. Using the commissioning in Matthew 28:16-20, Father Stylianopoulos argues the case that the Trinity has been a paradigm of faith, practice and community for Christian life from the beginning. Christians have understood themselves as living in, participating in, dwelling in, reflecting the life of God, the life of the Trinity, "with Christ," as the central truth, reality.

Father Myroslaw Tataryn argues that the doctrine of the Trinity is at the centre of Christian thought and life and is directly associated with the nature of the Church. He asks whether our images of the Trinity are adequate for humanity today and what the social implications of relational images of Trinity are for our collective self-understanding and relations to the world. He focuses on re-appropriating the doctrine of the Trinity through introducing the community of being as the image of God in humanity. He identifies our "capacity for relationship" as fundamental to a dynamic definition of being human, and claims that being is communal in its constitution, and as such emanates directly from the Trinity. The dynamic and essential quality of human relatedness flows from the *ekstasis* and *kenosis* of the eternal trinitarian love. Father Tataryn explores the implications of this definition for what it means to be God-like in the community of the Church and to be agents of social change in the world. This essential and dynamic relatedness of human persons and creation contradicts cultural individualism, which pits itself against community, regarded as constraint. It also embraces many with disabilities, whose marginalization has been justified by images of God based on rationality, and it binds us to each other and to the world.

1998 – Mary: Model for Christian Life and Ministry

The fifth "Windows to the East" revisits Mary as a model for Christians, against the backdrop of half a century of social and cultural change in North America, no small part of which has involved redefinition of and conflict over women's roles in the home, the workplace and society. Responding to the Windows committee's invitation, two women address the role of Mary in our lives today, both for Christian life and for ministry of service within the Christian community and in society. Their talks point not only to the importance of Mary in defining the role of women in the Church and society but also to Mary's importance in underscoring the reality and centrality of the incarnation for Christians.

In a devotional talk, Dr. Frances Colie prayerfully examines how Mary is archetype and exemplar for us today. Mary's central role in the incarnation is the basis of Dr. Colie's reflection on several titles of Mary. Focusing on Mary, the Theotokos, she examines Mary's response at the Annunciation, in bringing Jesus to the world, as a model for our response to God. Mary is also our model for prayer. Among the titles of Mary Dr. Colie explores are: Ever Virgin, Mother of God, *Panagia* – All Holy, and the New Eve.

In a talk directed at women's places and roles in church ministry, Khouriye Elaine Hanna asks what the history of women and the diaconate offers us today as churches. She begins by continuing Dr. Colie's reflection on images of Mary, taking up four of Mary's roles as Theotokos: Handmaid of the Lord, Spiritual Mother, Disciple, and Spirit-Bearer. These form the backdrop for a retrieval of women's roles in ministry illuminated in an historical overview of women and the diaconate. Basing her remarks on the Crete Consultation in 1988, Mrs. Hanna elaborates fourteen service functions in a proposed restoration of the diaconate for women in the Church today.

1999 – Meeting Christ in the Divine Liturgy

The sixth "Windows to the East" takes up the theme of the presence of Christ, a theme that appeared in previous talks. This conference specifically focuses on meeting Christ in the Divine Liturgy. In previous talks, the theme of relationships had emerged as being central to an Eastern Christian understanding of our presence in the world. The questions asked here are about relationship to Christ and what "meeting" Christ means.

Bishop Lawrence Huculak, O.S.B.M. asks what role the Divine Liturgy plays in encountering Christ. In a detailed description of the Liturgical celebration, he spells out the links between the various elements of Liturgy and our meeting Christ, not as a memory of something past, but as Christ truly present now, in and through the Liturgy and the community.

Father Daniel Guenther takes up the theme of meeting Christ by asking what it means to "see Christ." Through reflection on Scripture, Tradition, community, Divine Liturgy and Eucharist, he explores the paradox that seeing Christ involves becoming like Christ, being transformed into Christ to see reality through Christ's eyes.

2000 – Eastern Christianity in a Post-Modern World

The seventh "Windows to the East" explores the relevance of Eastern Christianity for contemporary society and culture. Sometimes called "post-modern" in its fragmentation, its competitive individualism, its multiple, contradictory and relativizing perspectives, our world emphasizes the particular and specific as opposed to overarching or meta-narratives like Christianity and to instrumental rationality. Post-modernism speaks of a world troubled, maybe even possessed, by questions of meaning. It represents losses of faith in the myth of progress, the perfectibility of the human and even the value of human agency. It signals lost hope. It bespeaks longing frustrated and human relationships become problematic. To consider these existential questions of our times, the Windows committee enlists two vantage points from within the Eastern Christian Tradition, that of a scholar-teacher in English literature and that of an artist-iconographer.

As a scholar in English literature, Father Anthony Ugolnik engages in a dialogue with and critique of the debate on gender. He challenges a Christian spirituality that excludes maleness and a contemporary culture that distorts sexuality in its absorption with self and the auto-erotic. He asks why the male voice, heard in theology, cannot be heard in the discourse of spirituality and prayer in which even the soul itself has been feminized. If male bodiliness appears to be a scandal and excluded from religious meaning, how are men to give genuine expression to who they are – mind and body – in prayer? This is a twofold problem for men: language style and bodily experience. As a way of opening up this question and providing a critique of popular culture, Father Ugolnik explores the sexual union in marriage as a sacrament that expresses male and female sexuality while evoking complementarity, mutuality and commitment – self and other. He finds in this mutuality and union of male and female a sign of the likeness to God in the Trinity and a way of taking the incarnation seriously.

In two presentations at the seventh "Windows to the East," Marianna Savaryn, an iconographer, shows slides of the icons she has written and describes the various aspects of iconography and the icons themselves. A number of her icons are found in this book. As background to iconography and the meaning of icons, Maria Truchan-Tataryn provides for this volume an orienting article entitled "Iconography: Windows of Life."

Professor Jaroslav Skira's epilogue, "Opening Windows to a Dialogue of Charity," rounds out this collection. He begins by thoughtfully asking about the meaning of the window metaphor, what it represents and points to, as well as what its limitations are. Too easily readers might be tempted to think that "Windows to the East" is an isolated initiative, peculiar to its Saskatoon, Canadian Prairie grassroots setting. Professor Skira suggests, however, that this local effort can only be properly understood as part of something that has been happening worldwide since at least the mid-1960s. As an effort toward unity through dialogue and worship, "Windows" is within the contexts of historical, theological, cultural, media and increased communication between East and West. The "Windows to the East" conferences are one of many manifestations of a major ecumenical movement of changing attitudes and approaches among Orthodox, and between Orthodox and Catholic Eastern Christians. "Windows" is itself part of promising developments.

A glossary of terms follows the epilogue. It provides readers with a concise description of key terms of the Eastern Christian Tradition used by contributors, terms that may be unfamiliar to some readers. The terms are arranged in alphabetical order so they can be easily looked up while one is reading the text.

John Thompson
Department of Sociology
St. Thomas More College
University of Saskatchewan

---

[1] Statistics Canada, *Religion in Canada* (Ottawa: Statistics Canada, 1993), 93-319.

[2] This image in fact comes from Yves Congar, *Diversity and Communion,* trans. John Bowden (Mystic, CT: Twenty-Third Publications, 1985), 89 & n. 17.II.

II. Exploring the Heart of Eastern Christianity (1994)

Chapter 1

Strangers on the Same Pilgrimage

ROBERT BARRINGER, C.S.B.

Fr. Barringer has a doctorate in Eastern Christian Studies from Oxford University. He has held a number of academic appointments, most prominently, President of St. Joseph's College, University of Alberta. He has published English translations of the work of Romanian theologian Dumitru Staniloae, Theology and the Church *(1980), and* The Experience of God *(2000). For a number of years Fr. Barringer served on the North American Roman Catholic–Eastern Orthodox Consultation. After concluding his term as Superior General of the Congregation of St. Basil, he became novice master for the Congregation in Cali, Colombia, where he now resides.*

Let me begin with an image from the book of the prophet Amos (3:3): "Do two people walk together on the road unless they have agreed?" Perhaps we can all identify with the human experience lurking behind this text. When we walk in a crowd of strangers there is little self-consciousness, but if we find ourselves walking with only one other person, a stranger, it becomes almost an imperative to "break stride" if by chance we find that our rate of walking is the same. We fall back or press forward as a way of denying any connection with the other, precisely because that person is the other, is "stranger" to us. And indeed there is no connection unless we deliberately establish some basis, some invitation which enables us to walk

31

on together. Yet we Christians, Eastern or Western, are all on a pilgrimage and the image of pilgrimage, of course, is Biblical. One of the classic places where it is found is in the Letter to the Hebrews (11:13-16):

> By acknowledging themselves to be strangers and foreigners on the earth, they showed that they were seeking a homeland. If they had been thinking back to the place from which they had come, they would have had the opportunity of returning there. But they were searching for a better, a heavenly home. Wherefore God is not ashamed to be called their God, for he has prepared a city for them.

East and West as Strangers?

This is true of all Christians. All of us are in some sense strangers in a strange land and in as far as, Western or Eastern, we are Christians at all, we are on a pilgrimage towards God and that is the critical thing. We need to be able to speak of this experience of God, of what we know, to those around us, to our fellow human beings in this world. This is the whole project of evangelization. However, an important question for consideration is whether we are on pilgrimage *together* as Eastern and Western Christians. Have we agreed to walk together? Or, are we strangers to one another? In the English language "stranger" means more than just "foreigner." In many other European languages "stranger" and "foreigner" are really the same thing, something outlandish, but in English "stranger" implies a more or less conscious decision not to get involved with someone else, not to care. I think our present reality as Eastern and Western Christians reflects this. There is a "strangerly" quality in the sense that we do not know much about one another; there is a lack of basic knowledge; there is a lack of deeper understanding and empathy that could come from better knowledge. However, there is also a lack of concern, a lack of care for the other. We have become strangers to other pilgrims. We are on the same pilgrimage and we are strangers.

Having thus introduced the problem we need to ask: Have we always been strangers to one another? If you think of kids at a dance, there is a natural reticence and difficulty, at least at a certain age when they ask one another to dance, especially if they do not know one another very well. We have all had a moment like that, of getting up our courage to get involved with someone else, whether it is a dance or any other social moment. Have Eastern and Western Christians always been strangers like that? Are we simply witnessing a natural reticence? Or have we become estranged at some point in our past? Do we in fact have a common past?

In both our collective memories as East and West, we each have some sense, some memory, of a time when a common unity existed. However, we are out of touch with this common life now. We often refer to this as the early Church, the Church of the first three or four centuries. Occasionally, when Eastern Orthodox and Catholics are talking they will sometimes say that the Church of the first millennium had a common life in some fashion. Each side, East and West, has a slightly different picture of how this common life was lost: who is at fault, or at least, more to blame. Yet perhaps the most important thing of all is that we have grown accustomed to living without the other. We have come to treat our own lives and our own resources and capabilities as if they constituted all that could be, all that should be. Today each side has come to define Christianity in terms of its own experience, not including the other side in that definition.

I propose to look at the story of our estranged relationship and I will try to emphasize the shape of the story rather than the details. Then I will examine the extent of our interaction as churches, the geography as well as the history of that relationship, and, more importantly, the patterns that we see when we look at ourselves in the mirror and when we begin to look at the other.

First, though, I would like to place my presentation in a personal context: I am a Western Christian who has a great love of Eastern Christianity and a great gratitude toward Orthodox and Eastern Catholic Christians who have figured prominently in my life. Over twenty years ago, I had the opportunity to spend a year at the Romanian Orthodox Seminary in Bucharest and that experience has marked the rest of my life. I have always wanted to make Eastern Christianity known in the West, but not as a kind of specialty. Unfortunately, some Western Christians have a rather esoteric interest in the Christian East. I have always wanted to see Eastern Christianity as normal, as bread and butter, as part of every Christian's heritage and not just a cultivated taste or a particular style. I am convinced that increased contact with the Christian East on the part of the West, particularly the Roman Catholic West, can change us. It can change the Catholic West enough to make the problems that now look insurmountable surmountable and, frankly, the most difficult problem of all separating us is the question of the Papacy. As long as there is little or no contact between us, as long as we break stride whenever we realize we are walking together, there can and will be no change in the way that Western Catholics exist or, to a large degree, in the way that Eastern Christians also exist.

One last introductory note: in the liturgy of the Christian East, February 2, the Feast of the Presentation of Christ in the Temple, is the Feast of the Meeting of the Lord, the day in which the Lord came to the temple, as it says in the prophecy of Malachi (3:1), to *meet* his people. Whom did he meet? Well, he met Simeon and Anna in that temple. These were his people, the Jewish people, but they also represent the entire human race because through him, through Christ (this child in the arms of his parents, this child who is the Word of God), all of us and everything has been made. The question that occurred to me in thinking about this was the following: Did Simeon and Anna know one another before this event? Here they were: Anna had been coming day after day for years and years, praying in the temple and Simeon (you get the same sort of impression that he was an old man looking to his death) had been hoping to see the Messiah before he died. They might well have been passing one another every day without ever having exchanged a word. Maybe they were usually in different courts of the temple. But here the Lord, who had come to meet his creation and his people, brought them together: two different lives that might never have otherwise touched. On this Feast of the Meeting of the Lord, Christ brings us in touch with one another, with our different lives and our different worlds. Ultimately all this is for the glory and praise of God. We should not be too quick to break stride again, to defend our own identities or our own agendas; we should let God be God and trust enough that if God is the cause of our meeting, then soon that will become clear, along with the divine purpose.

The Birth of the Church

The story of Christianity, of the Christian Church, begins in Jerusalem with the first Christian community gathered together in the upper room, preaching on the streets of Jerusalem on the Feast of Pentecost. This image, of the apostolic preaching going out from Jerusalem to the Roman Empire and to other parts of the world, accurately represents the spread of the Gospel. But what was the Church of Jerusalem like before it spread? We tend to think of it as one Church, but I think we need to see it in slightly different ways. Was it a local church? Was it the Church at or of Jerusalem? What we know, from Acts, is that those people in the upper room, those people on the streets, were Galileans. They did not belong in town. They were from somewhere else. They were strangers. Three thousand were added to their number the very first day when they actually started opening their mouths and talking about Jesus (Acts 2:41). Some of those people, at least Acts suggests, were from all over the world. They had homes to go back to as well. We see then that the local community of Jerusalem was already a kind of universal Church. Catholics looking at that community might think of it primarily as a gathering, a universal gathering, which represents the diversity of the rest of the world. Orthodox Christians might emphasize more, or be more empathetic to, the sense of the particular place, the particular community at a particular time. Although not playing a critical role in Christian history, Jerusalem nonetheless figured in the initial separation of Christianity from Judaism. After the first century destruction of Jerusalem, it did not really recover as a Christian centre until the fourth century.

From Jerusalem, the apostolic Church spread into the Roman Empire. The first major city for Christians beyond Israel was Antioch. Antioch was where Christians were first called Christians (Acts 11:26). It was a base of preaching for Paul and an important centre from which Christianity spread to the hinterland. There is evidence from a number of sources that Alexandria was an important and early Christian centre, as well as Rome itself. Therefore, already within the Roman Empire, places like Rome, Antioch and Alexandria are from a very early date important places. All three are associated in different ways with the name of Peter the Apostle. Antioch and Rome are closely tied with the name of Paul. However, the apostolic preaching found its way beyond the Roman Empire as well. Even many of the people mentioned in Acts have names from areas outside the Empire.

We do know that Christianity was not limited to the Roman Empire. Very quickly it began to spread to places like Armenia, perhaps India, certainly east of Syria into Persia, perhaps even into Ethiopia. Thus the Armenians claim that some of the apostles went to Armenia: Thaddeus and Bartholomew, for example. Although hard historical evidence of this growth is not available, local custom and tradition speak to very ancient origins.

Now what should be clear is that already in the first Christian century the Church of Christ is already diverse. The language of growth and of many of the Christians is Greek, even in what we think of as Rome. However, once you get outside the Roman Empire towards the East into Persia, the language becomes Syriac. These places are also asserting their identity. Christianity is growing in different forms. There is community, *koinonia*, but also a great deal of diversity.

Christianity and the Empire

A second period begins in the early fourth century, that is to say, about three hundred years after the resurrection of Jesus. This second period starts with what we call now the conversion of the Roman Emperor Constantine and, gradually, the conversion of his Empire. This period inaugurates a new relationship between Christians of the Empire and the Imperial authorities themselves. One of its most important dimensions is that Christians all of a sudden have responsibility for the Empire. Now the Emperor wants to use them as a means of binding the Empire together, of strengthening it. But this new relationship causes tension between the Christians inside the Empire and those outside. The Persians and others are the natural enemies of the Roman Empire and they thus become the natural enemies of the Christians. It is in this period that the Christianity of Rome, Latin Christianity, begins to form its identity.

During this period Christians come to struggle with the need for larger structures for this empire-wide community. Thus, councils of the Church emerge as a mechanism for resolving problems and difficulties which arise in the far-flung and ethnically diverse communities. Gradually specific centres of historical, political and ecclesiastical authority are established and as human institutions are wont, they jockey for power and primacy. Rome, Antioch, Alexandria, Jerusalem and Constantinople constitute the venerable Pentarchy of leading centres of Christianity. Notwithstanding this ordering of relationships they are also at times in conflict or even division. Thus begins a process of estrangement.[1] A significant motor for estrangement was language. The East and the West, respectively Greek and Latin speaking, grow apart. However, the East is also a very diverse area. Within the Empire Greek dominates. Yet, the East, which is older and only partly within the Empire, is Syriac-speaking or Persian or Armenian, and they come to define themselves without any reference to the Greek- or-Latin-speaking Christians. Today the word "estrangement" is regarded as the most accurate way to describe a gradual process, an historical drifting apart, and a cessation of understanding and caring which characterized the Christian experience from the fourth century.

Estrangement, Not Schism

There are two images of estrangement. The first comes from a volume entitled, *One in 2000?* in which an article by Hugh Wybrew, entitled "How Two Worlds Drifted Apart," gives us the following image of estrangement:

> In any family, children born to the same parents may turn out to be quite different in character and temperament. They may grow up to have apparently little in common. If they go to different schools and then make their lives in different surroundings, they may well end up having little to do with one another. Not infrequently a quarrel over the family inheritance finally sours family relationships and brings all contacts to an end. That may serve as a passable analogy for what happened in relationships between the two dominant members in the Christian family, the Greek East and the Latin West.[2]

That is one image of estrangement based on a family setting. The second image is that of husband and wife in a marriage drifting apart, eventually heading to a divorce, a complete separation.

In the period from the fourth century, for the next six or seven hundred years, and some would say down to the present day, the Christian East and West drifted apart and became estranged. This estrangement was encouraged by a number of factors. Constantinople was the new world, an upstart that had set itself up to replace and dwarf the ancient capital of Rome. With the division between the empires of the East and West, varying perspectives developed on relations with those outside the Empire. Increasing cultural diversification meant that the dominant language of the given region varied from Latin to Greek or Syriac; different approaches to law developed; different categories for understanding spirituality, with different theologies and theological vocabularies became manifest. Even a kind of racism arose: the Greeks regarded the Latins as latecomers, almost barbarians, while the Latins passionately believed in their own superiority over the Greeks.

All of this drifting apart in so many different areas created a climate in which particular differences were aggravated and led to serious confrontations beginning in the fourth century. Christianity quickly sub-divided into families of Churches: the Assyrian Church of the East in contemporary Iraq; the Oriental Orthodox Church in Armenia, Egypt, Ethiopia, Syria, and parts of India; the Eastern Orthodox Churches; and finally, from the sixteenth century on, the Eastern Catholic Churches.

The first of the various fights and divisions was in the middle of the fifth century at the Council of Ephesus in 431. A debate arose around the definition of the person of Jesus. There was a great concern that some had lost the sense of the human-divine unity of Jesus. After some very serious confrontations, a group rejecting the definitions of the Council of 431 came to see themselves as entirely separate from the other Christians. This is the Assyrian Church of the East, although some called them Nestorian Christians because they purportedly followed the deposed Bishop of Constantinople, Nestorius (d.451). Nevertheless, we should also recognize that part of the cause for the division was the political opposition between the Roman and Persian Empires.

In 451 further debates over the nature of Jesus culminated in the Council of Chalcedon. At this council those Christians inside the Empire accepted the definition of Christ as possessing both human and divine natures in one divine person. Other Christians, mainly on the periphery or outside the Empire, felt this was a betrayal of the earlier way of speaking about Christ as of one divine nature. They asserted this without denying his humanity. As a result, by the mid-fifth century at least three groups of Christians had become estranged from one another.

The third period I would propose is from 451 to 1453, the year of the final victory of the Muslim Turks over the Christian capital of Constantinople. This is a very complicated period. At times relations seemed good between East and West, yet at other times the Latins and the Greeks were not talking to one another at all. There were reconciliations that followed these periods of silence but they were typically superficial in nature. The means of communion, the being in one another's life that had been characteristic of those first couple of centuries, started to atrophy. The signs of real care and interest in one another started to fade. When meetings were arranged, they were often disastrous. They tended to accentuate differences rather than create community. The different communities regarded their understanding of God as different from that of the others. Ritual particularity became commonplace. The understanding of authority and its use and place in the Church began to be interpreted quite differently.

The fourth period stretches from 1453 and the fall of the great city of Constantinople down to 1958. This is a very difficult period and in many ways a period of inequality. The inequality did not necessarily start in 1453; it went back to earlier days. For our purposes we can focus on the period from the middle of the fifteenth century to the middle of the twentieth century. In this period, the Latin West is growing in wealth, in learning, in the force that it can bring to bear upon the world around it. Everything that we think of as "our history" – the rise of nation-states, the world of technology, the Renaissance, the Reformation – all of that is part of the Latin experience during this period. On the other hand, the Greek East and other Eastern Christians are having a radically different experience. The states of the East are in a period of political decline; their ability to control their own fate is not in their hands, and they are under the foreign control of the Muslims and other powers. Even Russia had a very difficult history through this period; even when it was powerful, it was also reacting to strong Western influence. As a result of the strength of the West and weakness of the East, areas of Eastern Christianity became objects of Western influence and expansion.

It is during this period that certain Eastern Christian communities, for various reasons, chose to break their bonds with other Eastern Churches and enter into closer ties with the Roman Church. This is the genesis of the Eastern Catholic Churches. Around these communities a certain sense of betrayal has crystallized among the Eastern Orthodox Christians. Some Orthodox have come to regard these Churches as an attempt to divide and conquer the East by the powerful Western Latin Christians. As a result, during this period there occurred a very definite hardening of the heart, coming ultimately to the point where either side would re-baptize the other. Neither was convinced that the other was truly Church. Each side claimed that it alone could lay claim to the whole Tradition.

A fifth era is from 1958 to today. This is a much shorter period – only two generations – in which these two communities, after a long period of drifting apart, of hardening of heart, have begun to rediscover themselves on the same road.

Today we are in this period of rediscovery, refamiliarization and it involves two aspects: the first, learning more about each other, and the second, dialogue – recognizing that we do share things in common and can speak civilly about what we do not share.

Families of Eastern Churches

I now proceed to a brief discussion of the various families of Christian Churches. The first, the Assyrian Church of the East, is a community of about two hundred thousand Christians. The community exists in its heartland, what used to be called Assyria and is now parts of Iraq and Iran; however, elements of the community are also found in India and other parts of the Middle East. Typically, as with all these communities, they also exist in the diaspora, which for most of these churches tends to mean the English-speaking world of North America, Australia, and at times other English parts of the globe. Western Europe is sometimes

40

part of the diaspora, and occasionally Latin America. This Assyrian group is not in communion with any other Christian group. It itself is split into two smaller groups because of internal problems and difficulties. Some of these communities divided over "family squabbles" and various problems without losing the same faith and the same understanding of God, Christ and the Church.

The second family of Churches, the Oriental Orthodox Churches, refers to communities in Armenia, Egypt, Ethiopia, Syria and India. In addition, of course, there is a large diaspora. The Ethiopian Church in recent times, because of political upheavals, has developed a very large diaspora. There are about 32 million Oriental Orthodox Christians. As a body they are in communion with one another but they are not in communion with Western Christians, neither Catholics nor Protestants. In recent years there has been a serious theological dialogue that is drawing the Orthodox Churches, and often some Western Christians, into bilateral discussions with each of these communities. Today a surprising amount of agreement has been achieved at the theological level by theologians representing these communities and those of the Orthodox Churches and of the Roman Catholic Church. Generally agreement has been reached by stating that when we look back to the fifth century when the theological disagreements began, we can recognize that the reasons for the disagreements, no matter how apparently serious then, no longer have the same weight or significance. The disputes of the fifth century do not seem to bear the same meaning, pastorally, spiritually or theologically, to us today as they did then. Today we can listen to one another and not be outraged and furious at what we hear. Today people are less defensive about the formulas, more ready to see limits and faults on both sides and to find a way forward. In some ways, the deeper problem ecumenically is how to interpret the lived experience of the period of over fifteen hundred years since these communities first became aware of a separate identity over against each other. The saints in one tradition have at times been anathematized as heretics by the other tradition. There have been centuries and centuries of accumulated experience and definition based on separation, not commonality. Each has simply lived a different kind of life which has not had to take into account statements by councils or movements in spirituality of the other group. History has created a second kind of division over and above the initial agreements and battles.

The third group, the Orthodox Church, has fourteen or fifteen autocephalous churches: churches that have their own head, their own patriarch or primate. The primary group of four ancient Churches (Constantinople, Alexandria, Antioch and Jerusalem) formed with Rome the ancient Pentarchy. They are completely self-sufficient and are ranked above the others since each has a role to play in the life of the remaining autocephalous churches by naming or confirming the election of its head or primate. In addition, there is another level of Orthodox Churches which have not yet developed to the point of autocephaly and are thus dependant upon a "Mother Church," for example the Greek Archdiocese of North America.

One of the characteristics of Orthodox Churches is that they have a strong dimension of national and ethnic identity. Culture and language are often perceived as integral components of the community's life. These communities are found in the Middle East, in the Balkans, in Eastern Europe and of course, the diaspora. Virtually all of them have a diaspora dimension in which precisely the ethnic and national dimension faces the challenge and, at times, the outright problem of assimilation.

These Churches also have a mission dimension. "Mother Churches" have spread Orthodoxy to Finland, Japan, China and Africa. In fact the first Orthodox Christians in North America were part of a mission movement from Russia. The relationships among these Churches are often dominated by the politics of nationality as much as by religious considerations. There are great tensions today between the Greek Orthodox and the Macedonian Orthodox, not because of doctrine or even ritual, but rather because of the historic antagonism between the two peoples. Many of the communities on the tier below Constantinople, Alexandria, Antioch and Jerusalem have had to achieve their autonomous status through struggles because the "Mother Church" was not eager to let them go their own way. Communities like Romania, and Bulgaria in recent times, have had to fight to be recognized by other Orthodox Churches and by the "Mother Church" in Constantinople before they could be recognized as autocephalous. Unfortunately, it seems to be a phase in the development of autonomous Churches that they must go through a period in which they are out of communion with some other Orthodox Churches before their autonomy or autocephaly is finally recognized.

The last group is the Eastern Catholic Churches. Precise figures are difficult to ascertain but there seem to be ten to twelve million Eastern Catholics, that is, about ten per cent of the Eastern Orthodox total. However, this does not mean that each Orthodox Church has a ten percent Catholic counterpart.

There are, however, also Eastern Catholic Churches with no Orthodox counterpart. First there are the Maronites, a Church centred in Lebanon, although it too has a diaspora in the Western world. If you were to ask Maronite Lebanese Christians about the history of their community you would discover that they have their own sense of what that means; they hold the view that their community has always been a supporter of the Catholic and Orthodox councils of the Church. In their own self-understanding, they were always in communion with the see of Rome, even though they were isolated from giving any practical expression to that communion for centuries. They came out of their isolation at the time of the Crusades to come back into an explicit communion with the Church of Rome that had now become an important player in the Middle East after the Crusades. It is a most interesting community, although it only has sixty thousand people.

There is also a fascinating Italo-Greek Catholic Church. There were many Greek-speaking Christian communities in Italy, not only at the time of the beginnings of the Christian Church, but for the next fifteen hundred years. In fact they have their historical roots in the Greek community of Italy which dates back to six or seven hundred years before the Christian Church. These communities, as far as we know, before the rise of the city of Constantinople, were in some kind of loose sense part of the Italian Christian reality, Italian in the sense of the contiguous land mass, and the patriarch of the West, the Pope of Rome, would have had some relationship to these communities. Later on these communities became a bone of contention between Rome and Constantinople and were declared to be under one or the other of the cities by emperors and others. But in the curious history of the relationship between the East and the West, they never really left communion with their fellow Christians, Latin-speaking and Italian. The Italo-Greeks never saw themselves as separated from the other Christians of Italy. So here we have an Eastern Christian community, a Greek community, which has always in one form or another been in communion with, although not always under the immediate jurisdiction of, the Pope in Rome.

Modern Ecumenism

I would now like to turn our attention to the fifth historic period: 1958 to today. It is our current period of, so to speak, reacquaintance. It is the age of ecumenism. However, it is very important to recognize that in this century the real origins of ecumenism, in its practical expression, have not been in the Orthodox Church or in the Roman Catholic Church – it was predominantly the work of the Protestant Christians. It has been Protestant Christianity that over the past century has simply refused to accept the status quo of a divided Christianity. They in many ways have simply insisted and shamed the Catholics and Orthodox into renewing a conversation, and now, a true and heartfelt Christian dialogue.

Although initially, in the twentieth century, relations between Roman Catholics and Orthodox were frosty at best, gradually, and mainly on the Catholic side as a result of Vatican II, this was overcome.[3] From 1963 to 1979 the Roman Catholic Church of the West and the Eastern Orthodox Church – particularly through figures like Paul VI (1963–78) and Athenagoras of Constantinople (1948–72), later on John Paul II (1978–) and Patriarch Demetrios (1972–91) – were looking for ways to show respect, to show love to one another in what came to be called the "Dialogue of Love."[4] It was felt that before there could be any kind of substantial discussion about problems that apparently still separated the communities, they had to show respect and love for one another. As a result, a whole series of customs developed which continue to this day: annual visits back and forth, gestures of friendship, exchanging letters and gifts, rebuilding the relationship which had been discontinued for so many years. Clearly, the deepest motivation for this transformation of attitudes and hearts is the Spirit of Christ, the Holy Spirit of God, seeking the unity that Christ himself prayed for, and finding ways around our resistance. But there was also a lot of preparation by individuals and groups within the Protestant churches and also, increasingly, among individuals and groups in the Catholic and Orthodox world. One cannot underestimate the influence of the personal visions of each of those two leaders, Paul VI and Athenagoras, who reached beyond the interests of their own communities and risked much for the new good of healing old wounds. Those first steps were tentative and unclear, but these pioneers, acting in good faith, were able to overcome the initial obstacles.

From 1979 to the present we have been witnesses to a profound dialogue of truth between the Orthodox Churches and the Roman Catholic Church. Although the gestures and rituals of a renewed relationship continue, we have also moved to a genuine dialogue about the way to achieve unity. We are now actually talking about substantive questions of faith. This dialogue of truth began with a joint planning committee and has moved on to a Joint International Commission for Theological Dialogue, leading to a series of meetings aimed at accumulating over time a group of agreed statements about how we understand Church, our relationship to God and our common views of salvation.[5] Finding ways to overcome the differences that we have inherited from the past is not easy. However, we have had some consensus. We now have a series of common statements on important theological matters. Recently difficulties have arisen, but even these are not insurmountable.

The International Dialogue still needs to deal with what one could argue is the central problem between the Orthodox and the Catholic parties: conciliarity and the papacy. How do these two dimensions of Christian experience in a community relate to each other? How do we as Christians combine what is a universal institution (the papacy) with an institution that expresses the autonomy and life of the local church (the council)? The hard walk still lies ahead. But that future is not just in the hands of the international committees. It is also fed and encouraged by local grassroots initiatives, such as this "Windows" series. Much movement has occurred, much more needs to be done, and the endeavour begun here will be an important contribution to the future reconciliation of Christians.

For Further Reading

Congar, Yves. *After Nine Hundred Years: The Background of the Schism Between the Eastern and Western Churches.* New York: Fordham, 1959.

Fahey, Michael A. *Orthodox and Catholic Sister Churches: East Is West and West Is East.* Milwaukee: Marquette, 1996.

FitzGerald, Thomas. *The Orthodox Church.* Denominations in America 7. Westport, CT: Greenwood Press, 1995.

McPartlan, Paul, ed. *One in 2000? Towards Catholic–Orthodox Unity.* Middlegreen, Slough: St. Paul's, 1993.

Meyendorff, John. *Rome, Constantinople, Moscow: Historical and Theological Studies.* Crestwood, NY: St.Vladimir's, 1996.

Roberson, Ronald G. *The Eastern Christian Churches: A Brief Survey.* 6th ed. Rome: Orientalia Christiana, 1999.

---

[1] This approach of understanding the separation between East and West as estrangement was first argued by Yves Congar in *After Nine Hundred Years: The Background of the Schism Between the Eastern and Western Churches* (New York: Fordham, 1959).

[2] Hugh Wybrew "How Two Worlds Drifted Apart." In Paul McPartlan, ed. *One in 2000? Towards Catholic–Orthodox Unity* (Middlegreen, Slough: St. Paul's, 1993) 101-115.

[3] Orthodoxy was clearly open to ecumenical conversations much earlier than the Roman Catholic Church. Important examples of this readiness for dialogue were the patriarchal encyclicals of 1902 and 1920. They can be found in Gennadios Limouris, ed. *Orthodox Visions of Ecumenism: Statements, Messages and Reports on the Ecumenical Movement,* 1902-1992 (Geneva: WCC, 1994).

[4] A very important volume chronicling this period is John Borelli and John H. Erickson, eds. *The Quest for Unity: Orthodox and Catholics in Dialogue: Documents of the Joint International Commission and Official Dialogues in the United States, 1965-1995,* (Crestwood, NY : St. Vladimir's; Washington, DC : United States Catholic Conference, 1996).

[5] The agreed statements thus far are "The Mystery of the Church and of the Eucharist in the Light of the Mystery of the Holy Trinity" (Munich, 1982); "Faith, Sacraments and the Unity of the Church" (Bari, 1987); "The Sacrament of Order in the Sacramental Structure of the Church with Particular Reference to the Importance of Apostolic Succession for the Sanctification and Unity of the People of God" (Valamo, 1988); and "Uniatism, Method of Union of the Past, and the Present Search for Full Communion" (Balamand, 1993). They can be found in *The Quest for Unity,* op. cit.

Chapter 2

The Ethos of Byzantine Christian Spirituality

DANIEL J. SAHAS

Professor Sahas is Associate Professor of Religious Studies at the University of Waterloo. He has published extensively in the area of Iconography and Orthodox–Muslim relations. His book Icon and Logos *(1986) is a valued source for the study of the Iconoclast controversy.*

This is certainly an ambitious title on a very broad topic. How can one summarize a religious experience, which extends for eleven centuries (323–1453) and beyond, of the Byzantine empire (in reality the religious experience of Eastern Christendom), let alone analyze the quintessence of this experience? The challenge then, even at the risk of becoming a generalist, is to find certain trans-historical characteristics which describe this inner quality or ethos of Byzantine spirituality. The Christian community in general, and in this instance "Eastern" Christianity in particular, must always be in a position to reflect upon itself, and form some kind of recognizable and reliable "Table of Contents" of its essentials, if it wants to be taken seriously and be meaningful to present and coming generations.

On this huge assignment, therefore, and as a way of introducing these talks, I would like to mention how some other scholars have outlined the historical Byzantine Christianity. I will restrict myself to three of them. Harry Magoulias, in a monograph titled *Byzantine Christianity: Emperor, Church and the West,* presents the topic (the subtitle betrays externals) in four chapters under the following headings: "Byzantine

Christianity and the Imperial Cult"; "Byzantine Christianity and the Heresies"; "Byzantine Christianity and Mysticism"; and "Byzantine Christianity and the West."[1] It seems to me that these headings aim at drawing our attention to the following characteristics: a) the departure and distinctiveness of Byzantine Christianity from the imperial cult; b) the theological divergence within the Christian community in general and the Byzantine community in particular, manifested in trends, movements, schools of thought, and heresies; c) the mystical element which Byzantium cultivated and experienced in its faith; and d) the relations and contrast between the Greek East and the Latin West on these matters, consciously implying that such a contrast between the two expressions of Christianity *can* be made.

The monograph of Joan M. Hussey, *The Orthodox Church in the Byzantine Empire,* offers the second survey.[2] In her highly respected book, the eminent British Byzantinist provides us with a valuable, albeit strictly historical, description of the evolution of the Byzantine Church with insightful comments on particular personalities and events.[3] The messages which one gets by paraphrasing these headings may be the following: a) that Byzantium made its debut with a theological preoccupation in mind, in fact, with a chain of debates over the fundamentals of its belief in Christ or, more precisely, about the Godhead as a Trinity of persons – debates which lasted until the eighth century, if in fact they have ever stopped; b) that those "theoretical" controversies had yet another "practical" existential turn in the 120-year debate over the appropriateness of making and venerating icons – a question which was dealt with also as a purely Christological matter; c) that the Byzantine Church had its own moments of renaissance, of high intellectual and ecclesiastical self-assurance, exemplified by such personalities as Patriarch Photius (858–67, 877–86); and, d) that in Byzantium, ecclesiastical authority, although associated with imperial authority, differed with it when crude politics and expediency wanted to prevail. This was the case of Emperor Leo VI (866–905) and Patriarch Nicholas Mysticus (ruled 901–907, 912–925) over the Emperor's demand for a fourth marriage. Clearly, Henry VIII had a counterpart in the East, with the difference that in the East the matter did not end up with a splinter national Church as in England. Let us continue with the subsequent points: e) the

Constantinopolitan Bishop enjoyed, as the Patriarch of the capital city, moments of predominance, but found himself embroiled in a competition with the Bishop of the senior Rome over what, in the earliest Church, was a "presidency over love," which evolved in subsequent centuries into a matter of "authority"; f) at the time when the West was emerging from the disasters of the "barbarian invasions," Byzantium was losing its Eastern provinces to the "sons of Ishmael" and entering an era of long and passionate struggle with a new rival, Islam; g) Byzantine Christianity itself tasted the fury of the Western Crusades equally, if not more vehemently, than the "infidels"; and finally, h) attempts at reconciliation between East and West remained precisely that – attempts – which did not help Byzantium to survive in the end. Having bled badly from the wars with the Arabs and the Crusades, particularly the Fourth Crusade (1204–1261), Byzantium succumbed to the Ottoman Turks (1453). The empire fell, and with it, the Church (although not the Tradition) of an empire. Hussey retells this familiar history with a punctuating accuracy and authoritative skill.

The third survey is *Byzantine Theology: Historical Trends and Doctrinal Themes* by the late John Meyendorff (1926–1992), a prominent Russian priest, scholar and spiritual teacher.[4] In this book, Meyendorff discusses the events and the themes that shaped Byzantine Christianity, especially after the Fourth Ecumenical Council (Chalcedon, 451), namely, the Iconoclastic crisis, which brought monks and humanists in conflict with each other; the Schism between East and West; and the encounter of Byzantine Christianity with the West. The issues with which Byzantine theology preoccupied itself are, again according to Meyendorff: Creation, Man,[5] Jesus Christ, the Holy Trinity or the Triune God, Sacramental Theology, the Cycle of Life, the Eucharist, and the Church in the World. The sequence of issues in itself is a meaningful insight into Byzantine theology and spirituality; and, it is interesting that the book concludes with a brief chapter called "Antinomies." Byzantine life and theology is, indeed, a phenomenon and an experience of antinomies, not contradictions. Antinomy is the recognition of finding balance and meaning in seemingly contradictory categories; in fact, this is the inherent finesse and the essence of apophatic theology.

The overriding sense which one collectively gains from these three expositions is threefold: firstly, that faith and theology permeated and were organically intertwined with all aspects of Byzantine life, politics, culture, intellect, ideology. Secondly, in living, articulating, expressing and defending its faith, Byzantium demonstrated, by temperament and conviction, a high degree of commitment, even a passion. Thirdly, Byzantine Christianity, with a natural predisposition towards the experiential, made mysticism become the pervasive characteristic of its religious expression and spirituality. All three characteristics are, in fact, behind the very survival of Byzantine Christianity and its spirituality, even at the absence of an empire – and, possibly, *because* of it! The Romanian Byzantinist Nikolae Iorga (1871–1940) has written about this continuity under the catching title *Byzance après Byzance* [Byzantium After Byzantium],[6] which is not necessarily a continuation of a history of Eastern mediaeval emperors, patriarchs, armies and courts, but of a whole civilization and a religious experience.[7] Byzantine spiritual experience continues to exist not only in historical research or in museums, but also in the faith and spirituality of Orthodox countries, in Orthodox communities everywhere, and among people all over the world who have discovered Orthodoxy. The Byzantine ethos is alive and well today, and not in the context of a theologically loaded society like in Byzantium, but in the midst of a pluralistic, diversified, fragmented and secularized world. It makes even more sense in such a world. Such a spiritual tradition is found not simply in libraries and institutions of learning, in manuscripts, books and artistic resources, in buildings, museums and specialized exhibitions,[8] but more importantly, in human beings, in small communities and parishes, in brotherhoods and sisterhoods, in places where they form the official "majority" and in places where they are an "ethnic" or religious "minority." Indeed, the Orthodox Church, as the heir of this tradition, has long ago ceased to be sociologically and geographically "Byzantine" or "Eastern." But we must also admit that certain moments, mentalities and expressions of its ecclesiastical institution, distinguishing between the theandric ontology of the Church and its historical human-cultural dimension, have become largely irrelevant precisely because some of its people in places of decision and administration are longing to resuscitate that

Byzantium which long ago died: the imperial, despotic, avaricious, intriguer Byzantium.

For students of Byzantium and for those who feel they are its heirs, it is important to demythologize Byzantium, to lift out layer after layer of its mundane, ordinary, and even demonic, elements that every human society breeds in itself, to discover its inner quality and to concentrate on its core and the essence of its spirituality. Byzantine spirituality, as not an angelic but a human experience, makes sense and makes a difference in the context of its history and beyond, and not in a vacuum. The grand schemes, structures and institutions may not be here, perhaps fortunately, but the ethos and the soul of Byzantium can be easily detected by the objective and discerning eye.

What is, then, the organic material that makes the fabric of Byzantine ethos and spirituality? I will summarize it, with some elation for its strength and with a sense of contrition for any deficiency today, in three broad, antinomical but complementary pairs of adjectives: the monastic-social ethos, the liturgical-synodical ethos, and the mystical-epistemological ethos. The seemingly unrelated or antinomical adjectives form their own synthesis and integration. The essence of Orthodoxy is to deal with antinomical categories, which together strike the *isorropon*, that is, the balanced, upright, or *ortho*-dox position, as the Fathers of the Seventh Council at Nicaea (787) put it.[9]

The Monastic-Social Ethos

The word "monastic," from the Greek *monos,* thence *monachos* in Greek, or "monk" in English, means "solitary," "alone," and even "unique." However, "solitary" in the Orthodox Tradition and experience does not imply "self-centred." Monasticism is essentially a communal life with other persons, with the entire human community, and with creation, in communion with God. Monasticism does not exist for its own sake, nor does it concentrate on or glorify the individual for his or her own sake, even though it is a life of personal exercise and struggle for one's personal salvation and for the salvation of the world. For a self-centred individual, the Greek language uses the word *atomon* ("atom"), which is radically different from a "person."[10] An individual can be more properly applied to an "it" in its minimalist state when something can no longer be "divided" into any smaller denomination or molecule. Individual and individualism is the rendering of a human being to merely matter. How little have we contemplated the implications of this cherished idea and notion in our modern secular, materialistic and consumerist world, where "individual" rights take precedence over personal rights and social obligations, and where every weird individualistic desire and lifestyle is fortified behind the schizophrenic notion of "individual" rights of such-and-such "community"! For Byzantine spirituality, accentuated by its monastic ethos, a human being is first and foremost a *person*, a notion whose etymology (in Greek *pros-opon*) and meaning connote reciprocal relationship with one's own self and with others. The notion "individual" applied to humans betrays the cruel distortion of our nature, which the materialistic view of man and life has imposed upon each one of us. The monastic view of man, on the other hand, begins with the affirmation of *prosopon*, as the unalienable image of God in every human being, and of its dynamic to become a "likeness of God" and thus share in the divine life with divine grace, by human initiative and struggle. In its essence the monastic ethos of Byzantine spirituality begins from the value of the human nature as a given, and concentrates on rendering it deified; it is the application of the Christian belief in God as a matter of human existentialism.

The belief in God in Trinity was not fought and defended in Byzantine Christianity as an intricate novel theory, or as a "doctrine," but as an *experience* of a *personal* Being, who exists and relates with Himself, his Word and Logos, and with his Spirit, "eternally and in love," as Maximus the Confessor (c.580–622) put it, and who shares his life with the world he created. This personal God, from here and now, is the life whom human beings are called to experience. In Orthodox Christianity the ineffable God, who is "one substance, one Godhead, one virtue, one will, one operation, one principality, one power, one domination, one kingdom," becomes "known, in three perfect persons and adored with one adoration, believed in and worshiped by every rational creature, united without confusion and distinct without separation, which is beyond understanding" (John of Damascus c.655–749).[11] Christian life as a way of life in general, and monasticism in particular, make sense only within the context of the Trinitarian theology and of Orthodox anthropology, which make the human a person, in the fullest sense of the word, and a participant in the divine life. Monasticism, even in its strictest ascetic form of Anthony (c.251–356)[12] and Pachomius[13] (c.292–346), does not constitute an isolation or celebration of the individual; it manifests the Christian communion of saints and the ontological reality of the Church, in its most intimate and sacramental sense, as the very Body of Christ whose members are in communion among themselves and with Christ. Monasticism is neither independent from the life of the Church nor a substitute, but rather, an affirmation and a celebration of the redemptive nature of the Church. The monastic community is the microcosm of the Church in all its functions. Monasticism was not invented as an alternative to the Church; it was constituted as a paradigm of the life, catholicity (meaning, truthfulness and wholeness), fellowship, worship and witness of the Church.[14] Thus, while *extra ecclesiam nulla salus* ("outside the Church" – meaning outside the mystical Body of Christ – "there is no salvation") according to Irenaeus of Lyon (d. c.202), outside monasticism there *is* salvation; and Byzantine Christianity understood the difference perfectly well. Without duplicating monasticism's daily rigorous lifestyle, which was for the few, Byzantine Christianity allowed the monastic ethos to penetrate its own life as a guiding force and as a means of protecting the salt of the Church in the world from losing its taste. Orthodox Christianity has been preserved and has had a lasting influence through history precisely because of this cross-fertilization with the monastic ideals and ethos. Clearly, we have here a truly *social* ethos!

By its very nature, monasticism has a place, a responsibility and a mission within the Church, as every member has towards the "others." Even in its earliest anchorite form of departing from the world for the desert, not to mention its cenobitic form, monasticism was always in relationship with the world. Anthony left the world, but monasticism allowed the world to come to him, and he returned to the world to provide it with spiritual solace. Although not *of* the world and physically not *in* the world, monasticism is *part of* the world, for the sake of the world, "for the life of the world." The latter are words of the great monastic hierarch Basil (330–379) from his liturgy, which Orthodox Christianity has celebrated since the fourth century.

Monasticism sees the world as the domain of God that has to be claimed constantly from the evil one; for God's is "the Kingdom, and the power and the glory, for ever and ever." This world has to remain the *kosmos* of God as it was meant to be. To this end, monasticism, through prayer and other exercise, is devoted to the remembrance and affirmation of the Lordship of God alone. Prayer is interwoven with every activity, and every activity is prayer (even breathing itself for the advanced monk). The life of a monk revolves around a *liturgical* life which, as the word indicates (*leitos*=public + *ergon*=function), is a social function, in community and communion. Prayer, both personal and communal, is the heart, the breath and the *raison d' être* of monastic life. In the early days, before some monks were ordained to serve as priests in the monastic community (the *koinonion*) monks used to go out to nearby parish churches to participate in the liturgy and receive communion. Then the monastic *typika* (or orders of services), which evolved within monastic communities, were transplanted and became part of the liturgical order of the parishes. The frequent services of night and day at designated times and hours (midnight prayers, Hours, Matins, Divine Liturgy, Compline or after-dinner service, Vespers) punctuated and continue to punctuate the cycle of night and day in Orthodox monasteries. The same prayers were observed by the faithful living in the world. Thus, the monastic and the community living in the world were united in prayer. In reality, the entire life of prayer and the spiritual exercise and behaviour associated with it, like fasting, repentance, prostrations, candles, veneration of icons and relics of saints, have all been transplanted into the world; thence came the lasting "liturgical" contribution of monasticism in Orthodox spirituality.

Never was the monastery, its life and ethos, divorced from the life of society. The expression "in the desert" was for monasteries located outside the city limits in remote places, these being centres for "hermits" (from the Greek *eremos*, meaning desert) and ascetics (from Greek *askesis*, meaning spiritual exercise). Monastic communities in Byzantium were often located in urban centres, even at the heart of a city. Constantinople was embellished with public buildings but also with monastic communities.[15] By the year 536 there were some seventy monasteries in the capital.[16] Where temples once stood during classical times with statues of deities and emperors, now crosses, churches and monasteries dedicated to Christ and saints were decorating the cities. A city with a church possessing the relics of a saint or martyr, more often than not of a local man or woman from the monastic community, was considered to be particularly blessed![17] The sounds of the market and the city traffic were mixed with the bells, the hymns and the activities of monasteries; the smells of the city were mingled with the incense of prayer.

The gates of the monasteries were open not only for the faithful to come in and pray, but also for the homeless to find shelter, for the hungry to receive a meal, for the sick to be given medical care, for the persecuted to hide, for the orphan to find protection, and for the illiterate to learn how to read and write![18] The whole monastic ideal and life were integrated into the life of the world, for the life of the world. Orthodox Christianity in general, and Orthodox monasticism in particular, have nothing to do with the Manichean or dualistic view of life which polarizes and divorces the spiritual from the material. Byzantine religious life and spirituality were shaped by the ethos of the cenobitic community, an ethos which is intrinsically social, communal, based on humility, poverty, obedience, simplicity, love, interdependence, seeking of the essential, concern for the whole world, revolving around and nourished by prayer. Prayer (in Greek *pros-euche*) is an act of extension (*pros*) in petition and hope (*euche*); in itself, it is an act of communication and communion with God, with one's own self, with one's fellow human beings, and with the creation as a whole. Never can prayer be an individualistic endeavour, even when done alone. Even the Jesus prayer, "Lord Jesus Christ, have mercy on me, a sinner," is meritorious not only for the person who repeats it, but also for the rest of the world. Divine mercy has a redeeming value for the world as a whole, as do fasting, poverty and humility – even celibacy itself. These are penitential, human and thus societal, communal qualities and expressions shared with the rest of humanity. The monastic ethos denies, or rather, transcends the individualistic "atomic" self and embraces the whole person, the whole of society, and the whole of life; only then is monasticism truly monastic. Because of its denial of self, pride, and the vices of the old Adam, all of which the world refuses stubbornly to abandon, monasticism is a phenomenon of witness (*martyria*) and sacrifice (*martyrion*), two consequential and complementary categories. No wonder that since the early Church, the life of the monk and the witness of the martyr were considered as Baptisms, the one a Baptism of tears and the other a Baptism of blood: both expressions of an imitation of Christ and of true Christian life. One could remember here the words of Ignatius, Bishop of Antioch (c.35–107), pleading with the Christians of Rome not to interfere with his execution so that he "may be [called] Christian not merely in name but in fact."[19]

Therefore, the monastic ethos that began in the East became an integral part of Byzantine Christianity and continues to be so within the Orthodox tradition. This ethos is permeated by the following motivations and characteristics: a profound sense of the dignity of the human nature that, although taken captive by the evil one, remains in an undiminished way thirsty for, and able to be reunited with, the divine, on account of the incarnation of God-the-Word; a profound sense of an integral communion of the human community; a profound love and thankfulness (*eucharistia*) to God for the gift of his Son; a convinced affirmation of the sanctity of life and the value of the material creation; a sense of responsibility for witness and sacrifice (*martyria* and *martyrion*) for a world which prefers to live under the pangs of death. These characteristics are not abstractions; they derive from the history, literature, and the very life of Eastern monasticism and result in the monastic ethos and the social orientation of Orthodoxy. Byzantine Christianity did not develop monastic orders with a specialized mission to the world or to the Church, because its realm is the world and its function is the life of the Church.

Where and when this monastic ethos prevailed, it wrought enlightened figures of sanctity, leadership and letters. It cultivated a rich spirituality which has enabled peoples and societies to survive under lengthy and ruthless rule of anti-Christian or atheist regimes. Some societies emerged in the end victorious, as in the case of Greece under Ottoman rule and of Eastern European countries under communism. Particular monastic communities in Constantinople, Syria, Palestine, Athos and elsewhere inculcated, articulated and defended the Orthodox doctrine when political or ecclesiastical expediency and obscurantism syncretized or diluted this faith. They became themselves centres of learning when, especially after Justinian, the state closed public schools of higher education. Monasticism cultivated and fostered the ecclesiastical arts, iconography, hymnography, music, when the state and society turned iconoclast. Monasticism moulded ideal bishops and the leadership of the Church and, more often than not, monastic communities became the refuge for emperors and state bureaucrats. The example of Emperor Cantacuzenos (fl.1341–1376), assuming in the end the monastic habit under the name Ioasaph, comes readily to one's mind. In the seventh century, the century which Byzantinists claim ushered in the so-called "Dark Ages of Byzantium," academies were closed in Syria and Palestine, a region which had fallen into the hands of the Muslim Arabs. For approximately the next hundred and fifty years there developed a whole "circle" or school of reform-minded, monastically oriented intellectuals who transformed the Mar Sabba monastery in the Judean desert into a fertile oasis of spirituality, hymnography, letters, rhetoric, hagiography, systematic theology, apologetics, and a centre of liturgical renewal which determined the typicon of the Constantinopolitan Church, of Athos and even of the Jacobite Church. The intellectual and spiritual activity of "the circle of John of Damascus" permeated the life of Byzantium and prepared successfully the Christian population of the Middle East to withstand the Arab onslaught. This "circle" is a wide one and includes such personalities as Sophronius, Patriarch of Jerusalem (c.634–638);[20] Maximus the Confessor; Leontius of Neapolis (c.590–650); Anastasius Sinaites (c.640–700); Andrew of Crete (c.660-740); Peter of Maium (d. 743); Cosmas of Maium (c.674–751); and especially the towering figure of John of Damascus, [21] as well as the perpetuator of the latter's tradition, Theodore Abu Qûrra (c.750–820). One is tempted to mention here another great Syrian poet, Romanos the Melodist (d. after 555) only because Karl Krumbacher made, for a moment, an attempt to re-date his life from the sixth to the eighth century.[22] Thus the so-called "Dark Ages of Byzantium" may not, after all, be proven so dark considering this religious renaissance, not only for Syria and Palestine in the seventh century, but for Byzantium at large throughout its history. For this thanks is due, almost exclusively, to monasticism. What is quite fascinating is how monastic ethos and spiritual and intellectual enlightenment go hand in hand, especially when fasting and prayer overtake the library.

If Western and North American Orthodoxy are to recapture the spirit of Byzantine spirituality and produce an Orthodox renaissance and a spiritual renewal, North American Orthodoxy needs to recapture its healthy traditional monastic ethos.[23]

The Liturgical-Synodical Ethos

For the Byzantines, belief was not an abstraction nor was prayer a detached ritual. Belief meant an existential experience of God permeating and affecting every aspect of life; prayer meant the living expression of this faith embracing the whole of the person, one's mind, soul and body, and the whole creation. Both the belief and the prayer had to be *ortho*-dox – "orthodox" – meaning comprehensive, encompassing and thence truthful. Eastern Christendom had understood the "belief in one, holy, *catholic* and apostolic Church" of the Nicene Creed as pointing to the wholeness (*kath-olon*) and truthfulness of the Church by preserving the wholeness (catholicity) of faith, not by maintaining its coincidence with the political borders (universal) of the Roman Empire. Interestingly, from the seventh century onwards, the expression "Orthodox" was used as a substitute for "catholic." "Orthodox" is not a claim to a status quo but to a dynamic state of being. "Orthodox," from the Greek *orthros*, meaning upright, claims the uniquely and finely defined position that inclines neither to the right nor to the left, as the Fathers of the II Nicaea put it – the absolutely and delicately balanced vertical position among various individual inclinations, idiosyncratic expressions, or "preferences" (*haereseis*) of faith (the latter, in fact, is the literal meaning of the word "heresy").

As an existential experience, Orthodoxy is expressed in an upright *doxa*, which means both faith and glory, or worship of God. There can be no right faith without a right glory and worship of God, just as there can be no right worship of God if this is not the outcome of a right faith. Right faith results in right and true prayer, and right prayer cultivates right faith. "If you are a Theologian, you will pray in truth; and if you pray truly, you are a Theologian," says Evagrius of Pontus (d.399) in one of his maxims On Prayer.[24] Bishop Kallistos of Diokleia comments, "Dogmas are nothing else than the crystallization of that which the saints have experienced in prayer, while prayer in its turn is the dogmas of the faith affirmed existentially."[25] Christianity is a redemptive religion whose message and experience culminates in the resurrection. For the Byzantines the liturgical life is a celebration of the resurrection, the experience of heaven here and now. This is the natural expression of Christianity and this is how, allegedly, the envoys of Volodymyr reported to him their impression of the liturgy they attended at St. Sophia in Constantinople: "We knew not whether we were in heaven or on earth, for surely there is no such splendour or beauty anywhere upon earth . . . We cannot forget that beauty"! In the magnificent celebration of the Eucharist, Byzantine Christianity was not looking for a panacea; it was truly celebrating the event of God on earth and reaffirming life in its true and ontological sense. Its faith and liturgical experience and legacy were that of the reality of God's dispensation in flesh, Christ's redemptive work and his resurrection. Because of this organic connection between faith and worship, or prayer, in these presentations there has been no suggestion of a "theological" ethos, as an independent expression, being characteristic of Orthodoxy. From this relation one can discern the characteristics of Orthodox theology.

Byzantine religious life and theology were captivated by the event of the Resurrection, and Orthodox spirituality was saturated by the event of the risen humanity, of the light, colour and the transfiguration of the material creation. Orthodox worship, then, was animated by that spark of the Resurrection and incorruptibility, which enlightens and gives meaning to this speck of the universe of ours. Earliest Christianity and, subsequently, the Orthodox world, replaced conscientiously the Sabbath with the *Kyriake*, the "day of the Lord," in which Christ with his Resurrection manifested that he is, indeed, the Lord of life. One should certainly remain mystified by the fact that on "Sunday," the day of the Lord, the whole world, including the Christian world, is still honouring some pagan sun god!

For the Orthodox, the whole religious experience revolves around, culminates and finds its meaning in the celebration of Christ's triumph over death. The Resurrection makes the Church not an institution (and an intransigent one at that) but an earthly, *as well as* an eschatological body – the Body of the risen Christ! The eucharistic community finds its integrity and solidarity in the liturgical celebration of the Resurrection, in which also the material creation participates as humanity's thankful celebration and shares in the event of redemption and restoration. This eucharistic-liturgical experience is what the Orthodox bring to their life and to the life of the world.[26]

From the liturgical experience of the Resurrection, all other services and prayers emerged with the aim of prolonging the celebration from night throughout day. The intense prayer cycle that the monastic life introduced and preserved begins from the evening, the forerunner of the day, and progresses through the night to the following day; it is God's own process of creation: "And became evening, and became morning, day one . . ." (Gen. 1:5)! All Orthodox prayer services are either a celebration, or an antecedent, consequence, foretaste or aftertaste, of the paschal eucharistic service. In these services the material creation participates in the forms of water, bread, wine, icons, candles, light, incense, gold, silver, wood, flowers, leaves . . . Without losing identity, everything is transfigured and finds its ontology as part of God's *cosmos*. Also with commemorations, prayers and actions, those "who have fallen asleep" join the living members into one Church. Nothing in the liturgical life that Orthodoxy inherited from Byzantium has come from the individual or the "private sector." Everything has arisen out from the experience and the practice of the Body. Only later, as an uncritical adaptation of custom, are "private" liturgies (a contradiction in terms) celebrated. Alternatively, "private" services and sacraments are performed, or "private" churches are built for individual persons or families. All sacraments, with the possible exception of the holy unction, the service of "blessing of oil," or *euchelaion*, were public services taking place in the context of the eucharistic liturgy. Even the sacrament of holy unction is performed at least once a year, on Good Wednesday, for the entire congregation in preparation for Holy Communion either on Good Thursday, the day of the institution of the Eucharist, or on Easter Sunday – a forceful reminder that every service is a communal, *liturgical* and *synodical* action, not a separate or individual one.

The central act of worship of the Church was meant to be truly communal and participatory. Hence its name *liturgy* – a Greek word from *leitos*, meaning people, or public, and *ergon*, or function, that is, a work *of* the people *for* the people, in the context of which the Eucharist and the act of coming together, the communion *par excellence,* take place. That is why the liturgical must be combined with the synodical ethos of Christianity.

Eucharistic liturgical communion is the source from which *all* prayer services and all Church functions, structures, institutions, activities and arts derive. Byzantine spirituality and the entire Church life are liturgically-eucharistically founded and oriented; otherwise, there is not in them a shred of authentic Christian characteristic. Church integrity and Christian fellowship derive from the liturgical-eucharistic ethos of the Church. Apostolicity, continuity and catholicity, dogma, spirituality, repentance and reconciliation, social action, ecumenical dialogue and, most importantly, *authority* all derive from the liturgical-eucharistic ethos of the Church. The ranks of the sacerdotium, deacons, presbyters and bishops, are first not managerial, or judicial-authoritarian ranks, but liturgical-eucharistic functions. "Authority" in the Church is exercised and manifested as a truly *liturgical-synodical* process, not as an individual, or a seemingly collective function.

All Church art, iconography, architecture, hymnography and music are not merely aesthetic pieces but intentionally liturgical expressions. They were executed by various people (the Church in action) who were less "artists" and more persons of prayer, and used as a means of prayer, preservation of faith, cultivation and maturation of the spirituality of all members of the Church. The Church's aesthetic-liturgical elements are meant to be instruments of *catechesis*, a word literally meaning "tuning according to the echos," or tone and ethos of the Church, and an aid to one's meaningful participation in the life of the Body. Leontius of Neapolis (c.590–650) and later John of Damascus, for example, called the icon an open book for the illiterate. Indeed, the icon is theology in colour![27] The liturgical-eucharistic essence, character and ethos of the Church give meaning and substance to the reality of the Church as the *Body* of Christ. It cultivates communion of the members with each other, and promotes a responsible participation in the life of the Church. Thus, the opposite of these has been rightfully termed eucharistically as "ex-communication," that is, severing from the liturgical-eucharistic bond!

There is also another inherent and dynamic connotation in the liturgical life and ethos of the Church. Every liturgical-eucharistic communion is a living experience of that "walking together" towards Emmaus between the two disciples and the risen Jesus, their offering of hospitality at the journey's end, and experiencing a full realization of the risen Christ "in the breaking of the bread" (Luke 24:13–35)! Such is the ground and the essence of the "synodical" ethos (in Russian, *soborni*) of Byzantine Church life and spirituality. There are crucial implications and a profound meaning behind this metaphorical expression of "synodical" vis-à-vis "conciliar" life of the Church. "Walking together" (in Greek *syn-odos,* or synod) points to an active, standing and moving process. Eastern Christianity consistently employed metaphorical expressions to speak of the mystery of theology and of the life of the Church, thus transcending the rational convention of language.

The Biblical expression for the earliest Christian community was "the Way" (Acts 9:2); thus the synodical ethos, or the experience of "walking together," is the natural outcome of Christian life. It connotes a physical, existential participation, a personal commitment, effort, sacrifice and pain, and it implies a sense of direction and a hope towards achieving a goal. The Semitic culture expressed in Judaism is centred around and expressed in the notion of household, or family. Christianity, which began as a movement, exceeded that. That which was "a household" of Abraham and a "nation" of Israel, Christianity transformed into a *Body*, the mystical Body of Christ: something organic, indivisible, dynamic, in motion! The "synagogue" or gathering together became an *ekklesia* (from *ek-kalein*), or "those called apart." The first official activity of the Church was an Apostolic *synod*, a walking together, in Antioch, 50 A.D. The earliest anchorites "those who departed [from the world]" formed *cenobitic* (living-together) communities of fellow ascetics and athletes, each *coenobium* being the microcosm of the universal Church. Every local church, no matter how small, was the catholic Church and every liturgy an act of and for the entire Body.

The ultimate unity of the Church was manifested in the partaking of communion taking place always at the liturgical, eucharistic gathering. The celebrant of the Eucharist was the bishop and on the local level an *elder*, a presbyter, whose title implies that there is a broader family which includes other junior celebrants and members. The bishop was an *episkopos* (an overseer) over the well-being of the flock, presiding over and manifesting the eucharistic unity and catholicity of the Church. Rather than a "manager," let alone a "despot" of the Church, the bishop was the chief celebrant of the Eucharist! An "archbishop," a word that implies other bishops acting in concord with the first among equals, headed each larger diocese. Larger regions were called "Metropoleis" and "Patriarchates," derived from the words "mother" and "father" respectively, implying a broader ecclesial family consisting of archbishops, metropolitans, bishops, presbyters, deacons, monks, nuns and lay people. Lastly, but not least, the Church's catholicity and orthodoxy, two interwoven and interchangeable notions, were manifested and expressed in "synods." Thus, the Church's definitions were measured by synodical consensus and catholic acceptance.

All these expressions and manifestations show how real and lively the eucharistic-synodal ethos was in the Byzantine Church and how it produced a meaningful sacramental communal life, and a meaningful role for each member within the Body. In today's rationalistic corporate mentality we have paid little attention to the practical consequences that the mystical and theological concept of the Church as "Body" implies, and much less to the notion and the implications of the notion "synodical" for the decision-making process, authority, roles and functions, hierarchy, personal rights, group "rights," etc.

Considering dangers, distance, impediments, cost and all the negative logistics of those days, synods during the Byzantine era were numerous and frequent. With the passing of time and the elimination of such impediments, the Church has become much less synodical. Of the many such synods, undivided Christendom acknowledged only seven as "Ecumenical," that is, as binding upon the universal Church – a rather discerning, critical and discriminating way of measuring authenticity! Byzantine Christianity was, one could say, elitist about that which had to do with faith and salvation. As "Ecumenical," those councils dealt with and defined the fundamentals, rather than the incidentals, of faith and of Christian life. Even these seven Councils must be treated not as *seven* councils, separate the one from the other, but as a total and integral phenomenon – the synodical process and voice of the Church. Each Council defined the *horos*, that is, the border of faith, on a given issue after reciting the *horos* of the previous council and then adding to it or making its own clarification. The process by which a Council reached its *horos* is in itself instructive and interesting, although time-consuming to fully describe here. Some of its elements were an examination of the credentials of the participants; an opportunity for those who deviated from the *catholic* faith to repent from their heresy; an examination of the heretical nature of a position, refutation, presentation of living witnesses of both sides of the argument; the reading of synodical letters from all Patriarchates of the Pentarchy or their representatives; another opportunity for repentance of the heretics and re-alignment with the faith of the Church; the reading of previous definitions and *florilegia* or anthologies pertinent to the subject; and eventually reaching a consensus on a definition at hand. Doctrinal definitions were never the result of a judicial process of a majority vote on a motion! The mystery of God's personhood in Trinity, or the mystery of the incarnation of God-the-Word in Christ, or the mystery of the two natures in the one person of Christ, are not matters of motions and of a majority vote. The synodical ethos of the Byzantine Church gave primacy to the *consensus*, the liturgical, eucharistic and organic cohesiveness, more so than to a judicial authority, to the "unity of faith and communion of the Holy Spirit," rather than to uniformity. By-zantine Christianity has shown an unreserved confidence, and risk, in the real presence and work of the Holy Spirit within the Church and an immense amount of trust towards its people.

A synodical ethos is reflective of fundamental convictions, something which means that the absence of such an ethos abrogates such convictions. This ethos affirms that the Church is a Body in motion, not a static institution or structure. The life of the Church is an experience of walking *together* with the risen Christ and with fellow communicants towards a union with God the Father, under the guidance of the Holy Spirit. Such an ethos affirms that the faith of the Church (or *dogma*) is the very experience of the Body lived and expressed in a way that "it seems good to us *and* the Holy Spirit," rather than an experience of an abstract directive imposed by some authority. The Church in Synod does not produce doctrines but identifies individual "preferences," abolishes inclinations ("heresies"), and affirms "what everywhere, what always, and that which has been believed by everyone," to use the expression of Vincent of Lérins (d.c.445), defining thus the *isorropon,* that is, the balanced and the *orthodox*. Finally, a synodical ethos affirms the Church as a divine-human reality that has a self-awareness of her unique integrity and authority and neither depends upon, nor seeks the approval of, the secular politically motivated authorities.

Councils did not convene in a vacuum or simply for the purpose of meeting. Behind the definitions made by Councils, there was the mind and sensitivity of the Church manifesting the mind of the Gospel, the uninterrupted and living Tradition, and the ethos of the Fathers, without promoting any personal theology. Therefore, behind the councils of Nicaea (325) and Constantinople (381) and the ingenious expression that the Son is consubstantial (*homoousios*) to the Father may stand the thought of Athanasius of Alexandria (c.296–373) and of the Cappadocian Fathers. Behind the Council of Ephesus (431) one may discern the thought of Cyril of Alexandria (d.444), or behind Nicaea II (787) the theology of John of Damascus. However, none of the synodical *horoi* were issued under the name of these theologians, or on their behalf. The participant bishops, presbyters, monks and even lay people (few though these may have been) did not get together in order to invent new doctrines, nor were they presuming that they could explain the mystery of God in Trinity and his dispensation in Christ.[28] They articulated in synod the trans-historical faith of the Church under the guidance of God-the-Holy-Spirit. The synodical ethos, enacted upon vigorously by Byzantine Christianity, is a celebration of faith in the living reality of the Holy Spirit "who proceeds from the Father," "the heavenly king, the Paraclete, the Spirit of truth."

A doxological, prayerful, *liturgical* disposition, in the full meaning of these words, leads naturally to a synodical living of the Christian experience, and the two together encompass and "define" the mystery of Christian ecclesiology. The one separated from the other deteriorates into ritualism on the one hand, and religious organization on the other. We must admit that in the post-Byzantine Orthodox Church nothing has suffered more than its liturgical-synodical tradition and ethos: a tragic legacy of Turkocracy and communism. Orthodox Christians have a unique liturgical-synodical experience and ethos to offer to the Christian community at large; but they also need to recapture this ethos of the one undivided Church, the Church of the pre-Ottoman or non-imperial Byzantium, that, unfortunately, they have let wither!

The Mystical-Epistemological Ethos

This topic has to do with knowledge: what it is and how it is attained; how the Orthodox Church is working and what makes her work; how the Church is "thinking"; what, and of what kind, are her experiences; and how she understands and projects herself. In trying to describe the "mental" ethos of Eastern Orthodoxy, I would consider and touch upon three topics which highlight what I have termed the mystical-epistemological ethos of Byzantine Christianity: the Cappadocian patristic legacy; the phenomenon of Iconoclasm as an Eastern Reformation; and hesychasm, the Christian existentialism and epistemology *par excellence*, or theology of the heart. In addition to being central subjects in the cultural and spiritual history of Byzantium, these topics include in themselves deeper and essential matters of Byzantine Christianity. Thus in discussing the topic of the Cappadocian Fathers one should try, in essence, to discern in it the inherent notion of "Tradition," its meaning and role in Byzantine Christianity. In discussing Iconoclasm, one should allow oneself to also hear what religious and spiritual "renewal," or responsible, personal and manifest faith meant to the Byzantines. In discussing Hesychasm, one should try to sensitize oneself to the fundamental in Byzantine spirituality, the eloquence and rhetoric of "quietness" *(hesychia),* and then pursue it!

The Cappadocian Patristic Legacy

The Roman province of east-central Asia Minor, Cappadocia, proved fertile ground for the spreading and flourishing of Christianity. The list of earliest converts to Christianity on the day of Pentecost includes Cappadocians (Acts 2:9). The salutations of the first "catholic" epistle of Peter (1:1) include the Cappadocians among the "chosen ones of the diaspora." Christians of the diaspora, of any diaspora, have had through the ages the best chance (if they understood their role properly) to be proven "chosen"! The fourth century saw the flourishing of Cappadocian Christianity and Christian thought in the persons of Basil of Caesarea, known as "the Great," his brother Gregory of Nyssa (331/40–c.395), and their friend Gregory of Nazianzus (c.329–90), one of only three figures upon whom the Church bestowed the title "the Theologian." It is neither coincidental nor insignificant for the evolution of the Patristic ethos that there are several connecting links among these Fathers of the Church. They were bound by a physical relationship and by a profound bond of natural love: all three became hierarchs of the Church; all three stood up against secular and sectarian forces; all three made charity and social responsibility the centrepiece of their personal life, and of the office of the bishop which they held; all three were admirers and supporters of the monastic life and its ethos; and all three were lovers of learning.[29] All this makes for a fatherly position in the Church and for an effective and lasting impact on it. Attuned to precision and balance, they sought to find the underlying cause of Arianism and its implications. They left their mark on the Church by treating doctrine as a *redemptive experience* and a way of life, rather than as an intellectual mental exercise. This is exactly what was lacking in Arianism and Pneumatomachianism (the heresies which questioned the consubstantiality of the Son, and of the Holy Spirit to the Father, respectively).

However, under the rubric "Cappadocian Patristic legacy," one should not confine oneself to or presume just three specific Fathers of the Church and great hierarchs but, again, discern the phenomenon and the ethos they represent. The entire Christian East has been wrought by the influence of the Cappadocian Patristic legacy. What bestows the title "Father" to a theologian are the following qualifications: that of sanctity of life, orthodoxy of thought, and universal acceptance along with an uninterrupted influence upon the Church. As it is impossible to give manifestation of these qualities for each of the three Cappadocians, I will restrict myself to the third qualification, that of continuity and acceptability, as it speaks of the character of Byzantine Christianity and its ethos in relationship to history and culture.

Although scholars are polarized on this matter, it seems that the Cappadocian Fathers, deeply rooted in the Hellenistic mind and culture, strove neither to Hellenize Christianity nor to Christianize Hellenism. This is a useful reminder for those who strive to acculturate Christianity, thus making Christianity a feature of their own culture, or to Christianize culture, thus pursuing a chimera – in both cases diluting Christianity. The vision of the Cappadocian Fathers was the evolution, the maturation, or, to put it theologically, the redemption of classical Hellenism rather than its change, let alone its destruction; and this is something distinctly different. Christianity transfigures; it does not destroy persons, societies, civilizations and cultures. In his incarnation, God-the-Word assumed up to himself the fallen nature and deified it. He did not destroy it, nor did he re-do it *ex nihilo.* To the Fathers of the East the pre-eternal Mind and Word of God, the *Logos,* meaning both reason *and* utterance – each being a manifestation of the other – existed in a "spermatic"[30] way before Christianity, even within pagan Hellenism. Justin the philosopher, apologist of Christianity, martyr (d.c.165), and a proud disciple of Plato, regarded reason as closely tied with Christian faith: "those who had lived by reason [meaning in truth] are Christians, even though they have been considered atheists"![31] One should note here the verb *lived.* Thus, now that "the Word became flesh and dwelt among us" (John 1:14), the Logos of God, and truth *par excellence,* had to be experienced and inculcated with the whole of the person's existence, *including the flesh!* For the Cappadocians, as it was earlier with Ignatius of Antioch (c.35–107), the designation "Christian" did not connote a "believer in" or a "follower of" Christ, but an imitator of Christ, and Christianity implied the experience of one's association with the incarnate Logos. Therefore, for the Cappadocians, Hellenism needed not to be destroyed but to be brought into the orbit of Christianity and transfigured. The Biblical story of the transfiguration (Matthew 17:1–9), the penultimate miraculous manifestation of Christ, is not only central to the Gospel narrative in unlocking the meaning of the ultimate miracle, the Resurrection, it is also the foundation of Orthodox spirituality, epistemology, and even of Christian culture. Three disciples are selected, brought up by Christ to a higher place, and there they experience even physically that which they thought they knew but could never have known on their own, which opened their eyes and also transfigured their own lives for ever!

Byzantine Christianity at its best moments strove to express the mind and the ethos of the Church in living categories of Greek thought, so that Hellenism might experience Christ. Behind this was the enlightened ethos of the Cappadocian legacy of conversion or, actually, transfiguration. Not everybody aspired to the same ethos and the same driving force. Constantine's conversion and his reign (306–323) brought about a radical change to the Christian community, moving it from the catacombs to an institution under the auspices of the empire.[32] But this may have been an ambivalent transformation; while it freed the Church from physical persecution, it let Christians become themselves enslaved into a rational-imperial mentality about the Church as a physical and visible *civitas Dei* on earth, something which Christianity itself never meant to be. The golden era of Patristic thought began with the Cappadocians and with the victory of Christianity over a different mentality, that of paganism and imperial worship of any sort. Emperor Justinian (reigned 527–65) may have been too insecure and unaffected by the Cappadocian spirit when he ordered the closure of the academies of Athens, Alexandria and other centres for breeding paganism. The Cappadocian Fathers were less fearful of the power of paganism and more confident in the power of the cross. They had, in fact, studied in those schools, learned from them, and left the mark of their own influence upon them, as they did on various aspects of Church life. Archaeology, for example, has shown that many early churches were built on sites of former pagan temples, using the stones from the same temples, not as a way of conserving material, but as a way of demonstrating the transforming power of Christianity. It is interesting that it was the *state*, especially Emperors Theodosius (379–95) and Justinian (527–65), not the Fathers or the Church, who suppressed the previous way of life and "knowledge coming from the outside" (*ten thyrathen gnosin*) since it was the *state* that originally had persecuted Christianity. The point that needs to be made here is that Byzantine religious experience and spirituality contain inherently that "Cappadocian" quality, first in terms of an awe towards the ineffable existence and power God, and then of a profound respect for humanity, in its ontological sense, its history, and culture.

The Cappadocians were at home with the Eastern mind, as well as with the ethos that produced the New Testament. Little attention has been paid to the fact that Christianity was, after all, born in the Middle East and developed in the context of the desert, with all those characteristics of an open, inclusive, optimistic, existential, mystical, lucid and spontaneous attitude towards the Wholly Other and towards life. Christianity would have been a very different religious experience if Palestine, Syria, Egypt or Asia Minor had never played a formative role in its early stages. An exercise at looking at "Windows to the East" must include a concerted effort at opening such windows and gaining through them a glimpse of the spiritual, cultural and psychological makeup, or the DNA, of the region and thus of the essence of the Christian Tradition.

Byzantine Christianity retained what could be retained from this "oriental" Tradition, even after the fall of its Eastern provinces to the forces of Islam. In fact, the cultural, religious and intellectual development, which from the middle of the sixth century had been halted in Byzantium proper, continued in a robust way for some one hundred and fifty years and beyond in the same Eastern provinces, under Islamic rule, with towering figures from within the Syro-Palestinian monastic communities of the region. They were the ones who cultivated the Greek letters, systematized the Christian theology, invented new forms of hymnography like the *kondak* [33] and the canons (a kind of elaborate *catecheses*, or systematic theology in hymns), wrote lives of saints which became the text books of the time, and renewed the order (*typikon*) of worship. They challenged the role of the state on matters of faith, developed and articulated a theology of icons, thus building a safety net for the survival of the Christian community under Muslim rule, and they prepared the ground for the Photian renaissance that arrived in the ninth and tenth centuries. Little of this "oriental" element of the desert, of the spirit of precision, of simplicity, spiritual discipline, and of deification, inherent in the very fabric of Christianity and characteristic of Byzantine Christianity, has been studied.

Christianity in general, and Byzantine Christianity in particular, its interaction with the Greco-Roman cultural notwithstanding, has more to do with the filial Semitic and Hellenistic metaphysical experience than with the Roman judicial-rational view of God. Byzantine Christianity is concerned more with unity and less with uniformity, more with

Tradition and less with conventions, more with ethos and less with definitions. Emphasis is placed on grace as opposed to law, spirituality as opposed to scholasticism, participation in a theandric and living Body as opposed to membership in an institution. Its vocabulary and categories are metaphorical, symbolic, parabolic, and fearlessly antinomical: *synod* (walking together) for "council"; *catechesis* (tuning-up) for "instruction" or "induction"; *mystery* for "sacrament"; *anaphora* (elevation from the ordinary to the unique) for the act of sanctification of the gifts of communion; *metabole* (trans-portation, or change of state of these gifts) for "transubstantiation"; *chrism* (ointment, or "making one a Messiah, Christ") for "confirmation"; *metanoia* (change of mind) for "repentance"; *liturgy* (public function) for "service"; *icon* (literally, "that which has been rendered the same") for "image"; *horos* (border) for "definition"; *dogma* (that which seemed good [to humans *and* to the Holy Spirit]) for "doctrine"; *mystical* (pertaining to God who is the mystery *par excellence*) for "systematic" theology; *Father* of the Church for "Doctor" of the Church; *holiness* for "justice"; *deification* (or *theosis,* i.e. partaking in the divine life) for "redemption"; Christ the *Victor,* for Christ the "Victim", etc. These are but a few examples of the Orthodox vocabulary over which ecumenical dialogue often stumbles. All of these aspects contrast the inner and the essential with the functional and the external.

The Cappadocian-Byzantine legacy, in letters, thought and ethos, has all those elements of mysticism, antinomy, sense of the reality of metaphysical powers, and especially the sense of the knowability of the unknown and of the existential experience of the ineffable through association and union. Byzantine theology maintains that magnificent "theocentric" view of man. In the words of John Meyendorff:

> The central theme, or intuition, of Byzantine theology is that man's nature is not a static, "closed," autonomous entity, but a dynamic reality, determined in its very existence by its relationship with God. This relationship is seen as a process of ascent and as communion to God.[34]

The Fathers of the Christian East were not "analysts" of exotic ideas, but persons who lived and taught theology as a matter of personal experience and redemption. They had something fresh and existential to say that came out of their own personal experiences. They expressed their reflections in eloquent homilies, in delicate verses and poetry, in hymns and apologies, in meditations and in prayers, and especially through their own lives. Athanasius held Arianism at bay by exposing the logical but non-redemptive value of the Arian argument. John Chrysostom (c.347–407) set the standards of social responsibility for the Church. Thomas Aquinas (1225–1274) once said that he would give all Paris for a homily written by Chrysostom.[35] Basil, the hierarch, the defender of faith and a Church philanthropist, became also the father of monasticism as an organized and integral part of the ecclesial community. Gregory of Nazianzus changed the course of understanding Christmas and Easter with five sermons delivered in a private house, and Cosmas the Melodist and John of Damascus, talented hymnographers that they were, made them into hymns for the entire Christian East to sing. John, the writer of the fourth Gospel, Gregory of Nazianzus (329–89), and Symeon the New Theologian (959–1022), the singer of union with God, were given the title "Theologian," not for their "systematic" theology, but for their experience and praise of the divine. Such are the manifestations of the mystical-epistemological ethos of Eastern Christianity.

Iconoclasm – The "Eastern Reformation"

In 726, the Byzantine Emperor Leo III the Isaurian (reigned 717–41) issued a decree forbidding the veneration of icons, declaring it to be an idolatrous practice. Little did anyone know that this unsophisticated military emperor was thus unleashing the forces of "reformation" in Eastern Christendom.[36] Iconoclasm (which lasted officially for some one hundred and nineteen years, but whose antecedents were in existence much before 726 and persisted much longer after the "triumph of Orthodoxy" in 843) was not an isolated and marginal incident in Byzantine history, nor was this controversy a matter of simply culture, art, or political expediency.[37] The lines were well drawn. Byzantine society as a whole viewed the offence against icons as a Christological, anthropological and ecclesiological heresy and it dealt with it accordingly as a continuation of the Christological controversies. Was the incarnation of God-the-Word in Christ real, imaginary or an apparition (docetism)? Does one compromise the belief and worship of a personal God when paying respect to an icon of Christ? Was human nature absorbed by, or annihilated, as a result of its union with the divine? Did human nature remain unaffected by its union with the divine? Is material creation alien to the event of the incarnation and redemption? Is it possible for humanity to know God or, even after the incarnation, for humanity to continue to remain ignorant and separated from the divine? Is human nature, which through the incarnation has been injected with holiness, able to manifest holiness through ordinary human beings, or is holiness something totally out of reach of human beings?[38] Dealing with Iconoclasm in this fashion, Byzantine Christianity underwent an examination of the application of its doctrine and expression. On this very practical level, and under the light of the theology of the icons, Byzantium brought about its own reformation from within, and, at the conclusion of this process, hailed it as "the triumph of Orthodoxy"!

Such a triumph was found not in the sophistry but in the simplicity, comprehensiveness, inclusiveness, existentialism, realism, common sense, and love for finesse and distinction of its synodical-ecclesiological experience. These qualities are manifested in the "*synodicon* of Orthodoxy" (again, a fruit of a synodical ethos) which the Council of Constantinople pronounced on that first Sunday of Lent, May 11, 843:

> As the Prophets have known; as the Apostles have taught; as the Church has received; as the Teachers have defined; as the universe has consented; as grace has made it shine; as the truth has made it manifest by lashing out at falsehood; as the wisdom has explicated; as Christ has praised thus we also think, thus we speak, thus we confess about Christ our true God and his saints: that we may honour them with words, with writings, with gestures, with sacrifices [meaning liturgical services of communion], with churches, with icons. And as far as Christ is concerned we may bow down to him and revere him as Lord. As for all the rest, we may honour them as true servants of his and *pay to them a relative veneration*; for all of us have one and a common Lord.[39]

On the topic of epistemology, there are three characteristics of Byzantine Christianity derived from this statement. First is the sense of a living, sacred, trans-historical, uninterrupted Tradition of God's reality and revelation, something which the Church cherishes (consider the litany of the "as is ...") and is keen to maintain (consider the litany of the "thus we, too, ..."). Second is the conviction that belief in, and knowledge of, God is a living endeavour at the centre of one's existence and culture, experienced and expressed in words, in writings, in physical and bodily movements, in services, in architectural structures, even in icons painted on boards with paints and brushes. Third, because of that, faith is not something crude and vulgar but actually something precious and delicate which the Church has to preserve and handle as a treasure so as not to lose its finesse, through great care, constant vigilance, discretion and distinction. The crucial distinction made in the synodical statement of Orthodoxy is between "bowing down" and offering worship (*latreia*), which belongs to God alone and to Christ as Lord and God, and "paying a relative honour" (*timetike proskynesis*) to the Theotokos and the saints. The distinction is crucial!

External or internal causes notwithstanding, Iconoclasm was the event that in the wake of its encounter with the dynamic Monarchianism of Islam, brought Byzantium face to face with the existential nature of its faith in God. History has proven that Iconoclasm became the catalyst for an inner renewal which facilitated the ultimate survival of Byzantine Christianity.[40] Iconoclasm was a comprehensive revitalizing phenomenon which affirmed both the reality of the incarnation and the relevance of the entire liturgical-spiritual experience of the Church – literally "in colour"! The iconoclasts did not simply desecrate and burn icons. They also attacked the veneration of the Theotokos, the Mother of God-the-Word in flesh, the veneration of saints and martyrs, prayer, and monasticism as a way of life and institution, as well as monks, nuns and monasteries, the ecclesiastical arts, the liturgical practice of the Church, and even the very rights of the individual or of the Church as a whole to express faith by means of the material creation. In essence, Iconoclasm raised some broader, crucial and fundamental questions: What is religion? What are the spectrum and the role of reason and revelation in religion? What is the nature of God's grace and how can one experience it, or can one experience it? What is the epistemology of Orthodoxy?

Byzantium, as an expressive society and culture, wanted its faith to be equally expressive. Byzantine Christianity did not pray to icons; it prayed with icons.[41] In the communion *with* icons, Christ's true human nature was manifestly affirmed. The icon served as a reminder of several things: that "the Word became *flesh* and dwelt among us" [not merely body but *sarx*] (what could be more existential and real?); that Mary was, indeed, the Mother of the one (Theotokos) who is truly God; that martyrs and saints are imitators of Christ; that on account of Christ's entrance into the world, the material creation – the water, the earth, the food, the animal and physical world, and the whole environment – shares in the event of redemption!

With its transcendent realism and its silent eloquence, the Byzantine icon has preserved Orthodoxy in the hearts, minds, bodies, lives, eyes and senses of the Orthodox people and has carried them through the darkest, most suppressive and bitter periods of their ethnic histories. Like living Christians, icons throughout history have become themselves martyrs and confessors of faith by simply being icons and witnesses to holiness, as the defiled churches and the defaced icons in the former communist USSR, the Balkans, and in today's Turkish-occupied sector of Cyprus demonstrate. Icons have inspired and challenged, taught and condemned, soothed and upset human minds of various degrees of sensitivity and disposition. With their eloquent silence, they have instructed and nourished the Orthodox and have made converts to Christ throughout time. The Orthodox *hagiologia* are full of stories of lively encounters between living humans and the not so lifeless icons! That is why the icon (and I refer here to the true, correct and authentic Byzantine icon, and not any religious painting) is an essential characteristic of Byzantine Christianity and of Christian epistemology.

Hesychasm

This is the last and culminating stage of Byzantine religious experience and spirituality. What the Cappadocian Fathers and their descendants wrote in books, what the Councils proclaimed in definitions, and what the icon proclaimed in colour – the unique event of the incarnation and God's dispensation in Christ and his entrance into history and creation – Byzantine spirituality made a way of life. If God assumed a human nature, then this human nature, even this flesh, has been granted the possibility of experiencing God, from here and now.[42] The disciples on Mount Tabor experienced God's energies, the divine light, physically, in their own eyes. What could be a closer and more direct knowledge of God? Again, one should be keen to notice the critical distinction the hesychasts made between divine *essence*, which is ineffable and known to God alone, and divine *energies* which are communicable. The distinction is crucial. There is heresy in professing that one experiences the sun when feeling its rays, its light and its warmth. Hesychasm is not an egocentric, psychological, mental exercise; it is a Christocentric experience of divine ascent presupposing a life of long spiritual struggle, prayer, concentration, fasting, humility, exercise and self-denial. The Christocentricity of hesychasm is manifested in the ceaselessly repeated prayer where the name of Jesus and his mercy become part of one's breath, or of one's heart: "Lord Jesus Christ, son of God, have mercy upon me, a sinner." The "person-centricity" of hesychasm is manifested in the integration of the mind, heart and body in prayer.[43] Hesychasm is a delving of the whole self into the divine *gnofos*, or darkness, by all means of human existence: a heart burning with love for God and at peace *(hesychia)* with the passions; a mind stilled and removed from the self and its material context; and a body tamed and desirous to come to a communion with the divine. Hesychasm seeks to experience deification of the human nature *(theosis)* and the beatific vision, here and now, in so far as it is accessible to human nature. The event of the Transfiguration points to the possibility of such an experience, even though it is not common. If the three disciples, the closest, most loyal and simplest ones, had to be taken aside by Christ himself, away from the ordinary, and be led to a high place to concentrate on Jesus (the disciples desired to prolong their experience by constructing "tents" for the transfigured Christ, Moses and Elijah), so too must the faithful who wish to partake in the experience of the divine in this life be taken aside.

Interested in and attuned to a living faith, Byzantium continually made Christianity a living experience; what came with hesychasm was not, therefore, a new idea. It is only because of the so-called hesychastic controversies of the fourteenth century – between Gregory Palamas, Archbishop of Thessalonica, and a later hesychast at Mount Athos, and Barlaam, a monk from Calabria, and Akindynus – that we are talking about and writing books on hesychasm as if it were a fourteenth-century phenomenon. In fact, this is a spiritual tradition that can easily be traced back to the early desert Fathers and the spiritual masters at Sinai.[44] Teachings on the pure prayer, reference to the Jesus prayer, and descriptions of the physical accompaniment of Jesus and other "monologic" prayers can be found in Evagrius of Pontus; Macarius of Egypt (c.300–390); Gregory of Nyssa; Gregory of Nazianzus (who said that we are to remember God more often than we breathe);[45] Diadochus, Bishop of Photike in Epiros (d. before 486); Barsanouphios and John of Gaza (early sixth century); Maximus the Confessor; John Scholasticos or Sinaites (d.c. 650), known as "Climacos" for being the author of a masterpiece on monastic spirituality, *The Climax* or *The Spiritual Ladder*; Symeon the New Theologian and many more. *Hesychia* and *hesychasts* emerge with the beginning of the Byzantine era, and are common terms in the fourth-century literature. Gregory Palamas's name (c.1296–1359) prevails in this movement as the one who made a thoughtful theological synthesis and defence of the hesychastic tradition.

Hesychasm sought its roots in the New Testament itself. Paul's statement, "Our Lord Jesus Christ, though he was rich, yet for your sake became poor, that you through his poverty might become rich" (2 Cor. 8:9), meant for the hesychasts precisely that: on account of the incarnation of God-the-Word and his entrance into the created world, the ineffable essence of God has now become accessible through his energies. This "poverty," or "emptiness," of God has made the person's sharing in the divine glory possible! This is what the hesychasts meant by *theosis* or deification; and this was not something new in Byzantine religious life and spirituality. Athanasius, in his treatise *On the Incarnation of the Logos*, had already stated in a most definite manner that "God became man, so that man [in the inclusive sense of human nature] may become God" (8.54). Again, addressing itself to the essentials, *theosis* is the Eastern Christian equivalent of salvation. What else, after all, can salvation be but the experience of God Himself? What Paul had also admonished the Thessalonians to do, "be joyous; pray ceaselessly" (1 Thess.

5:16-17), or "glorify God in your body" (1 Cor. 6:19), the hesychasts took literally to the heart and to the body itself. As breathing does not stop when the body is occupied with various endeavours, even at sleep, neither does prayer need to cease. Prayer becomes a bodily function embedded in the heart. What was new in Byzantine hesychasm was the making of inner quietness from passions *(hesychia)* and ceaseless prayer a way of life and a full-time endeavour.

Concluding Remarks

To distil the Byzantine religious experience and spirituality and to delineate their essentials into statements is not an easy endeavour. I chose, therefore, to speak not so much on monasticism and social life, liturgy, councils, Orthodox education or mysticism, but on the Byzantine and, by extension, the Orthodox *ethos* that permeates and expresses itself in such categories and functions. We discussed this ethos under three pairs of characteristics: the monastic-social, the liturgical-synodical, and the mystical-epistemological ethos. If each combination sounds contradictory, abstract or theoretical, it is not, because it characterizes and describes the underpinning Orthodox sense of the individual, of society, of responsibility, of community, of religion, of faith, of authority, of freedom, of knowledge, of reason, of culture, of human nature, of institutions and more – a wide range of topics of human experience and condition.

This certainly has been a quick and sketchy excursus aimed at opening a window to the East and allowing us in the West to glimpse it for the purpose of evoking and stimulating dialogue and contemplation among Orthodox and non-Orthodox alike. In fact, the East is found already in the West and such categories like "East" and "West" make little difference today except for the very discerning eyes. The problem is that, in spite of its lengthy history, Orthodoxy remains an unknown, or little known, reality in North America and possibly also in the East itself; and what is little known is usually little appreciated and much misunderstood! It is my conviction, however, that Orthodoxy remains the best-kept secret in the West. It will be tragic if it remains only a secret. It is always amazing how well the Orthodox side is received, how refreshing and relevant it sounds to the ears of others, and how influential it becomes when given the chance and the proper context to speak. This means that the onus is on the Orthodox people to seek opportunities to study, reflect, and enter into a meaningful dialogue with others – in this order of action.

The cultivation and flourishing of the hesychastic tradition and ethos during the entire Byzantine era says about Christian experience what we have repeated often here: faith is an existential way of life. Of course, all religious traditions profess to be and are ways of life. For Byzantine Christianity, however, "a way of life" was not enough. Christianity had to be *the* perfect way of life, in the ultimate sense of the word: deification, or participation in the divine life from here and now! Such an ideal had immediate, practical and visible implications. It broadened Christian experience and spirituality to become a matter for every person. It made faith an inner experience, not simply a matter of formalized ritual and externals. It made prayer a communal, personal and continuous enterprise as well. The faithful of the Christian East did not look only to outside means and sources, such as the *sacerdotium*, or even to the letter of the Bible, for inspiration or for models of law and discipline; they looked also into their hearts and into prayer for inspiration and God's grace. So on the popular level, where or when the Bible, or the *sacerdotium*, were not readily available, people knew that they could discover and experience God in their own hearts.[46] However, to avoid any misunderstanding, we must hasten to say that hesychasm and mysticism never were anti-Church or practised outside the Church; they were at the heart of the Church. Byzantine mysticism and the life of pure prayer are the yeast that has kept the Church fresh, alive, and rising! Monasticism, that incubator of Orthodox spirituality and preserver of the life of humility, obedience and hesychastic prayer, has been a central and vital component of Orthodox experience in the past, in the present, and it will be so in the future, even in the midst of the most materialistic and secularized moments of human history, as long it continues to preserve its ethos.

The monastic ethos is the true expression of communal and social life of the Cappadocian Patristic legacy as an authentic expression and manifestation of the sense of Tradition; of the liturgical and synodical ethos as the refined sense of human community and communion; of the Iconoclastic Controversy as a paradigm of spiritual renewal from within; and lastly, of hesychasm, as the expression and culmination of theological and spiritual epistemology – what true knowledge is and how this knowledge is reached! Such characteristics developed and matured, more or less, in this order. But there is another characteristic that completes the quintessence and recapitulates the picture and the ethos of Byzantine Christianity: Byzantine Christianity speaks lengthily and elegantly, argues forcefully, defines and distinguishes diligently, stands up proudly, celebrates magnificently, paints and chants gloriously. However, after all these things are said and done, simultaneously rather than disjointedly, it pauses silently, prayerfully, obediently, gratefully and longingly in front of the ineffable mystery of God. This is, indeed, what completes the quintessence of Byzantine religious experience and spirituality!

For Further Reading

Baggley, John. *Doors of Perception: Icons and Their Spiritual Significance.* Crestwood, NY: St.Vladimir's, 1988.

John of Damascus. *On the Divine Images.* Translated by D. Anderson. Crestwood, NY: St.Vladimir's, 1980.

Florovsky, Georges. "Bible, Church, Tradition: An Eastern Orthodox View." In *The Collected Works of Georges Florovsky* 1. Belmont, MA: Nordland, 1972.

Maloney, George, S.J. *A History of Orthodox Theology Since 1453.* Belmont, MA: Nordland, 1976.

Meyendorff, John. *Byzantine Theology: Historical Trends and Doctrinal Themes.* New York: Fordham, 1974.

Sahas, Daniel. *Icon and Logos: Sources in Eighth-Century Iconoclasm.* Toronto: University of Toronto Press, 1986.

Ware, Kallistos. *The Orthodox Way.* Rev. ed. Crestwood, NY: St.Vladimir's, 1995.

---

[1] Henry Magoulias, *Byzantine Christianity: Emperor, Church and the West* (Detroit: Wayne State, 1982).

[2] Joan M. Hussey, *The Orthodox Church in the Byzantine Empire* (Oxford: Clarendon, 1990). See also her more popular and brief monograph *The Byzantine World* (New York: Harper, 1961) which, along with historical information, touches upon some themes of these lectures.

[3] A glance at the chapter titles indicates the scope of this work: I. The Christological Problem in the Early Middle Ages; II. The Iconoclast Controversy 726–843; III. The Age of Photius 843–886; IV. Leo VI's Dilemma: Nicholas Mysticus and Euthymius 886–925; V. The Patriarchate (925–1025); The Predominance of Constantinople; VI. Increasing Pressures on Constantinople and the Widening Gap 1025-1204; VII. The Effects of the Fourth Crusade 1204–1261; VIII. Contacts: Failure and Achievements 1258–1453. The book ends with a brief Part II with the thematic title "Organization and Life of the Orthodox Church in Byzantium."

[4] John Meyendorff, *Byzantine Theology: Historical Trends and Doctrinal Themes,* rev. 2d ed. (New York: Fordham, 1983).

[5] The editors have refrained from making changes to the authors' texts relating to non-inclusive language. Although they recognize that today inclusive language is standard, it is noteworthy that non-inclusive language is still current within the context of Eastern Christian discourse.

[6] Nikolae Iorga, *Byzance après Byzance: Continuation de l'histoire de la vie byzantine* (Bucharest: Bucharest Association internationale d'études du sud-est européen, Comité national roumain, 1971).

[7] On the broader question of continuity/discontinuity of Byzantium, see Alexander Kazhdan and Anthony Cutler, "Continuity and Discontinuity in Byzantine History," *Byzantion*

52 (1982): 429-78; Robert Browning, "The Continuity of Hellenism in the Byzantine World: Appearance or Reality?" in *Greece Old and New,* ed. Tom Winnifrith & Penelope Murray (London: Macmillan, 1983), 111-28; and Warren Treadgold, "The Break in Byzantium and the Gap in Byzantine Studies," *Byzantinische Forschungen* 15 (1990), 289-316, where the broader debate is revisited and annotated.

[8] *Byzantine Art: A European Art* (Athens, 1964), *Byzance* (Louvre, 1992), *Byzantium: Treasures of Byzantine Art and Culture* (British Museum, 1994), *Byzantium: Late Antique and Byzantine Art in Scandinavian Collections* (Copenhagen, 1966), and the latest one *The Glory of Byzantium* (New York, Metropolitan Museum of Art, March 11–July 6, 1997).

[9] For surveys of Orthodox Christianity see: Jaroslav Pelikan, *The Spirit of Eastern Christendom,* The Christian Tradition: A History of the Development of Doctrine 2 (Chicago: Chicago, 1974); Timothy Ware, *The Orthodox Church,* new ed. (London: Penguin, 1997); Kallistos Ware, *The Orthodox Way* (Crestwood, NY: St. Vladimir's, 1979); Alexander Schmemann, *The Historical Road of Eastern Orthodoxy* (New York: Holt, Rinehart and Winston, 1963); Nicholas Zernov, *Eastern Christendom: A Study of the Origin and Development of the Eastern Orthodox Church* (London: Weidenfeld and Nicolson, 1961); John Meyendorff, *The Orthodox Church: Its Past and Its Role in the World Today* (New York: Pantheon, 1960); Sergius Bulgakov, *The Orthodox Church* (Crestwood, NY: St. Vladimir's, 1988); Tomás Spidlík, SJ, *The Spirituality of the Christian East: A Systematic Handbook,* Cistercian Studies Series 79 (Kalamazoo, MI.: Cistercian, 1986); Ernst Benz, *The Eastern Orthodox Church: Its Thought and Life* (New York: Doubleday, 1963); M. J. Le Guillou, O.P., *The Spirit of Eastern Orthodoxy* (New York: Hawthorn, 1962). The last three titles are by Roman Catholic scholars.

[10] Cf. John D. Zizioulas, *Being as Communion: Studies in Personhood and the Church* (Crestwood, NY: St. Vladimir's, 1985).

[11] *The Orthodox Faith,* 1.8. In *Saint John of Damascus: Writings, The Fathers of the Church* 37, trans. F.H. Chase, Jr. (New York: Fathers of the Church, 1958), 177.

[12] On Anthony, see Athanasius's translation of his *vita* in Athanase d' Alexandrie, *Vie d'Antoine,* Sources chrétiennes 400, sec. ed. and trans. G.J.M. Bartelink (Paris: Cerf, 1994).

[13] On Pachomius, his life and rule, see *Pachomian Koinonia: The Life of Saint Pachomius and his Disciples,* Cistercian Studies Series 45, trans. Armand Veilleux, vol. 1 (Kalamazoo, MI: Cistercian, 1980).

[14] For the origins of monasticism and its ideals, see the newer edition of a classic on the subject, Derwas J. Chitty, *The Desert a City: An Introduction to the Study of Egyptian and Palestinian Monasticism Under the Christian Empire* (Crestwood, NY: St. Vladimir's, 1966); also, Otto F.A. Meinardus, *Monks and Monasteries of the Egyptian Deserts,* rev. ed. (Cairo: American University in Cairo, 1989).

[15] See R. Janin, *La géographie ecclésiastique de l' Empire byzantin: Les églises et les monastères,* vol. 3, 2d éd. (Paris: Inst. français d'études byzantines, 1969).

[16] See the entry "Monasticism" in *The Oxford Dictionary of Byzantium,* 3 vols., ed. Alexander P. Kazhdan et al. (New York: Oxford, 1991), 2: 1392-94.

[17] Cf. the *vita* of John of Damascus and Cosmas the Melodist in Papadopoulos-Kerameus, *Analekta hierosolymitikes stachyologias,* vol. 4 (Bruxelles: Culture et civilization, 1963): 305; and Daniel J. Sahas, "Cultural Interaction during the Umayyad Period: The 'Circle' of John of Damascus," *ARAM Periodical* (Oxford/Leuven) 6 (1994): 35-66.

[18] For the social role of the Church and of monasticism in the Byzantine era, see D.J. Constantelos, *Byzantine Philanthropy and Social Welfare* (New Brunswick, N.J.: Rutgers, 1968) and the entries "Almsgiving," "Hospitality," "Orphanage," "Monasteries," and "Philanthropy" in *The Oxford Dictionary of Byzantium,* op. cit.

[19] Epistle to the Romans, 3: 2. In *The Apostolic Fathers,* The Fathers of the Church 1, trans. F.X. Glimm et al. (New York: CIMA, 1947).

[20] On Sophronius, see the monograph by Christoph von Schönborn, *Sophrone de Jérusalem: Vie monastique et confession dogmatique,* Théologie historique 20 (Paris: Beauchesne, 1972).

[21] On John of Damascus, see Daniel J. Sahas, *John of Damascus on Islam: The "Heresy of the Ishmaelites"* (Leiden: E. J. Brill, 1972).

[22] For a quick reference to each of these personalities, consult the particular entries in the three-volume *Oxford Dictionary of Byzantium.*

[23] In the last few years, and in spite of the resistance on the part of the official Church administration, a momentous monastic activity has been noticed in North America, thanks to the initiative and the personality of the former abbot of the monastery of Filotheou, Mt. Athos, Fr. Ephraim. At the time of editing these lectures there are some sixteen monastic communities flourishing in this continent. In Canada: in Bolton, Ontario and Brownsburg, Québec. In the USA: in Florence, Arizona; Kendalia, Texas; Lawsonville, North Carolina; Troy, North Carolina; Bartow, Florida; Reddick, Florida; Dunlap, California; Kenoshwa, Wisconsin; Weatherly, Pennsylvania; Saxonburg, Pennsylvania; Goldendale, Washington; Detroit, Michigan; New York City, New York; Chicago, Illinois. This is, indeed, a miracle and a bright ray of hope!

[24] Caput LX [PG 79: 1180B], and in *Philokalia* (London: Faber, 1979) 1.62. The title "Theologian" in the Orthodox Tradition refers not to someone whose profession is the study of theology as an academic discipline, but rather to someone whose life and teaching manifest an experience of God. Out of a long line of illustrious Fathers who spoke and wrote on theology, the Church of the East bestowed the title of "Theologian" to only three figures: John the Evangelist, the most mystical of the four evangelists; Gregory Nazianzen, writer of contemplative poetry; and Symeon "the New Theologian," the singer of union with God. Cf. Vladimir Lossky, *The Mystical Theology of the Eastern Church* (Cambridge: J. Clarke, 1968), 9.

[25] Bishop Kallistos of Diokleia, "Praying With Icons," in *One in 2000: Towards Catholic-Orthodox Unity: Agreed Statements and Parish Papers,* ed. Paul McPartlan (Slough, England: St. Pauls, 1993) 141-168, at 153.

[26] On the divine liturgy and its multi-faceted aspects as a sacrament, see Alexander Schmemann, *The Eucharist: Sacrament of the Kingdom* (Crestwood, NY: St. Vladimir's, 1987).

[27] I have borrowed this perceptive expression from the subtitle of three essays on icons by Prince Evgenii Nikolaevich Trubetskoi (1863–1920) published under the title *Icons: Theology in Colour,* trans. Gertrude Vakar (Crestwood, NY: St. Vladimir's, 1973). From the rich bibliography on the theology of the icon, see Leonid Ouspensky, *Theology of the Icon* (Crestwood, NY: St. Vladimir's, 1978); and Paul Evdokimov, *The Art of the Icon: A Theology of Beauty,* trans. Stephen Bingham (Redondo Beach, CA.: Oakwood, 1990); and the conciliar documents in translation in Daniel J. Sahas, *Icon and Logos: Sources in Eighth Century Iconoclasm* (Toronto: University of Toronto Press, 1986).

[28] Cf. T. Ware, *The Orthodox Church,* rev. ed. (Harmondsworth, Middlesex: Penguin, 1997), 20.

[29] A superlative study which places the Cappadocians within the context of classical learning and culture is Jaroslav Pelikan's *Christianity and Classical Culture: The Metamorphosis of Natural Theology in the Christian Encounter with Hellenism* (New Haven: Yale, 1993).

[30] Cf. Justin, *Second Apology,* 13. In *St. Justin Martyr: the First Apology, the Second Apology, Dialogue with Trypho* [etc.], Fathers of the Church 6 (Washington, DC: Catholic University of America, 1965).

[31] Justin, *First Apology,* 46. In *St. Justin Martyr.*

[32] Among the rich bibliography on Constantine, see Samuel N. C. Lieu and Dominic Montserrat, eds., *From Constantine to Julian: Pagan and Byzantine Views: A Source History* (London: Routledge, 1996), and A.H.M. Jones, *Constantine and the Conversion of Europe* (Toronto: University of Toronto Press, 1978).

[33] The *kondak's* invention is attributed to Romanos the Melodist (born in Emesa, he died after 555). On Romanos, see *The Oxford Dictionary of Byzantium,* 3:1807-8, and J. Grosdidier de Matons, *Romanos le Mélode et les origines de la poésie religieuse à Byzance* (Paris: Beauchesne, 1977).

[34] John Meyendorff, *Byzantine Theology,* 2.

[35] Robert Payne, *The Holy Fire: The Story of the Fathers of the Eastern Church* (London: Skeffington, 1958), 13.

[36] On Leo and his Iconoclasm, see Stephen Gero, *Byzantine Iconoclasm During the Reign of Leo III, With Particular Attention to the Oriental Sources,* Corpus Scriptorum Christianorum Orientalium 346 (Louvain: Secretariat du Corpus SCO, 1973).

[37] On the various aspects of Iconoclasm, see the volume *Iconoclasm: Papers Given at the Ninth Spring Symposium of Byzantine Studies* [Birmingham, 1975] (Birmingham: University of Birmingham, 1977).

[38] For the synodical theses pro and against icons, see Sahas, *Icon and Logos.*

[39] On this *synodikon*, see Jean Guillard, "Le Synodikon de l' Orthodoxie: Édition et commentaire," *Traveaux et Mémoires* 2 (1967): 1-316.

[40] I am fully aware that I am proposing a revisionist interpretation of history on this point, as Western historians of Byzantium treat Iconoclasm as the beginning of the fall of Byzantium (which came eight centuries later and because of entirely different reasons).

[41] Cf. Kallistos of Diokleia, "Praying with Icons" mentioned above.

[42] On mysticism and the world, see especially the chapters in the second part, "Transfiguration of the World and Life in Mysticism," of Nicholai Arsen'ev's *Mysticism and the Eastern Church* (Crestwood, NY: St. Vladimir's, 1979), 63-147.

[43] On this topic of Orthodox anthropology and spirituality, see Kallistos of Diokleia, "Praying With the Body: The Hesychast Method and Non-Christian Parallels," *Sobornost* 14 (1992): 6-35.

[44] On the subject, see John Meyendorff's monograph, *St. Gregory Palamas and Orthodox Spirituality,* trans. Adele Fiske (Crestwood, NY: St. Vladimir's, 1974); also his *A Study of Gregory Palamas* (London: Faith, 1964).

[45] *Oration* 27:4 [PG 36:16B] [See *Cyril of Jerusalem and Gregory Nazianzus,* A Select Library of Nicene and Post-Nicene Fathers of the Christian Church 7, second series (Grand Rapids, MI: Eerdmans, 1974–1983)] ; cf. Kallistos, "Praying with the Body," 9.

[46] Cf. R.M. French, *The Way of a Pilgrim* and *The Pilgrim Continues his Way* (New York: Seabury, 1965).

iii. Centrality of the Lord's Table: Eucharistic Perspectives (1995)

Chapter 3

Holy Communion:
Its Theological Foundation[1]

SERAPHIM STORHEIM

Bishop Seraphim is the Orthodox Bishop of Ottawa for the Canadian Diocese of the Orthodox Church in America.

I am beginning this consideration of "An Orthodox Theological Consideration of Holy Communion" with theological considerations. If this seems odd, it cannot be otherwise, because a theological foundation is necessary in order to understand how the Orthodox properly approach Holy Communion, or even how the Orthodox behave, which is often seen as a mystery in itself.

I am going to refer, in the course of my reflections, to some sayings of the Fathers of the Church. These Fathers are persons whose sayings, sermons, answers to questions and treatises help to shape our understanding of Holy Communion and all other aspects of our Orthodox life.

Some of the Fathers are early, especially the ones we generally recognize as the greater authorities, like Basil the Great, John Chrysostom, and John of Damascus. Others of the early Church Fathers are desert types. There are also Church Fathers who are more recent. Although we may almost automatically assume that this term "Fathers" applies only to the period of the Cappadocians,[2] for instance, and is limited to persons of that historical period, in fact, the term applies to significant persons in all ages, even to the present. In the same way as the age of miracles is not passed, so is the time of the Fathers not passed. Moreover, to keep us on our toes, some of the Fathers are Mothers!

Another important basic factor for us to note is that if one is looking in indices for references regarding Holy Communion or Eucharist in the patristic writings, they will find such references to be surprisingly limited. This is for a good reason: never in the history of the Orthodox Church has this matter been considered in isolation from the wholeness of Orthodox Christian life and experience. It is part of an interdependent and interrelated whole; it cannot be precipitated out for independent study and isolated analysis.

We find a concrete example of this in the introduction to the book *Holy Women of Russia.* The author, Brenda Meehan, says:

> I have had great difficulty writing this book, and I am convinced now that it is because the women I am writing about – vibrant, spiritually intense women – didn't like the way I was originally telling their story, making it part of a dry, scholarly analysis of the rise of women's religious communities in nineteenth-century Russia. It had been my intention to analyse in tidy chapters various aspects of these communities, including their origins, statistical profiles of their founders, the economic resources and institutional structures of the communities, the socio-economic characteristics of the members and their cultural significance in pre-revolutionary Russia, but these women jumped up from the pages, refusing to be neatly contained within my chapters and within a framework that stressed the socio-historical at the expense of the spiritual. [3]

In this context, I hasten to add to her words: "and at the expense of the personal." The word "spiritual" can be taken today in a distanced, isolated, detached way. However, the word "personal" demands relationship, relationship on the level of being itself – that is what is involved in our perception of the meaning of communion.

Theology and the Leap of Faith

As an undergraduate I did a course on metaphysics during which we studied Thomas Aquinas's *Summa Theologica* and his proofs for the existence of God. Although the whole experience was taxing, I have been happy for it, because those arguments have proven quite helpful in many a discussion with searching hearts since then.

However, Aquinas understood, and our very patient professor pointed out, that in spite of the proofs one still needs the leap of faith. Through the blessing of Irish humour, we were taught that although one may rationally achieve a logical acceptance of God's existence, in itself reason is insufficient. The leap of faith has to occur before "belief" is possible. Belief is like confidence or trust – such as that confidence or trust in a chair or table to hold up one's weight when sitting or leaning on it. It is the leap of faith that enables one to have confidence or trust in God's existence.

Philosophy is a useful tool, but it is not theology, and the topic at hand is an Orthodox theological understanding of Holy Communion. If we are treating the word "theology" as if it were some kind of philosophy, we will have trouble in understanding the Orthodox perspective. It is necessary to take another moment to remember what theology is. Theology, of course, means words about God, speaking about God. Nevertheless, it does not mean that we take a set of propositions about God and then begin to debate them, or even to adjust them according to our liking. Theology is the result of an experience of God. It is not just the result of my experience of God. It is the result of *our* experience of God – and not just the result of our experience, here and now – but the communal experience of those who have encountered Him. Most pointedly, Orthodox theology reflects the Orthodox, Christian, shared-in-communion experience of God for the past two thousand years and even more.

A theologian is not someone who necessarily knows a lot about God or about history, councils, debates, arguments, ecclesiology, soteriology, biblical Tradition, translations, hermeneutics and so forth. Moreover, a theologian is not someone who is an original! A theologian is a person who has had an experience of God and who follows the exhortation of

1 Peter 3:15: "Should anyone ask you the reason for this hope of yours, be ever ready to reply." In addition, the authentication of this experience and this defence is found in its conformity to the shared experience of Orthodox Christians at all times and in all places. In other words, and to quote the favourite Biblical passage of a holy Lutheran man who repeated it many times to me in my youth, "Jesus Christ is the same yesterday, today, and forever" (Heb. 13:8). Yet this understanding of the stability of the Godhead is not something new, since we see it as God reveals Himself to Moses first at Mount Sinai in Exodus 3:6: "I am the God of your father, the God of Abraham, the God of Isaac, and the God of Jacob."

Holy Communion in the Scriptures

With this theological foundation in place, we can begin to discuss the foundation of our Orthodox perception of Holy Communion and the results of it. Moreover, I would like to start by pointing out one of the most striking differences between the East and the West in their Christian experiences. The Orthodox, in the so-called East, have always given Holy Communion to infants. It is a fact of life from the moment of Baptism. In the West, for many hundreds of years, this has been withdrawn until a variously timed "age of discretion," reflecting the long-held requirement that a person must know and understand what is being received. For the Orthodox, there is not and has never been such a requirement. There is no distinction made in ability to reason or to perceive what is happening, for we have given, do give and will give Holy Communion not only to infants, but to those incapable for various reasons – to those in comas, and so forth – of having any intellectual ability to comprehend anything. On the other hand, among these very Orthodox, there are still many who do not receive and have not frequently received Holy Communion, and do this on the basis of the very acute awareness of the poisonous effects of sin.

Every day, near the beginning of Matins, we sing as a refrain, "The Lord is God and has revealed Himself to us! Blessed is He that comes in the name of the Lord!"[4] This phrase contains the foundation of the Orthodox theological approach and the fundamentals of our understanding of Holy Communion. I will add that here we find our real roots: in our Semitic, Judaic, Middle-Eastern background interpreted through Hellenism.

From the very beginning, on the initiative of the One who is the Source of all Being, the Creator reveals Himself to the created. We see it in the beginning, in Genesis. However we may choose to take the details, the foundation of Genesis can be found in God's revealing Himself to mankind, his creation. He walks and talks with mankind before the Fall, and yes, even after it. Nevertheless, there is an interesting detail for us to notice. In Genesis 1:26 we read: "Then God said: 'Let us make man in our image, after our likeness.' " It is repeated again in Genesis 11:7, as God interrupts the handiwork of our pride: "Let us then go down and there confuse their language, so that one will not understand what another says." A little further along, in chapter 18, we have the well-known appearance of God by the oaks of Mamre. Here, we have the Lord repeatedly speaking in the singular, but visibly presented in the form of three men or angels during the encounter with Abraham, and later appearing in the form of two angels for the encounter with Lot in Genesis 19.

God reveals Himself as a Community of Being, not only in language but also in visible form both in the Old Testament and in the New Testament. In the latter, it is most particularly so at the moment of the Baptism of our Lord, as we hear in the Gospel according to Mark (1:10-11): "Immediately on coming up out of the water he saw the sky rent in two and the Spirit descending on him like a dove. Then a voice came from the heavens: 'You are my beloved Son. On you my favour rests.' " God reveals Himself not in a mere abstract community of being, but in a Community of Persons with whom there is interaction and interrelationship. This community of persons, Augustine of Hippo (354–430) and all the Fathers admit, is founded in love and is not self-enclosed. It reaches out. It creates life and invites the created into a relationship with the Creator.

The life of the Holy Trinity begets life in love and then maintains a similarly loving and personal relationship with the created. So God reveals Himself to us and, as the Lord, intends that this revelation should bring about "relationship." That "relationship" is, in fact, communion and that communion is the communion of love: the communion of life-giving love that invites imitation. Human beings will imitate the selfless, life-giving love of God; their obedience is motivated by this very love.

Revelation and the Liturgy

It is for this reason that we rehearse the great moments of this revelation at more important liturgical moments. In the anaphora of Basil the Great, for instance, we participate in this repetition of the historical revelation, as also in Baptism and at the Great Blessing of Waters at Theophany. God reveals Himself to us in creation, at Mamre, at the Red Sea, at Sinai, in the Judges and the Prophets, in holy persons in all ages, and then in culmination in the incarnation of our Lord, God and Saviour, Jesus Christ, the Word of God Who takes flesh, and in the Descent of the Holy Spirit. What this all comes down to is, that in celebrating the Divine Liturgy, we bring into the present moment all the past saving acts of the Holy Trinity. However, it does not stop there. We bring not only the past saving acts of the Lord into the Divine Liturgy but also future acts, including a commemoration of the Second Coming.

We celebrate all these past, present and future events because we participate in them and we have a personal relationship with them. This personal relationship with the Holy Trinity and all the saving acts of history is not, as one might think, a mere facet of our existence, something we do as just a part of all the rest of what we are. This personal relationship is enacted on the level of our very being. It is the substance, the foundation of who we are; for who we really are as persons can only be discovered in the perfection of the relationship with the One Who created us. The more deeply we are identified with God – the living out of His love, the imitation of Him – the more we are really ourselves, because we are more approximately what God created us to be. The more we insist on lives of our own choosing and neglect our communion with God in living our lives, the more distorted we become from what we should be and become parodies of our true selves.

In order to understand the Orthodox theology of Holy Communion, one must continually take into consideration the Mystery of the Body of Christ as described by Paul in 1 Corinthians

12-31. At the same time, the very purpose of the Eucharistic assembly must be recalled, as Father Alexander Schmemann (1921–1983) points out at the beginning of his book, *The Eucharist,* quoting the Apostle Paul in his disciplinary comments in 1 Corinthians 11:18-33:

> "When you assemble as a Church..." writes the Apostle Paul to the Corinthians. For him, as for all of early Christianity, these words refer not to a temple, but to the very nature and purpose of the gathering. As is well known, the very word "Church" (*ekklesia*) means "a gathering" or "an assembly," and to "assemble as a Church" meant, in the minds of the early Christians, to constitute a gathering whose purpose is to reveal, to realise, the Church. This gathering is eucharistic – its end and fulfilment lies in its being the setting wherein the "Lord's Supper" is accomplished, wherein the eucharistic "breaking of bread" takes place .... Thus, from the very beginning, we can see an obvious, undoubted triunity of the assembly, the Eucharist, and the Church, to which the entire early Tradition of the Church, following Paul, unanimously testifies.[5]

We believe that, for the sake of love, for the sake of enabling us to be restored to the personal communion with God which we ourselves had rejected and broken, the Word of God took flesh, lived, died at our hands, rose again destroying the power of Hades, and ascended into heaven. He left us the Divine Liturgy of his Body and Blood in order to feed us, and to maintain and increase the unity and identity between ourselves and Himself.

The Fathers and Holy Communion

Bearing all this in mind let us attend to what is written about Holy Communion by some of Fathers of the Church.

John Chrysostom

John Chrysostom spoke of Communion in his *Homily* 24.3-4 on 1 Corinthians 10:

O blessed Paul ... do you give the title of "cup of blessing" to that fearful and most tremendous cup? Yes, he says, and the expression is no mean title. For when I call it "blessing," do I mean thanksgiving, and when I call it thanksgiving, I unfurl all the treasures of God's goodness and call to mind those mighty gifts .... I am giving him thanks for having delivered the whole race of mankind from error. Being far off, he made them near, so when they had no hope, and were without God in the world, he constituted them his own brethren and fellow heirs. So when we approach, giving thanks for these and all such things ... we communicate not only by participating and partaking, but also by being united.

For what is the bread? The Body of Christ. And what do they become who partake of it? The Body of Christ: not many bodies, but one body ... so we are conjoined with each other and with Christ... "For the multitude of those who believed," says the text, "were of one heart and soul." (Acts 4:32). ... He brought in, as one may say, another sort of dough and leaven, his own flesh – by nature indeed the same, but free from sin and full of life – and he gave to all to partake of it so we might be blended with life and eternity by means of this table.[6]

I will add here parenthetically that John, when he used the word "blending," was not suggesting a wadding-together or a blending of us into some sort of indistinct life. He was saying that while being united to life, the Source of Life, that is, God, we remain the particular persons, the unique creations that we are.

Again John Chrysostom wrote in *Homily* 3 on Ephesians 1:

Look, I entreat: a royal table is set before you, angels minister at the table, the King Himself is there, and do you stand gaping? Are your garments defiled, and yet you make no account of it? Or are you clean? Then fall down and partake .... You have sung hymns with the rest; you have declared yourself to be of the number of those who are worthy by not departing with those who are unworthy.

Why stay and yet not partake of the table? I am unworthy, you will say. Then are you also unworthy of the communion you have had in prayers? For it is not by means of the offerings only, but also by means of those canticles, that the Spirit descends all around .... So I may not then be the means of increasing your condemnation, I entreat you, not to forbear coming, but to render yourselves worthy both of being present, and of approaching .... And what then is our hope of salvation? We cannot lay blame on our weakness; we cannot lay it on our nature. It is indolence, and nothing else that renders us unworthy.[7]

John Chrysostom further elucidated Holy Communion in *Homily* 30 on 2 Corinthians 13:

We are the temple of Christ; we kiss the porch and entrance of the temple when we kiss each other .... And through these gates and doors Christ both has entered into us and does enter, whensoever we communicate. You who partake of the mysteries, understand what I say: for it is in no common manner that your lips are honoured when they receive the Lord's Body. It is chiefly for this reason that we kiss.[8]

Cyprian of Carthage

Cyprian of Carthage (d.258) commented on Communion in his Treatise "On the Lord's Prayer" (18):

"Give us this day our daily bread." These words may be taken either spiritually or literally, because in the divine plan, both readings are helpful for your salvation.

The bread of life is Christ; now this is not everyone's bread, but it is ours .... We call this "our bread" because Christ is the bread of those who partake of his Body. And we ask that this bread be given us daily, lest we, who live in Christ and receive the Eucharist every day as the food of salvation, be separated from his Body by some grave sin that keeps us from communion and so deprives us of our heavenly bread.[9]

Cyril of Jerusalem

In his lectures on the sacraments, Cyril of Jerusalem (c.315–386) wrote about the Body and Blood of Christ:

> With fullest assurance, let us partake of the Body and Blood of Christ, for in the figure of Bread is given to you his Body, and in the figure of wine his Blood, that you, by partaking of the Body and Blood of Christ, might be made of the same body and blood with him. For thus we come to bear Christ in us ... thus it is, according to blessed Peter, we become partakers of the divine nature (2 Pet. 1:4).

> Christ on a certain occasion discoursing with the Jews said, "Unless you eat my flesh and drink my blood, you have no life in you" (Jn. 6:53).... Contemplate therefore, the bread and the wine not as bare elements, for they are, according to the Lord's declaration, the Body and Blood of Christ.... Let faith establish you.[10]

Hesychius of Jerusalem

Hesychius of Jerusalem (d.c.451) reflected on the operation of Holy Communion upon communicants in his texts on *Sobriety and Prayer:*

> Whenever we unworthy ones are thought worthy to be admitted, with fear and dread, to the Divine and undefiled Mysteries of Christ, our God and King, then let us all the more show forth sobriety, watchfulness of mind and strict attention, so that our sins and our small and great uncleanness may be destroyed by the Divine Fire, that is the Body of our Lord Jesus Christ.

> For when it enters into us, it straightaway drives from our heart the spirits of wickedness, and it does away with our sins of the past, and the mind is left empty of the restless importunities of evil thoughts. If, after this, we guard our mind strictly, and stand in the gate of our heart, each time we are again counted worthy, the holy Sacred Divine Body will more and more brighten the mind and make it shine like a star...[11]

Symeon the New Theologian

In his *Ethical Chapters,* Symeon the New Theologian wrote,

Just as Eve was taken from the flesh and bones of Adam so the two formed one flesh, so Christ, in giving Himself to us in communion, gives us his own flesh and bones. This is indeed what he gives us to eat. Through communion he makes us one with Himself.

All those who believe in Christ become akin to him in the Spirit of God, and form a single body.... United to him spiritually in this manner, each of us will form a single spirit with him, and likewise one body, since we corporally eat his body and drink his blood.... One I say, not according to the person but to the nature of the Deity and the humanity: according to the divine nature, since we, too, become god through adoption....

Before all ages, [God] has predetermined that those who believe in him and are baptised in his name (the name of the Father, and of the Son, and of the Holy Spirit), and eat the sinless flesh of his Son, and drink his precious Blood, would be justified by this, that is, glorified and would become partakers of life eternal....

If you want to know whether I am speaking the truth, become a saint by practising the commandments of God, and then partake of the Holy Mysteries. Then you will understand the full import of this statement.[12]

Nicholas Cabasilas

In *The Life in Christ,* Nicholas Cabasilas (b.c.1322) wrote about the action of Eucharist:

But when Christ dwells in us, what else is needed, or what benefit escapes us? When we dwell in Christ, what else will we desire? ... What good thing is lacking for those who are in such a state? What have they to do with wickedness who have entered such brightness? What evil can withstand so great an abundance of good? What evil thing can continue to be present or enter from without when Christ is so evidently with us, and completely penetrates and surrounds us?

The Eucharist, alone of the sacred rites, supplies perfection to the other Mysteries.... So perfect is this Mystery, so far does it excel every other sacred rite, that it leads to the very summit of good things. Here also is the final goal of every human endeavour. For in it we obtain God Himself, and God is united with us in the most perfect union; for what attachment can be more complete than to become one spirit with God?[13]

Understanding and Practice Today

Because of our selfishness we retreat from our call to perfect communion. We satisfy ourselves with limited, cheap, even dark substitutes and alternatives. St. Nikolai Velimirovich (1880–1956), in his *Prayers by the Lake,* reflected,

[My soul], repent of your yearnings for this world and all that is in this world. For the world is the graveyard of your ancestors, which is gaping and waiting for you. Just a little longer, and you will be ancestors, and will yearn to hear the word "repentance," but will not hear it.

Pontius Pilate asked our Lord, "What is truth?" He asked the wrong question, for truth is not a what, but a Who. Very often, in trying to understand the Mysteries of God, we are caught in the same kind of bind by asking the wrong questions. Moreover, if we dare to think that we can ever fully understand the Mysteries of God, and most particularly the Mystery of the Eucharist, we will do nothing but ask the wrong questions.

Hopefully, we are beginning to see that in the Orthodox understanding of the Mystery of Communion, everything is interrelated. Everything and everybody is connected to and influencing, and influenced by everybody and everything else! So much is this so, that if we are asked, "How many sacraments are there?" our answer will be "God knows." It is one or numberless. All of what we commonly distinguish as separate sacraments are, in fact, linked tightly to each other, all knit together so as to be inseparable, albeit distinct, acts. Every time God confers grace upon us, we should perceive this event to be a sacrament (including the holy kissing that John Chrysostom described). The sacraments are multitudinous. It is all a reflection of the life of the Holy Trinity, and we are back where we began.

The bishop, as the chief celebrant of every eucharistic Liturgy in his diocese, focuses in his person the perpetuation of the Tradition of Christ, the true belief in the Holy Trinity.

"And how do you believe?" asks the presiding bishop to the one being consecrated. The future bishop responds,

I believe in one God, the Father Almighty, maker of heaven and earth, and of all things visible and invisible;

And in one Lord, Jesus Christ, the Son of God, the Only begotten, begotten of the Father before all ages; light of light, true God of true God, begotten not made, of one essence with the Father, and through Whom all things were made; Who for us men and for our salvation came down from heaven, and was incarnate of the Holy Spirit and the Virgin Mary, and became man; and he was crucified for us under Pontius Pilate, and suffered and was buried; and the third day he rose again, according to the Scriptures, and ascended into heaven, and sits at the right hand of the Father; and he shall come again in glory to judge the living and the dead, whose kingdom shall have no end.

And in the Holy Spirit, the Lord, the Giver of Life, who proceeds from the Father, who with the Father and the Son together is worshipped and glorified, Who spoke by the prophets. In one holy, catholic and apostolic Church;

I acknowledge one Baptism for the remission of sins; I look for the resurrection of the dead, and the life of the world to come. Amen.

This is the Nicene Creed which we daily reaffirm, and which we confess from our baptisms. The presiding bishop blesses the new bishop with the Grace of the Holy Trinity. Then, to clarify, the bishop-to-be is asked to speak in more detail about his trinitarian and Christological faith, and he responds aloud with the Second Confession:

I believe in one God, the Father Almighty, maker of heaven and earth, and of all things visible and invisible; who is without beginning, unbegotten and without cause, but is Himself the natural beginning and cause of the Son and of the Spirit.

I believe in his only-begotten Son, without change and without time begotten of the Father, being of one essence with him, by Whom all things were made.

I believe in the Holy Spirit, who proceeds from the same Father, who with him is glorified as co-eternal and co-enthroned, being of one essence with him, of equal glory, and the author of creation.

I believe that the only-begotten Word, one of that same superessential and life-giving Trinity, came down from heaven for us and for our salvation. He was incarnate of the Holy Spirit and the Virgin Mary and became man; that is, he became perfect man, yet remained God, in no manner was his divine essence changed by his participation in the flesh, nor was he transmuted into anything else. Without change he assumed man's nature, in which he suffered and died, although in his divine nature he was free from all suffering. On the third day, he rose from the dead; he ascended into heaven, and he sits at the right hand of the God and Father.

Furthermore, I believe and proclaim that Christ is one and the same in two natures after his incarnation, preserving those things which were in them and from them. Therefore, I also adore two wills, in that each nature retains its own will and its own action.

I believe those traditions and teachings of the one catholic and apostolic Church which have been received from God and men of God. I reverence, but not in the way of worship, the icons of Christ Himself and of the all-pure Birthgiver of God, and of all the saints, holy and worthy of reverence. The honour that I address to them, I direct to their originals. I reject and deny those who think and teach otherwise as persons ill-advised. I confess truly and sincerely our sovereign Lady, Mary, the Birthgiver of God, as having given birth in the flesh to one of the Trinity,

Christ our God. May the same Birthgiver of God be my helper, protector, and defender, all the days of my life. Amen.

This is the foundation of what Orthodox Christians at all times and in all places believe. Further, this foundation of faith permeates the whole of our life. It participates in our assembly as the Church; it undergirds our status as the Body of Christ. It penetrates our thanksgiving and our offering of ourselves and the whole of our being. It mingles with our commemoration of the living, the dead, the saints, the saving acts of God, and our participation in Holy Communion. It profoundly affects every aspect of our life as we step out to meet people and events that will put our relationship with Christ to the test.

For it is about our relationship with Christ, being in love with Christ, being one with Christ, being found in Christ, being alive in Christ, that this is all about. It is, as these great phrases from the Divine Liturgy indicate, "Your own, of Your own, we offer to You, on behalf of all, and for all." This "all" is not just us standing here; it includes all: everyone and everything.

And again, when we come to the end of our commemoration of the departed and the living, we remember our bishop, asking that the Lord will protect him in all things, and enable him "rightly to define the word of Your truth." And the faithful respond, "And everyone and everything," revealing the interdependent unity of the faithful and the bishop, and the assembly and all of creation.

Orthodoxy and Orthopraxy

To further our understanding of the sacrament of Holy Communion we must also turn to practical and historical considerations regarding Eucharistic participation in the Church. First, let us look at Holy Communion as it is documented in the Early Church. *The Canons of the Holy Apostles,* while they are not exactly that, derive from the experience of the Early Church, from sub-apostolic times.[14] Significantly, the influence of the *Canons* on the Church's interior life remains to the present day. Let us examine first *Canons* 8 and 9 relating to Holy Communion:

If any bishop, presbyter or deacon, or anyone on the sacerdotal list, when the offering is made, does not partake of it, let him declare the cause; and if it be a reasonable one, let him be excused; but if he does not declare it, let him be excommunicated as being a cause of offence to the people, and occasioning a suspicion against the offerer, as if he had not made the offering properly (*Canon* 8).

All the faithful who come in and hear the Scriptures, but do not stay for prayers and the Holy Communion, are to be excommunicated, as causing disorder in the Church (*Canon* 9).

The above sentiments were reiterated in *Canon* 2 of the Synod at Antioch in Syria in 341.

What the quoting of these canons reveals is not that the Early Church liked to excommunicate people, but rather that a great deal of importance was placed on complete participation in the Eucharistic Offering, particularly on the Lord's Day. At this point, it is necessary to say that excommunication as mentioned here does not in any way imply a permanent condition. In the early Church, and in the Orthodox Church until now, if anyone is excommunicated for whatever reason, it is considered as a temporary medicinal treatment for a spiritual malady. In apostolic times, we have evidence that people might have received Holy Communion every day. In addition, there was the strong sense of need to receive the Holy Communion of the Body and Blood of our Lord God and Saviour, Jesus Christ, every Sunday. It is well known that in those days, if anyone was absent from the Liturgy without good excuse for three Sundays, the person would be excommunicated for treating the sacrament lightly, and would remain in such a state until they repented.

Eucharistic participation did not and does not carry the sense of simply receiving Holy Communion. Reception as such is "part of the whole" and cannot be understood without the whole. In early Church times, even receiving Holy Communion as a sick person unable to attend the liturgy was taken seriously as a "part of the whole." It was customary for a presbyter, or more often a deacon, to take Holy Communion to the sick immediately after the celebration of the Sunday liturgy. In fact, to this day this is standard practice among Egyptians who, for the sake of safety, do not keep Communion in reserve.

Now you might be ready to ask, "Part of the whole what?" The first answer is "part of the whole Divine Liturgy." However, this cannot be the complete answer, because the Divine Liturgy is not an end in itself, or isolated in any way. We see in the Divine Liturgy the greatest example of inclusiveness. It makes present all the saving acts of God. It makes us partakers of the Divine Nature. It includes and affects all the faithful, past, present and future. It realizes the Body of Christ in the fullest sense of the term. It encompasses and enables the renewal of all creation. It puts us in the Kingdom of Heaven, in the paradise of God. It makes visible what was quoted from the Apostle Paul's letter to the Corinthians earlier (1 Cor. 11:18-33) – "When you assemble as a Church..." – the coming together of believers in unity, in order and in love for the receiving of the Body and Blood of Christ in a worthy manner. All of this may sound fine in theory, one might say, but for the Orthodox Christian, there is no sense of abstraction or disconnection with the so-called practical reality in all of this. It must be understood that there is no division between what we believe and what we do: to use an expression in vogue these days, Orthodoxy is inseparable from Orthopraxy.

The whole life of an Orthodox Christian is expected to be focused on the Eucharist, both preparing for it and working from it. As John of Kronstadt (1829–1908) says in his work, *My Life in Christ,*

> Both public and private prayer are necessary in order that we may lead a truly Christ-like life, and the life of the Spirit should not become extinct in us. It is indispensable that we should attend divine service in Church with faith, zeal and understanding just as it is indispensable to provide a lamp with fuel or power if it is to burn and not go out....

> [And:] What does the Holy Church instil in us by putting into our mouths during prayer, both at home and in Church, prayers addressed not by a single person, but by all together? She instils in us constant mutual love, in order that we should always love one another as our own selves – in order that, imitating God in three Persons,

constituting the highest unity, we should ourselves be one formed of many. "That they all may be one, as You, Father are in Me, and I in You, that they also may be one in Us" (John 17:21).

Common prayer on the part of all teaches us also to share the things of earth with others, to share our needs, so that in this life also we may have all things in common – that mutual love should be evident in everything, and that each of us should use his ability for the good of others, not hiding his talent in the ground, that he should not be selfish and idle....

[He continues:] By means of its divine service, the Orthodox Church educates us for heavenly citizenship...by giving "unto us all things that belong unto life and godliness" (1 Pet. 1:13). Therefore it is urgently necessary for us intelligently, reverently and willingly to assist at the divine services of the Church, particularly on festivals, and to make use of the sacraments of Penitence and Holy Communion. But those who withdraw themselves from the services of the Church become victims of their vices, and are lost....

[And:] If the Lord gives us Himself in his divine mysteries, every day, ought we not absolutely to give freely, for nothing, perishable goods, such as money, food, drink, clothes to those who ask them of us? And how can we be angered with those who eat our bread for nothing, when we ourselves partake freely of the priceless and immortal food of the Body and Blood of the Lord?[15]

The utter centrality in and necessity to the life of the Orthodox Christian of the Divine Liturgy and *ipso facto* the receiving of Holy Communion, is thoroughly underlined in what John of Kronstadt has said. Not only does it unite us to Christ and to each other, Holy Communion enables the Christ-like, selfless, loving life that is the expression of this union described by the Apostle Paul in his Letter to the Ephesians, chapter two. It also reveals and makes present the fact, as the same Apostle says in chapter three of his Letter to the Philippians, that our citizenship is in Heaven. Of course, this is not to say that every Orthodox Christian is always aware or conscious of all of this all of the time: far from it. However, the Orthodox Christian, aware of his or her sins, will nevertheless sense much of this, almost by instinct.

Augustine of Hippo says, in his commentary on the Psalms,

> Many, it is true, approach the altar you see here, unworthily, and God permits his sacraments to be profaned for a time. Nevertheless, my brethren, will the heavenly Jerusalem resemble these visible walls? By no means; you many enter with the wicked into the walls of this Church, you will not enter with the wicked into Abraham's bosom. Have no fear therefore: wash your hands clean.[16]

Not only is Holy Communion the object of our life in Christ, it is also the means to that end. It is that spiritual food by which we are enabled to hope to come into the Kingdom of Heaven.

Once again, Basil the Great sets before us the proper standard and at the same time reveals the practice of the fourth-century Church (quoted from his *Letter* 93):

> Daily Communion and participation in the Holy Body and Blood of Christ is a good, helpful practice. He [that is, the Lord] clearly says, "The man who eats My Flesh and drinks My Blood has eternal life." Who doubts that to partake of life continually is really to have a life of abundance? For myself, I communicate four times a week, on the Lord's Day, on Wednesday, on Friday and Saturday, and on the other days if there is a commemoration of a martyr. If in times of persecution, individuals, under this compulsion, give themselves communion with their own hands, without the presence of priest or minister, this raises no difficulty. In fact, there is no need to point this out, since long-established custom has sanctioned the practice under pressure of circumstances.
>
> All the hermits in the desert, when there is no priest, keep the communion at home and give it to themselves. And in Alexandria and Egypt it is the general rule for each member of the laity to keep the communion at his own house.

For once the priest has completed the sacrifice, and has given the sacrament, he who has received it as one entire portion is bound to believe, as he participates day by day, that he rightly partakes of it and receives it from him who gave it. Even in the Church, the priest gives a portion and the recipient retains it, with complete power to do what he will, and brings it to his mouth with his own hands.[17]

In addition, I quote from *Letter* 57.2 of Cyprian of Carthage, whom I cited earlier:

As the Eucharist is appointed for this very purpose, that it may be a safeguard to the receivers, it is needful that we may arm those whom we wish to be safe against the adversary with the protection of the Lord's abundance. For how do we teach or provoke them to shed their blood in confession of his name, if we deny to those who are about to enter into warfare, the Blood of Christ? Or how do we make them firm for the cup of martyrdom if we do not first admit them to drink, in the Church, the cup of the Lord by the right of communion?[18]

We see here, first in Basil, the very strong sense of the utter importance and centrality of receiving Holy Communion very often, even every day. In addition, we see that in some places the laity might have the Holy Communion at home for daily reception. At the same time, we see that Cyprian has exactly the same attitude toward its value, its utter necessity for the life of the Christian, whether it be in a time of persecution or not. However, he gives hints in his language, just as did John Chrysostom in a previous quotation, that not everyone of the faithful was so prepared. There have always been those who have fallen prey to sin and are tempted to take the receiving of Holy Communion and, by extension, their participation in the community of the faithful, lightly.

We see the Apostle Paul rebuking those in Corinth who abused the sacramental feast by turning it into a picnic. We see John Chrysostom complaining that some are partaking of the Sacrament without proper reverence or regard. And we have yet another quotation from Martyrius, a Syriac Father of the early seventh century, in *The Book of Perfection:*

I shudder to mention something else that is the most dreadful thing of all done by people who show contempt: at the dread moment which makes even the rebel demons shake, I mean at the awesome point when the Divine Mysteries are consummated, when angels and archangels hover around the Altar in fear and trembling, as Christ is sacrificed and the Spirit hovers, many of these people will, on occasion wander about outside, or...will come in according to their whim and stand there showing their contempt by yawning as though at their excessive burden, being tired of standing up.

At that moment when the priest is making this great supplication on their behalf, deep sleep gets the better of them; so slack are they; at this moment which causes even the dead to awaken, here are these people, fully alive and supposedly running after perfection, nevertheless sunk in sleep, or wandering about expectantly for when they can quickly leave their place of confinement; for the Jerusalem of light and life is like a prison to these people – the place where Father, Son and Spirit dwell, when spiritual beings and the bands of saints together give praise and glory before in holy fashion (Heb. 12:28).

Again, we see the awe with which the sacrament of Holy Communion was and is held, and the sinful response of some. There has been a tendency to find blame for this attitude in the fact that pagans were admitted to the Church in large numbers in the fourth century. They are blamed also for the decreasing numbers frequently receiving Holy Communion, particularly from about the seventh and eighth centuries.

Some have come to suggest that the rise of allegorical interpretation of Christian liturgy has been problematic. The allegorical interpretation of the Divine Liturgy, as being a re-enactment of the life of Christ by the priest, betrays, they say, an influence of pagan mystery religions. In addition, it is added that the movement into allegory has served to distance the celebration of the Eucharist from the people. Also, some like to say that because of pagan influence, and to protect the Mysteries from profanation, the Church discouraged people from receiving Holy Communion frequently and thus it became less and less frequent. At the present, I think I see rather the continuous dark thread of sin throughout. I think I see that, in the light of the Lord's saying, "Many are called but few are chosen" (Matt. 22:14), there are some throughout all of Christian history who deeply love the Lord and want to be pleasing to him and to be like him and to obey him and therefore to feed on him. However, there are others who, when they are confronted by the brightness of the glory of the love of God in Christ, recoil in pain and rebellion. Thus, they shy away from receiving the Divine Food necessary for the Life in Christ.

Let us examine the quotation from Martyrius just cited. He condemns all disrespectful wandering around and late arriving. Moreover, what characterizes modern Orthodox Christians? For what behaviour do they even gain the admiration of some? For exactly this inattentive wandering around and this disrespectful late arriving and early departing from the holy place of worship. So much is this so, that we think we can allow ourselves to be disrespectfully casual. In our barbaric boorishness, we think it is acceptable to come late to the Lord's Banquet, to wander around, in and out, not to eat anything and to head off early. I can imagine the reaction we would get if we did this at a banquet of the Queen or the Lieutenant-Governor! And is the Lord less than they?

Liturgy, Hymns and Epistles

When the Orthodox hear the readings from the Holy Scriptures – from the Gospels or from the Epistles – and when the Orthodox celebrate feasts of the Lord, all of this is done and heard in the *present*. What is spoken by any of the Apostles, or recounted in the Acts, is taken to be spoken by us, here and now, in the present. The proper response is not, "Oh, those naughty Corinthians," or "Oh, those Thessalonians," or whoever! It is, rather, that we hear the Apostle addressing our sin or exhorting us to zealous, active faithfulness. The letters are written to us who stand there hearing the words. That is why we call the Epistles "the Apostle."

It is the same with readings from the Gospels. We who hear the words participate in the events, in the works of the Lord. We hear the Lord Himself speak to us in the here and now. Moreover, in Holy Week, when we reread all the events of the Passion, we are not just hearing about it and kind of remembering it; we are participating in the very events. We are with the Lord in everything, both acclaiming and betraying him (yes, betraying him, since we are all sinners, and every sin is a betrayal, and we could all be Judas), and we are at the Last Supper with him, and condemning him, and by the Cross, and at the Tomb, and at the Resurrection. Then we are with the Apostles during the forty glorious days of Pascha, and at the Ascension, and with the Mother of God and the Apostles at the Descent of the Holy Spirit. We are present at other kinds of events, too. We are at the Nativity and we are at the Baptism. We are at the Presentation, the Annunciation, the Transfiguration and the Dormition. Look at how we are praying. On the Sunday of the Prodigal Son, in pre-Lent, we identify ourselves with the Prodigal: "I have recklessly forgotten Your glory, O Father.... And *now I cry to You as the Prodigal:* 'I have sinned before You, O merciful Father....' " On the day of the Entrance of the Lord to Jerusalem, we say to him: "Like the children with palms of victory, *we cry to you,* O Vanquisher of Death: Hosanna in the highest."

On Great and Holy Thursday we pray, "Of Your mystical Supper, O Son of God, *accept me today* as a communicant..." and we identify with the repentant thief. On the Day of the Resurrection, we do not say that this is the day "Christ rose," but rather we use the present tense – "Christ is risen." Thus, the Resurrectional Tropar declares in song, "Christ *is risen* from the dead, trampling down death by death, and upon those in the tombs bestowing life." Our identification with events continues past the Paschal cycle. It shows itself in such feast days as the Entrance of the *Theotokos* into the Temple: "*Today* is the prelude of the good will of God.... The Virgin *appears* in the temple of God.... Let *us* rejoice and sing to her...." On the day of the Lord's Nativity we sing, "*Today* the Virgin gives birth to the Transcendent One." Moreover, at the Baptism we sing, "*Today* You have appeared to the universe, and Your light, O Lord, has shone on us." At the Annunciation we sing, "*Today* is the beginning of our salvation...."

All of this shows concretely how we understand the telescoping, the compression of time, much in the way the Exodus is celebrated at the Passover. It also reveals that in celebrating the Eucharist, we encompass not only God's saving acts in all of history, but also every act and event of our daily lives. What separates us from this perfection? Sin and rebellious pride. In all of this, I could have gone on at length about the exterior details of how we have adjusted our manner of serving the Divine Liturgy, and how the receiving of Holy Communion has likewise adjusted to cultures, circumstances and so forth. But if we are truly to understand any of the adjustments, which are readily available in all sorts of books in English and even more in French, it all has to be seen in light of the adage that the more things change, the more things remain the same. From the Council of Carthage (256 A.D.), Lobosus, Bishop of Vaga, says, "In the Gospel the Lord says, 'I am the truth.' He said not, 'I am the custom.' Therefore, the truth being manifest let custom yield to truth."

Regardless of how much we progress technologically, we human beings are in fact no different from our forefathers, for good or ill. In our time, there are zealous faithful who diligently fulfill the will of God. There are also those who are bound in sin and there are those who betray. Indeed, it can be very ugly, but bad as it is, we should remember God's word to Elijah at Horeb: "Yet I will leave 7,000 in Israel, all the knees that have not bowed to Baal and every mouth that has not kissed him" (1 Kings 19:18). In the midst of all, it is still through the Divine Liturgy, through the receiving of Holy Communion, that our Lord Jesus Christ, who is indeed "the same, yesterday, today and forever," unites us to Himself, feeds us, enables us to live in him and enables us to serve each other in him. It is he who brings unity to the whole of our life, and indeed to the whole cosmos!

When the Orthodox do anything, it is understood that God's blessing and participation must be invited into all activity. Thus, we make the sign of the cross on bread before cutting it. After all, it is not simply bread from the supermarket we are eating here. The bread is connected to the Bread of Life. We certainly do not sit on tables. Why? Because the home is the "small Church," and the table in it is like the Holy Table in the Temple. We treat the table with the same respect as we do our eating at it. Moreover, Martyrius, from the source already cited, speaks to us again:

Indeed, anyone who has enjoyed the good things of an ordinary meal ought to render thanks for this enjoyment, otherwise he will be reckoned as animal-like and lacking in discernment. As one of the saints said, "A table from which the praise of God does not ascend is no different from an animal sty," and it is not the table that is reckoned to be like a sty, but rather the person eating from it resembles an animal, owing to his lack of thanksgiving.

One of the characteristics of Orthodox Christians, one that makes us sometimes appear foolish or naive, is the readiness to take the Gospel, most particularly, quite personally and even literally. For example, when someone is struck by Paul's exhortation to the Philippians to "pray unceasingly," it is taken as a personal admonition by God – a personal call via the apostle – and the person seeks to respond. Another person might be struck by the Lord's admonition to "sell what you have, and give it to the poor, and follow Me," and proceed to do so.

Messages of repentance in personal encounters are abundant. They are the fruit of the experience and expectation of communion. It does not matter whether the person is a simple, uneducated person or a very well-educated scholar. For instance, a person such as John Chrysostom knows well about the literary criticism of Scriptural texts, but that does not in any way conflict with or inhibit his understanding of the same Scripture's ability to convey God's personal communication with and call to us, each and all. Our behaviour might be called radical obedience. We tend, as the Gospel directs, to put our relationship with Christ into concrete practice. Out of love, we try to serve persons. Hospitality, for which the Orthodox are known, comes from our loving desire to serve Christ, Who comes to us in all visitors. Sometimes they are angels, like the guests of Abraham and Sarah. Care for neighbours, friends, the poor and the needy likewise springs up from the love of Christ. Tender care for and communication with our environment are the "ecological expressions" of this same loving relationship. As God in His saving love for us takes flesh for our salvation, so for the salvation of the world, we reveal, we carry Christ in our flesh. We concretely and materially bring our being in love with Christ into every part of living.

Conclusion

In closing, I bring to you two final quotations on Holy Communion and the relationship of love it entails. The first is taken from *The Lives of the Desert Fathers:*

> When the Father saw us, he was filled with joy, embraced us, and offered a prayer for us. Then, after washing our feet with his own hands, he turned to spiritual teaching, for he was well-versed in Scriptures, having received this charism from God. He expounded many key passages in the Scripture for us, and having taught the Orthodox faith, invited us to participate in the Eucharist. For it is a custom among the great ascetics not to give food to the flesh before providing spiritual nourishment for the soul, that is, the Communion of Christ. When we had communicated and given thanks to God, he invited us to a meal.[19]

The second quotation is an extract from Maximus the Confessor's *Centuries of Love,* taken from *Drinking from the Hidden Fountain: A Patristic Breviary*:

> Do all you can to love everyone. If you are not yet able to, at the very least do not hate anyone. Yet you won't even manage this if you have not reached detachment from the things of this world. You must love everyone with all your soul, hoping, however, only in God and honouring him with all your heart. The friends of this world are not loved by all, but neither do they love all.
>
> Christ's friends persevere in their love right to the end. The friends of this world persevere only so long as they do not find themselves in disagreement over worldly matters. A faithful friend is an effective protector. When things are going well, he gives you good advice and shows you his sympathy in practical ways. When things are going badly, he defends you unselfishly and he is a deeply committed ally.
>
> Many people have said many things about love. However, if you are looking for it, you will find it only in the followers of Christ. Only they have true Love because their teacher is Love. This is the Love about which it is

written: "If I have prophetic powers, and understand all mysteries and all knowledge, but have not love, I am nothing" (1 Cor. 13:2). "Whoever has love has God, because God is Love" (1 John 4:16).[20]

For further study, I would like to recommend to you Bishop Kallistos' book *The Orthodox Church,* [21] in which he outlines this whole "theology of communion" as being based on the understanding and teaching of the sub-apostolic bishop and martyr, Ignatius of Antioch. As he tells us, what he says is not new, or an invention, but merely a passing on of what he had already received, just as the Apostle Paul had done.

How does one draw a conclusion on so deep, so pertinent, so alive a topic as Holy Communion? Perhaps only with some thoughts from our perspective – that this life-giving Mystery should have powerful effects upon our lives, for we cannot participate in the Holy Communion of our Lord God and Saviour, Jesus Christ, and then go about life as if nothing happened.

By the sacrament of Holy Communion, we are changed. We are citizens of the Kingdom of Heaven. We are in the world but not of it. Whether we live as Orthodox Christians in the first, fourth, fifteenth, twentieth or thirtieth centuries, we must live out, in the very practical ways that Maximus described, the reality of God's love for us, of the redeeming and saving acts of our salvation wrought by the Word of God, Who took flesh for us and for our salvation.

For Further Reading

Archbishop Paul of Finland. *Feast of Faith.* Crestwood, NY: St. Vladimir's, 1988.

Schmemann, Alexander. *The Eucharist: Sacrament of the Kingdom.* Crestwood, NY: St. Vladimir's, 1988.

Sheerin, Daniel J. *The Eucharist.* Message of the Fathers of the Church 7. Wilmington, DE.: M. Glazier, 1986.

Ware, Kallistos. *The Orthodox Church.* New ed. New York: Penguin, 1993.

---

[1] By permission of St. Thomas More College this paper appeared under separate cover as a publication of Holy Resurrection Parish, Saskatoon. Some editorial changes have been made to that text.

[2] The Cappadocian Fathers were the three great defenders of the faith of Nicaea at the Second Ecumenical Council at Constantinople in 381. Basil the Great, Archbishop of Caesarea; Gregory, his brother, Bishop of Nyssa; and Gregory the Theologian, Bishop of Nazianzus (later Archbishop of Constantinople), were all from the region of Cappadocia in Asia Minor, hence the name. To this day, all Christendom is indebted to them for their precise articulation of trinitarian theology. See D. Sahas's discussion in the second article in this volume, "The Ethos of Byzantine Spirituality."

[3] Brenda Meehan-Waters, *Holy Women of Russia: The Lives of Five Orthodox Women Offer Spiritual Guidance Today* (San Francisco: Harper San Francisco, 1993).

[4] Psalm 117:26–27 (See Psalm 118 if not using an Eastern psalter).

[5] Alexander Schmemann, *The Eucharist: Sacrament of the Kingdom* (Crestwood, NY: St. Vladimir's, 1998).

[6] See *St. John Chrysostom: Homilies on the Epistle Paul to the Corinthians,* A Select Library of Nicene and Post-Nicene Fathers of the Christian Church 12, 2d series (Grand Rapids, MI: Eerdmans, 1974–1983).

[7] *Saint John Chrysostom: Homilies* [on Galatians, Ephesians, Philippians]. A Select Library of Nicene and Post-Nicene Fathers of the Christian Church 13, 2d series (Grand Rapids, MI: Eerdmans, 1974–1983).

[8] *St. John Chrysostom: Homilies on the Epistle Paul to the Corinthians.*

[9] *St. Cyprian: Treatises,* Fathers of the Church 36. (New York: Fathers of the Church, 1958).

[10] Lect. 22.3–5 in *St. Cyril of Jerusalem and St. Gregory Nazianzen,* A Select Library of Nicene and Post-Nicene Fathers of the Christian Church 7, 2d series (Grand Rapids, MI: Eerdmans, 1974–1983).

[11] For some of his homilies, see *Homélies pascales* [cinq homélies inédites], ed. and trans. Michel Aubineau (Paris: Cerf, 1972).

[12] See *On the Mystical Life: The Ethical Discourses,* trans. Alexander Golitzin (Crestwood, NY: St. Vladimir's, 1995-c1997).

[13] See *Life in Christ,* trans. and notes Margaret Lisney (London: Janus, 1995).

[14] The Apostolic Fathers is a title given since the seventeenth century to the Fathers of the era immediately succeeding the Age of the Apostles, who represent the Apostolic Faith

they inherited from them, such as Ignatius of Antioch and Clement of Rome. "Sub-apostolic" is used more broadly to refer to the era immediately beyond Apostolic memory. To this period is dated *The Didache,* or the "Teaching" of the Apostles, upon which is based the concluding article of the Apostolic Constitutions, a work whose final form dates to the latter half of the fourth century. For an excellent treatment of these and other early documents of early Church liturgy and governance, see Lucien Deiss's work, *Springtime of the Liturgy* (Collegeville: Liturgical Press, 1979).

[15] See *My Life in Christ,* 2 vols. (Jordanville: Holy Trinity Russian Orthodox Monastery, 1957).

[16] See his *St. Augustine: Expositions on the Book of Psalms,* A Select Library of Nicene and Post-Nicene Fathers of the Christian Church 8, 2d series (Grand Rapids, MI: Eerdmans, 1974–1983).

[17] In a slightly different trans., see *Ep.* 93 in *St. Basil: Letters,* The Fathers of the Church 13 (New York: Fathers of the Church, 1951).

[18] *St. Cyprian: Letters,* The Fathers of the Church 51 (Washington: Catholic University of America, 1964).

[19] Norman Russell, trans., *The Lives of the Desert Fathers,* with an introduction by Sister Benedicta Ward (London: Mowbray, 1981).

[20] Thomas Spidlik, *Drinking from the Hidden Fountain: A Patristic Breviary* (Kalamazoo, MI: Cistercian, 1994).

[21] Bishop Kallistos (Ware), *The Orthodox Church* (London: Viking, 1993).

Chapter 4

The Centrality of the Lord's Table: Eucharistic Perspectives

NICHOLAS SAMRA

Bishop Nicholas is the auxiliary Bishop of Detroit for the Melkite Archeparchy of Newton.

The Church and the Trinity

The Church is a mirror of the Holy Trinity. We also call it a spiritual body, the spiritual Body of Christ. Christ lived on earth for a short period, but he left the earth physically and left in his place a body, his own body, which becomes his mystical presence, the Church. As the Church is the image of Christ, it is also the image of the Trinity, because Christ is inseparable from the Father and the Spirit. The best image of Church in visual form is the Pentecost icon. We see the twelve disciples seated; sometimes Mary is placed in the icon also, but always below them is another figure called Kosmos. This is the symbolic representation of the world. It was at the great event of Pentecost that the Trinity was manifested, fully manifested, to the Christian community. In our Tradition Pentecost Sunday is called Trinity Sunday. We celebrate the creation of the Church in the world as an image of the Trinity.

In the Old Testament, the Trinity was only partially revealed. In Genesis, we note the presence of the Trinity in the creation account: "Let us make man in our image, after our likeness" (Gen. 1:26). God speaks in the plural. The Father creates all by means of the divine Word. He also creates by the means of the Holy Spirit, who according to Genesis moves upon the face of the water (Gen. 1:1). Thus, we see the prefiguration of the Trinity. The presence of the Holy Trinity is also given to us or shown to us in Psalm 33: "By the word of the Lord the heavens were made, by the breath of his mouth all their host" (Ps. 33:6). Once more, the Word and the Spirit are used by the Father in creation. God reveals himself once again in trinitarian form to Abraham and Sarah in the form of three angels (Gen. 18:1-15). Again, it is only a prefigurement.

The New Testament coming of Christ changes everything. The incarnation reveals to the world the fullness of the Trinity. John tells us in his Gospel, "Not that anyone has seen the Father – only the one who is from God has seen the Father" (John 6:46). Therefore, it is Christ who reveals God to the world. Christ makes the Trinity known in various ways and at various times. At the beginning of his public ministry, Jesus approaches John at the Jordan River; he is baptized by John and we are told that the heavens open and a voice says, "You are my beloved Son" (Luke 3:22) and the Spirit appears in the form of a dove. At the Last Supper Christ prays for his followers, asking the Father "that all may be one" (John 17:21). Christ speaks of God as Father while promising to send the Holy Spirit to enable us, his followers, to become God's adopted children. Then at the end of the ministry, the coming of the Spirit at Pentecost, the Spirit is revealed and the gift of the Father and the Son completes the image of the Trinity.

Trinity means tri- or three-unity. We see a community in God, or a communion in God: three in union with each other. In our finite and simple minds, we need to distinguish and to define a little about God so we try to break down the work of God in the different persons, the Father, the Son, and the Holy Spirit. Scripture helps us a bit with that, but when one person acts, all three act; when one wills all three will; they all do things together. One does not act separately from the other. Therefore, we speak about "God" as Father. Most generally, when Scripture uses the word God it is speaking about the Father. We see the Father as the Source of all things. God loves; thus God creates – all three persons are creators. Similarly all three redeem: the Father sends the Son, Jesus Christ, the only-begotten one of the Father. He becomes man yet remains God. Christ, the Saviour, sends us God, the Holy Spirit, in order to sustain us. He leaves the world physically, but leaves a strong presence by allowing the Spirit to be more present, to be the Sanctifier, to be the Inspirer, to be the Consoler, the Comforter. It is the Spirit who enables us to maintain our relationship with God. Thus, we arrive at the foundation of our trinitarian faith: one God, a divine unity, yet distinct and perfectly united in three; one God because all three are one divine nature in their being; one God since whatever one person wills each wills; one God because whatever action one takes, each takes the same action. We speak of one God, both divine knowledge and love, yet three divine persons, and one God, who is a community of being. A community of being exists where the three are one. The Trinity is the model for the Church; it is the foundation of our whole faith.

When we think about Church as a body, many difficulties arise in our minds because of the dominance in our society of notions of individualism. In the past people grew up in one home, and maybe two, three, and four generations stayed in that home. Today people move from apartment to apartment, from town to town – communities are constantly changing. Stable communities are rare. All emphasis is placed on the individual: his or her rights, his or her choices, and his or her whims. We have a society of disconnected individuals.

God's plan is different from this. Humanity was created to be like God – a community. The Church, as community, is rooted in Genesis: "It is not good for man to be alone" (Gen. 2:18). A community is at the very core of the Genesis account. We are made to be connected, to be community. This, however, breaks down because of sin: Adam separates himself from God and from Eve. However, God works to re-establish this plan, to reunite humanity with the divine life through the covenant, the plan of salvation. The first covenant was meant for the Hebrews – the chosen people. The New Testament opens membership in the chosen to those who believe in Christ. They are no longer a tribe or a race, but a community of faith. All who trust in God as Abraham did, as stated in Romans 9, are the new Israel. This community of faith is the Church.

The Church that is given to us by Jesus Christ is, in a sense, Eden revisited. The first Eden was a place of happiness, bliss, perfect life for man and woman, where there was no possibility of ever hating or disliking each other until they brought sin upon themselves by estrangement from God. However, the new Eden is the place where the happiness, the bliss and the perfect life can take place once again. The Church is the regrouping of the descendants of Adam and Eve, the body that gathers the many into one. The Greek word, *ekklesia*, from which we get our English word "Church," means "she who belongs to God." The Church is the body that belongs to God. The human race finds its pattern or its model in none other than God. "Let us make man in our image after our likeness" (Gen. 1:26). God creates family. Christ re-creates that family in the Church, in the community of believers. The great teachers of the Church saw this same fact pointing to the fact that God is family in Trinity. They insisted on speaking of this image of Trinity and Church as one. The gift of Christian life can only be lived fully in community, in the Church. Without the Church, we cannot have Christian life.

The Church is also the Body of Christ. What a beautiful image a body is. The brain is also the centre of energy and life. When it is dead, there is no more movement in my body. So when Christ is head, it is Christ who gives direction; it is Christ who energizes and gives life to the body. There is a real intimacy between Christ and Church: one life and yet many lives are affected; one life and many depend on it. We need Christ to be Church and Christ exists in his body, the Church. So, when we think of Christ today in the world we must think of the body of believers. How does this divine presence show itself in this Church? God's presence is manifested by a variety of gifts that Christ bestows on the Church. Paul tells us there are extraordinary gifts: healing, prophecies, miracles. We still see them in the Church today. There are some who are graced with being the channels of healing. There are so many prophets still speaking to us from the Old Testament until today. There are so many miracles taking place in our lives. Even if science can explain it, the birth of a child is still a miracle.

Paul tells us that there are ordinary gifts also in the Church. The Church is manifested by ordinary gifts: authority and headship – the bishops, apostles, pastors and teachers; people who do charity work, the helpers; and the martyrs who are the witnesses of the presence of God. "Martyr" and "witness" are the same word. Martyrs were the witnesses of the presence of God. How could somebody die if they did not feel the presence of God;

how could they die for their faith? They died for their faith because they believed in it; they were the presence of God for us.

Sacraments in the Church

Another way that the divine presence is manifested in the Church is by the Holy Mysteries or what we call the sacraments. The sacraments or the mysteries are God's action to transform a human situation into a vehicle of divine presence. That is the easiest way I can explain what a sacrament is. God is shown forth in every aspect of life.

In Baptism, the person baptized by the Holy Spirit is born into the humanity or into the community of Christ: born into humanity first and yet through Baptism born into the community of Christ. God uses this natural situation and transforms it into a rebirth, making that person a member of the Body of Christ. In chrismation, the person anointed becomes another *Christos*, Christ, the anointed one. They go into the world as a witness to Christ to proclaim their faith in him. In marriage, we see the unity of two making them one. They remain two, but with God in the centre of their relationship, we have a trinity, a community. Marriage blesses this new community, this new family.

In the Sacrament of Penance or Reconciliation, there is a renewal to live as children of God through the grace of Christ by the power of the Holy Spirit. We are reunited once again to the Church, again this being a communal action. For so long we have gotten away from the communal action of the Church because of individual private confessions, which developed through the influence of Irish monks and penetrated also into the East. Nevertheless, let us remember that when a person sins they hurt someone. He or she has hurt someone and it is not God. God cannot be hurt. We have sinned against what God wants us to do, but God is not hurt by it; we have hurt another person. Our sin has broken a relationship within the body, so when we reconcile, we reconcile with that person through the Church. In the early Church, people used to stand up and profess their sins very publicly. Sometimes it took place during different seasons of the year and the Church realized that it was a little difficult, and a little embarrassing. So, we gradually moved to private confession.

However, even now when one speaks to the priest he represents the community to which that person is being reconciled. It is a communal action: the Holy Trinity is present.

Unction, the anointing of the sick, is another one of the manifestations of the presence of God. The Spirit anoints the sufferer to be with Christ and to be healed and made alive for eternity. Sometimes the sick are healed physically and go on to live in life, but they are healed also for eternity. This communal prayer for healing is a sacrament or a mystery that is given to sick people and not just to the dying. We even offer this anointing to the whole body on Holy Thursday. Everyone suffers from some form of physical or spiritual ailment – we all need healing.

The holy orders of deacon, priest and bishop are ministerial roles that speak very strongly of the presence of Christ. The community needs ministers. To serve, *diakonia*, there are deacons; to preach the good news and to evangelize there are presbyters; and to oversee there are bishops. All the orders are based on serving the community. The gifts of ministry are for the entire body.

The Eucharist is the communion or the union with Christ by the power of the Holy Spirit, present in the Word and in Eucharist, and it forms and unites all of us into one body. When Christ inaugurated this aspect of his ministry and left us this mystery of his love, he did not use Scotch and crackers; he used bread and wine because he knew them as natural symbols, which still speak so vibrantly to us today. Wheat makes bread and many grains go into making that one loaf. The many become one. The cup of wine is made out of grapes. I do not know how many are crushed to make one cup. However, they all mingle together and they become one. So too in the sharing, the millions of us who partake of it become one. It is the mystery of the whole Church *par excellence.* Therefore, we see how the sacraments or the mysteries of the Church create this image of the Trinity, this community that is so very, very necessary.

We are gifted people. God has bestowed the divine presence upon us in our midst. When you get a gift, what do you do? You respond in care. When somebody gives you a diamond ring, you wear it, you polish it, you hide it in the bank sometimes and you respect it. You also give thanks to the giver of the gift. Yes, so does the Church. We are the stewards of God's presence. We are the stewards of the special gifts; we get together, and we give thanks. If we are members of this Church, we accept the gift and we respond to God. We care for the gift of the Church; we respect it and we give thanks to God for the gift. This is the Eucharist. Because of our broken human nature, the plan of God is not totally fulfilled because we are sinful people. Yet as Church, in the eucharistic assembly, it is possible to share the divine life.

The gift of God is still happening to us. Tradition has not ended with the death of the last apostle. Tradition continues in the life of the Church. There is an ongoing presence of God. Paul tells us very beautifully in his Letter to the Corinthians, "You are the temple of God and ... the Spirit of God dwells in you" (1 Cor. 3:16) and then he compares that body to a building being constructed but never totally finished. As long as the Church is in the society of humanity, and as long as the world exists, the Church will never be finished. It is constantly growing and constantly becoming increasingly like the Body of Christ, the real Christ; it is constantly becoming like God. Our goal on earth is to become godly and that cannot be finished while we are on earth. This we call *theosis*, a Greek word meaning to become more and more like God. So many evangelical people ask, "Are you saved?" But that is not the question we should ask others. Jesus Christ saved us all and as we live on this earth, we are called to become increasingly like God through this process of *theosis*. Our Church, our body, is still not complete.

The Local Church

We may not see the presence of God so easily in our personal experience. Why? Maybe because we treat the Church sometimes like McDonald's. McDonald's has a branch in every big city. It is a multi-national corporation with national offices and state offices and city offices and outlets in every little town. You get the same Big Mac and the same fries at each one. This is not the image of the Church that we need. This is not the image of the Church from Scripture or from Tradition or from our Christian East. There was an attempt in the West to make the Church into the McDonald's image, but it is not that. We have a local church and local church is not part of a whole. It is a whole. It is a complete Church. When I speak of the local church, I mean a diocese or an eparchy. This is an entire Church with a bishop celebrating the Eucharist, and once you have a bishop and the celebration of the Eucharist, you have a complete local church. You have the entire heaven and earth together. Christ is present in every broken particle, in every crumb of the Eucharist, in every believer. So the Body of Christ is present totally in every local church: the Church of Saskatoon, the Church of Ottawa, the Church of Newton, the Church of Winnipeg. He is present in every one and the unity of all of those churches comes from the Eucharist. The local church then is a group of believers gathered around their bishop, with their priests and their deacons, in communion with other sister churches and mirroring the Trinity because they are in communion with each other, like the Father, the Son and the Holy Spirit.

By this point, I think you can probably gather that when I speak of Church I do not speak of a "what." The question is not "what" is Church. But I speak of a "who": "who" is Church? The Church is those baptized in Christ and in whom the Spirit dwells with a variety of gifts, like those of the Trinity: the Father of creation, the Son of salvation and the Spirit of sanctification. The bishop oversees, presides, and by his presence gives identity to the Divine Liturgy and to the Eucharist. The Divine Liturgy becomes the focal point of unity. He chooses presbyters, elders, priests to advise him and to be his associates and his arms of ministry throughout the vast diocese. In the early Church every village was a diocese, but today we have narrowed them down and made the diocese bigger and the number of bishops smaller: fewer bishops, bigger churches. In the early Church it was different. Every village had a bishop. However, in the early Church the apostles did not have enough time to do everything so they ordained some men to serve as deacons. The deacons waited on the tables, giving freedom to the apostles to go out and preach. Of course, the deacons sometimes went with them too. They went out and began to evangelize, so they certainly shared in the ministry of orders. The various communities that were visited were all churches, and together they were the Church as well. We see local churches, then, in communion with each other like the Trinity. All the local churches were in communion with each other because of the Eucharist. All the dimensions of local church are realized in the Divine Liturgy: the celebration of the presence of God in our midst. This is a vision of the Church. If it is not realized in a concrete way, it will only remain a dream. Thus to know the temple of God, which is our local church, we must begin to look at the living stones from which it is being built, the people of the Church. This vision becomes real in the people who make up the Body.

Doxology and Communion

The Acts of the Apostles lays out for us a blueprint of how we are to realize this vision of Church.

> They devoted themselves to the apostles' instruction and the communal life, to the breaking of bread and the prayers.... Those who believed shared all things in common; they would sell their property and goods, dividing everything on the basis of each one's need. They went to the temple area together every day, while in their homes they broke bread. With exultant and sincere hearts, they took their meals in common, praising God and winning the approval of all the people. (Acts 2:42-47)

In this blueprint, we see five major elements. First, the Church is a community of praise. What were they doing? They were praising God, liturgizing, breaking bread. They were a community of instruction, learning, and teaching. They were a community of shared life. They shared things together, life was in common, and they put everything in a common fund. They were a community of service. We heard how they served the needs of everyone, especially those who had specific needs, like the poor. In addition, we saw that they were a community of apostolic ministry founded upon the apostles.

The Church is made up of the people of praise, because the Church celebrates the Divine Liturgy. I think one of the most beautiful statements of the Patriarch of Moscow, Alexei II (b.1929), was his reply to, "Can you give us one short sentence about what is the Eastern Church or the Orthodox Church?" He thought for a moment and he said, "We are a Church that celebrates the Divine Liturgy." That is not all that we do, but certainly it is the summit and it is our experience and our reason for existence. We are Church because we celebrate the Divine Liturgy. The Church pivots around the altar; it does not pivot around ethnicity, clubs, or groups, but around the altar. We are Church because of Christ. Liturgy, when we gather before that holy table, is when we feel most fully Church. We read in the Epistle of Peter, "You, however, are a chosen race, a royal priesthood, a holy nation" (1 Pet. 2:9), emphasizing to us that we are the people of God and it is around Christ that we pivot. In a sense Christ's liturgy is not yet finished. He stands before the Father offering his sacrifice for the salvation of his people. We, as his Body on earth, share in that same ministry before the Father's throne. When we gather as Church we celebrate the liturgy; we attempt to unite heaven and earth.

Liturgy must be the central experience around which our communities are built. So often, many of our churches are built around the ethnic cultures that our people come from and the liturgy is pushed aside. Sometimes the liturgy takes on the name of the country from which the people have come. They fail to realize that in the Church of Christ, as we hear in the Scriptures, there is neither Greek nor Roman nor Latin nor Ukrainian nor American, but all are part of the Body of Christ. We have to prepare well for the liturgy and its execution. Sloppy liturgy is no good. We must take time and educate clergy, readers, deacons, bishops, even singers, so that they all understand the importance of their role in liturgy. We must have informed liturgical communities.

A third important aspect of liturgy is understanding the context of the liturgical life. We have the daily worship cycles and the saints of the days whom we commemorate. We have the seasons of fasts and the seasons of feasts. All these cycles bring the liturgical life together into our home as well as in the Church building. We need a daily deepening of our faith. Prior to the Sunday liturgy, it might be healthy to check our calendars and to read over with our families the scriptural readings of that day, the Epistle and the Gospel, so that we are prepared for the celebration. Perhaps we should have a bible study group in the parish or group discussions of the feast or season. We can improve our understanding of the liturgical cycle in many ways.

Participating in Church

Our Church music, whether it is led by cantors or choirs, is very important and requires full participation of the community. Unfortunately many of our churches, both Catholic and Orthodox, have become very choral-oriented: choirs singing and people sitting looking at the altar or at the icon screen and just expecting a show to be put on for them. However, if there is an audience for the liturgy, it is God and we are the actors, performing this great show of thanksgiving for God. So we must participate in all aspects: our singing – everyone's singing – is essential.

The idea of using our creativity to prepare for liturgy is very important too. It is a very healthy thing for parishioners, talented people in the community, to make the altars, the cross, the fans, floral arrangements for the icons, the various elements that are needed for the liturgy, and certainly to make the bread and the wine. We have lost that a little bit today. We get a little lazy so we go to the local bakery and they bake all the bread for us, the *prosphora*, instead of the families baking, as they once did, and bringing it to the Church as their offering. Today they give a few dollars cash donation and they think they have done their job. All this leads to a distancing from the liturgy.

The second aspect of Church, an extension of liturgy, focuses on instruction: being steadfast in the teachings of the apostles. There was a commitment among the apostles to pass on the apostolic tradition, to pass on the teaching of Christ. We must be a Church that is devoted to passing on the Tradition. We have received wonderful gifts that God has revealed to us: the Bible, the liturgy, the icons, etc., and the process by which we pass these insights on to the next generation. Historically, the liturgy was the main place of instruction. Today we have developed other mechanisms for teaching: Sunday School for the youth or any youth programs; Bible study, liturgy study, group studies for adults. However, all instruction, for example, preparation for the sacraments, bible study to understand the references in the liturgy, etc., pivots around the liturgy.

We also need to focus more on evangelization, the giving of the Good News. In the early Church, evangelization was very important. Before a person was baptized, they studied for up to three or four years to learn about Christ. I think in many of our communities our people have lost the basic Christian message and they need to hear it repeatedly. Therefore, we need to evangelize first at home. After people are evangelized and they live the Good News, the next step is nurturing. Milk is for babies; solid food is for adults. Even Paul in Corinthians tells us, "I fed you with milk, and did not give you solid food because you were not ready for it. You are not ready for it even now" (1 Cor. 3:2). So we evangelize first, and then once evangelized, we begin nourishing the neophytes. And, of course, when you nourish you begin with the easy stuff and you make progress. Solid food is only for the mature. Religious education cannot end at the eighth grade. It must continue on to adulthood and to the day we die.

I like to involve families in this process. I find it healthy at a baptismal catechesis to take the parents who are committed in their faith and have them work with the priest or the deacon and with other couples to learn to share their faith as a family. This is also important for marriage preparation.

In order to teach and to serve we have to be prepared ourselves, so we have to educate our educators. We must educate our educators so that they can be people of faith and can share that faith with those they are teaching and to whom they are ministering. In the early Church, there was a ministry of teaching that was a special blessing. Not everybody taught. Certain people who were more prepared, and whom the bishop felt could pass on this education, were blessed as catechists. This is something that I think we should take more seriously. We need formation programs to spiritualize our people, to let them know that parish councils are pastoral councils. They have an important function for the entire body – they are not just there to hire or fire. We all need more instruction in the faith!

We now hear more and more of drive-in churches or televangelism. All these new forms of religiosity are signs of the individualism I spoke of earlier. They are popular, but are they Church? Something is lacking in these churches. There is no life together; there is no community. If you belong to a drive-in church or a TV ministry only, there is no support. In worship, we hear in our prayers one mind and one heart. Father Tom Hopko[1] from the Orthodox Church of America gave a Lenten mission in one of my parishes and he told us about an instruction series he had been giving on the Orthodox Church. After many, many sessions, he suggested to the people who were taking this course that, besides reading the theology, they might to go out to live it a little bit in the life of the parishes. So one of the men, after once or twice doing this, came back very angry and said, "I am not coming back to class. Everything you've been telling us is a lie." What the man had experienced was a group of people in this church who were too cliquish to welcome him. They never said "Hello" to him, or "Who are you? Welcome to our Church. Come back again if you'd like," because they never saw beyond the blinders they had on. They were part of a community, but had no concept of evangelization. Strangers must become insiders when they enter the Church. Therefore, a Christian community requires openness to others, a social life. Not everything should be social in a Church, but we require social life. As social beings, we cannot get together without having some fun. Birthdays and anniversaries should be celebrated in the parishes, along with the feasts. It is common in our Tradition that a particular family offer a specific feast day. Each family takes a feast. If the family's name, the name of one of the important ancestors, or the father's name is George, St. George becomes their feast day. They come to Church, they bring their friends, and that is their feast. We need occasions to celebrate and occasions to mourn. We need youth groups, associations, dinner dances, barbeques, and much more. All of these are so very important. They build that sense of community, the deeper relationships among people. They bring the Church into the home.

The Mission of Charity

The Church must become once again the centre of charity. In the early Church, the Church was the centre of the whole community. Therefore, it was the Church that cared for the needy. Today we have secular charities: Kiwanis Clubs, the Heart Association, the Liver Associations, and others. As a result, often the Church forgets that it has a responsibility to be with the needy. Too often, our communities focus on raising money – raising money to pay for the bills of the Church – and the poor go unnoticed. The Gospel of Meat-fare Sunday is the Gospel of the

Last Judgment, when Jesus tells the story of the sheep and the goats and their division:

> "Come. You have my Father's blessing! Inherit the kingdom prepared for you from the creation of the world. For I was hungry and you gave me food, I was thirsty and you gave me drink. I was a stranger and you welcomed me, naked and you clothed me...." "Lord, when did we see you thirsty and give you drink? When...." "I assure you, as often as you did it for one of my least brothers, you did it for me." Then he will say to those on his left: "Out of my sight, you condemned, into the everlasting fire.... I was hungry and you gave me no food, I was thirsty and you gave me no drink...." "Lord, when did we see you hungry or thirsty or away from home or naked or ill or in prison and not attend you in your needs?...." "I assure you, as often as you neglected to do it to one of the least of these, you did not do it to me." (Matt. 25:34-45)

This is how we will be judged: not based on our prayer habits, but on our treatment of others. The needs of the poor are our business! First, our parishes need charitable societies. Maybe we should consider giving a percentage of our income into a fund for charity. We must be a Church that identifies with the neighbourhood. We should not only be for our ethnic group; we should be there for everybody, and we must look at the needs of the neighbourhood. We should support the local soup kitchen. Every parish needs to attend to those confined to wheelchairs or to their homes. There are churches throughout the world that suffer; they need our support. The poor are around us and they need to hear our words and hold our hands. In New York City, we operate an outreach program at Emmaus House and many people are just shocked. This is a Melkite ministry to the poor in Harlem. We do not have any Melkites born in Harlem, as far as I know, but one of our priests felt called to work there. He started a soup kitchen and then eventually he bought a burned-out hotel, which was being used as a house of prostitution. He began to renovate it; the pimps tried to burn it down twice. Nevertheless, with the help of the city and the police the Melkites stayed and are slowly building community. If any persons really want to change their lives around, after spending a week there, they can commit to living with the community. They get fifteen dollars a week. In the food kitchen downstairs they cook for the other poor. Once their lives are put back together, they share their talents with others. We have started a cabinet-making workshop because one homeless man was a phenomenal cabinetmaker. We now have opened an AIDS centre for dying people with AIDS. We are in the midst of a community that needs our help.

Ministry and Community

The final aspect of the liturgical community is the ministry for the body. We have talked about worship, which is *leitourgia*; teaching, which is *kerygma* or *didache*; fellowship, which is *koinonia*; and service, which is *diakonia*. The oldest vehicle given for service in the Church is the apostolic ministry, given to serve the Church in a special way in an array of ministries, raised by the Spirit to keep the community on the path set for it for the Lord. It is the mortar of the building. The first order put in place was that of bishop or overseer, the one who holds the community together. In his letter to the Smyrnaeans, Ignatius of Antioch tells us "where the bishop is, there is the Church" (Ch. 8). The bishop is the head of the liturgy, the presider at the Eucharist. The second order in historical development was the diaconate or the *diakonia*. The apostles realized that they could not handle all the work of a growing community, so they chose seven men and ordained them as deacons for the ministry of service. Then, as the Church began to grow, the concept of the presbyter and elder developed as an extension of the episcopal office. Together sharing collegial responsibility for the whole Church, Bishops help us maintain the apostolic tradition. The presbyters or the priests also have a share in the corporate service of the bishops. They form a council with the bishops. We have other ministries also. The subdeacons were the ones who went into the holy place for the incense. The candle-bearers and the cross-bearers served outside of the iconostasis. All these ministries and many others are necessary in the life of the Church.

God has given us so many wonderful gifts. Liturgy is just our simple way of trying to say thank you. We have elaborate cycles of feasts, fasts and readings. We have many ministries. We need to learn and teach. In the Eucharist, we offer to God what is already God's – the gifts we offer are received and returned to us

WInDOWS TO THE EAST

as God incarnate. We receive, consume and commune with God. However, in the end we need to remember that the best thanks, the best response, we can offer is ourselves. We can be transformed by the divine presence. We are made into the Body of Christ. We become Eucharistic.

Conclusion

I will close with a story of one of the most recent *startsi* in the Russian Tradition. One day his disciples asked, "Holy Father, what is the most important part of the liturgy?" He said, "You tell me." So one said, "Oh, the Gospel because that is when Jesus is speaking to us." And the second said, "No, no, it is the time of the consecration when we call down the Spirit to transfer these gifts into the body and blood. That is the most important part." Another one said, "No, no, no, it is when I receive the Eucharist and put God in me; that is the most important part." And the *starets'* says finally, "That is enough; that is enough. You all have some right in you. But the most important part of the liturgy," he said, "is when you leave the Church and you take back into the world the God that is in you and make the world a godly place to live."

For Further Reading

Chirovsky, Andriy, ed. *Following the Star from the East: Essays in Honour of Archimandrite Boniface Luykx.* Ottawa: Andrey Sheptytsky Institute of Eastern Christian Studies, Saint Paul University, 1992.

Cyril of Jerusalem. *Lectures on the Christian Sacraments.* Edited by F.L. Cross. Crestwood, NY: St. Vladimir's, 1986.

Zizioulas, John. *Being as Communion: Studies in Personhood and the Church.* Crestwood, NY: St. Vladimir's, 1985.

---

[1] See T. Hopko's chapter, "The Christian Vocation: Being Prayer" in this volume.

IV. Prayer in the Modern World: An Eastern Christian Perspective (1996)

Chapter 5

The Christian Vocation: Being Prayer

THOMAS HOPKO

Father Hopko is Professor of Dogmatic Theology and Dean of St. Vladimir's Orthodox Theological Seminary (Crestwood, NY). He has been a member of the Faith and Order Commission of the World Council of Churches and a member of the North American Roman Catholic–Eastern Orthodox Consultation. Among his publications are: The Spirit of God *(1976),* All the Fulness of God *(1982), and the multi-volume* The Orthodox Faith *(1987).*

The Orthodox Tradition contains much that is debatable and often unclear, but there are certain things that are very clear and very convincing. Much in the Tradition is directly antithetical to the modern world, and especially to the modern mind and to the modern approach to spirituality, to God, and to Church life. Prayer for Christians and in the Christian Tradition has to do with God; thus there is such a thing as right prayer and wrong prayer, true prayer and untrue prayer. Not all prayer is according to the will of God. The key thing about prayer in the Christian Tradition is that there is God: God the Father, the Lord Jesus Christ, and the Holy Spirit. Secondly, the human being and the whole of creation are created for communion with God. All is created as an epiphany of God and is created to be in communion with God. All is created to glorify God, to praise God, to obey God, to delight in God, to know God; that is the very purpose of all existence. The human being, the human person, is made for communion. The very definition of human life is to model, express and realize the very communion that exists between God the Father, his only-begotten Son, and the Holy Spirit. This is the communion according to which we are created and it is the communion in which we are called to share and to participate, and which we are called to actualize in our own life.

It is the communion that we are called to receive as a gift from God, a grace coming from God to us. The particular gift or grace of that which we will be discussing is prayer. Prayer is life lived. Life as given to us by the living God is a life sharing in the divine life. Since human beings were created in the image and likeness of God, we have the possibility of saying "Yes" to that gift and thus we may accept the gift consciously. Thus the most important Christian prayer that exists is to say "Amen, Amen" to what God is saying and doing and giving to us. In the Eastern Christian Tradition and in the Christian Tradition generally, we affirm that we do not just respond to God, but we receive, we accept, we say, "Yes" to God. As a result, the Spirit of God becomes one spirit with our spirit and God in fact effects the prayer within us. God prays within us and we are thus drawn within the blessed life of the Trinity.

The Nature of Prayer

What is the nature of prayer, of God's action in us and of our own free will? This is a problem that has plagued Christians for centuries and to discuss it we must avoid the problems that have arisen throughout Christian history. People very often want to know, is it God's grace acting in me or is it I who act? Is it I in my freedom deciding to interact with God, or is God choosing me? In metaphysical terms, this is a problem between what is called pantheism (meaning everything is God and God is acting and doing everything) and some type of dualism (wherein I am a kind of autonomous creature over and against God deciding whether or not I will respond or react to God). Do we accept the fatalistic view that I mean nothing and God decides all, or do we become Pelagianist[1] and assert that I can decide whether I want to interact with God's grace and thus be the agent of my own salvation? I would like to insist that from a truly Christian perspective on the very nature of humanity and God, the manner in which we interrelate these juxtapositions is incorrect. In the

Christian view, I am who I am in the sovereign uniqueness of my dignity and freedom as a creature only when I say "Yes" to God and realize that this very "Yes" is inspired by the very grace of God that is within me. When God is fully realized within me then I am truly I. There is no me who is not God in me. There is no God acting in me who is not the sovereign freedom of the Holy Spirit within me. St. Theophan the Recluse said, "For those who pray and those who know God, they know that it is true. For those who do not, do not bother trying to explain it to them. They'll never understand." This is a very important insight because in our world we are dominated by a perspective that to be human is to be an autonomous, free individual who can pick and choose one's own gods, decide whether one wishes to pray or not, and be the ultimate source who judges, valorizes, and validates human life. Whether you are an atheist or a theist, all these decisions become a sovereign individual choice. I would submit to you that this position is fundamentally a lie. It is a demonic lie because it proposes that we have a life in ourselves, excluding God, but we do not! It is a fact that there is a God and that we are made in God's image and likeness and not God in ours.

This call to communion is given to all creation whether we like it or not, want it or not, know it or not. If we like it, want it and know it, it is called Paradise. If we do not want it, do not like it and do not care to know it, it is called Hell. However, it is a given; it is reality. Thus the human being's greatest glory and dignity is to say "Amen, Amen, Amen, Yes" to that reality and then to live a life in communion with God.

In Romans, Paul asserts that the original sin is the refusal of prayer. It is the refusal of God's gift of prayer; certain people had knowledge of God, yet they did not glorify him as God or give him thanks (Rom. 1:21). God's presence in the world is known to all; God's eternal power and divinity have become visible, recognized through the things he has made (Rom. 1:20). It should be the most natural thing in the world for a human being to see and to know God's activity in everything that exists. In fact in Christian terms a human being with every breath should be saying, "Holy, holy, holy, Lord God Almighty, heaven and earth is full of thy glory." However, we do not experience life that way because the human being created that way has decided to suppress the reality of God's image and likeness.

Humanity has chosen to conceive of life and to attempt to live a life without God, ignoring or denying God. That is impossible, and so humanity has created an irrational, insane, self-destructive state. With our futile attempt to try to deny God, we have created the Hell we know. This is the original, primordial sin. Paul condemns humanity as having wilfully rebelled against this God who is so clearly present in creation. Rather than glorifying God (doxology) and thanking God (*eucharistia*), humanity has chosen idolatry (Rom. 1:19-25). Father Alexander Schmemann would assert that human beings by nature are created by God as doxological, eucharistic beings. We are created to be doxological, to praise and to glorify and to say "Thank you" to God. Thank you for the gift that not only of the hundred thousand million galaxies with the hundred thousand million stars all of which have been given to us, but also thank you for creating us in your own image and likeness with the freedom to know you, to love you and to serve you.

Prayer and Communion

Prayer is total communion with God at every moment of our lives, with every breath of our mouths. All that we are serves to glorify God and the entire purpose of our lives is to do God's will. We now live for the Other, for God. We follow the example of God, not a uni-personal God, not a God who finds self-sufficiency in oneness. Rather, we follow the example of the trinitarian God, one who is constantly in love and loving another Person.The Father loves the Son, the Holy Spirit loves the Son, and the Holy Spirit loves the Father. Then the prayer that we are taught is one of forgetfulness of self, even the denial of self, for the sake of receiving love and loving. This prayer empowers and enables us to become love ourselves, to become by grace what God is by nature. That love, the love of the other, is the direct fruit of prayer. Prayer, as that great gift of receiving from God communion within the blessed Trinity, is the very gift that constitutes the whole creation. This is the very gift that makes humanity human and creation what it is created to be. This prayer is part of the very internal divine life as well: the Son from all eternity receives his life from the Father and the Spirit and returns it to the Father in gratitude and glory without any tragedy, without any cross, but within the very life of the Trinity itself. Salvation, life, the Church are the entrance and the participation in that eternal communion between the Son and the Father, the eternal prayer of the Son to the Father in the Spirit from all eternity. This is the true and full meaning of the Divine Liturgy.

We use the term, the Divine Liturgy, for the Eucharist. But the Divine Liturgy on earth, the *leitourgia*, which is the common activity, the common work, is divine because it is the work of God. It is a liturgy that goes on from all eternity, whether there would have been a created world or not. This is what is given to us in Christ and this is what the worship of the Church is in its sacramental gift. It is the entry into the Divine Liturgy of the blessed persons of the Trinity. Now, that liturgy is going on in the entire cosmos: the heavens are declaring the glory of God, the earth is showing forth the work of his hands. As we bless water on the Theophany we say, "Great art thou, O Lord, and marvellous are thy works, and there is no word sufficient to hymn thy wonders. The sun sings to thee, the moon glorifies thee, the stars meet together in thy presence." The prayer continues: "and with the angels and with the elements and with the whole totality of creation," we are glorifying God. This great blessing is a clear example of cosmic liturgy that is going on throughout creation. Simultaneously there is the celestial liturgy – the angels, the cherubim and the seraphim are glorifying God with the ceaseless song: "Holy, holy, holy." Within this magnificent act of praise, the human person emerges, made in God's image and likeness, as the microcosm and the mediator of everything.

This is the primordial song of creation, but we now live in a world dominated by the discordant noise of our human "No!" We are born into a world that has said "No" to God. We are born victimized by a world where glorification of the true God and gratitude to the true God are not the content of life. We are in need of salvation. We need to re-establish life as communion and to once more activate the gift of prayer. Salvation is about making us once more doxological, eucharistic, praying beings. This is what Christ gives to us when he comes into the world and conquers death by death.

Salvation makes it possible to pray always and everywhere. We pray because prayer is true life. We pray because prayer unites us to the source of our life, God. We pray because we know the Truth, God – the real God – not of our creation, but the God who has created us! Prayer is about hungering for Truth, about wanting to be in communion with the true God and letting go of all our preconceptions. Thus, prayer is letting go and becoming a child of God, not by nature but by adoption.

Now some people mistake knowledge of religious things for prayer. They learn to recite the Bible or the Fathers by memory; they learn the *ustav* [2] or the *typicon*.[3] They become databases of ritual minutiae. However, do they know God? St. Theophan the Recluse (1815–91) was asked once about this dilemma. There are so many people who are very religious, who pray a lot, who read prayers all the time, who go to churches, who know every hymn, every *tropar*, every *kondak*, everything that needs to be done. They know what the pure Eastern Tradition is, as opposed to that of the Latin West. They know all these things, yet they become worse instead of better. Instead of being more loving, they become more hating and suspicious. Instead of being more merciful and kind, they become more judgmental. Instead of being more open and free, they become more defensive and paranoid. The more they pray the worse they look. So St. Theophan was asked, "Why is this so?" His answer was very simple. He said, "Because they do not want God." They worship liturgy, or they worship our Tradition and rite; they worship our language and music, or they worship our type of iconography. They worship their particular agenda; they worship many things. However, they are not worshipping the living God. They are in the worst possible spiritual state called in Slavonic, *prelest,* a state of spiritual delusion. They have created an idol and they call the idol Father, Son and Holy Spirit, but it is not God. It is what they have created, what they have invented! Prayer, however, is about falling into the hands of the living God. It is about putting oneself into the hands of the living God. St. Theophan quotes the letter to the Hebrews, "For our God is a consuming fire" (Heb. 12:29). We are called to be consumed by God just as a fire consumes everything it touches. We must want God so much that we let go of our reality and take on God's. We must enter God's realm, God's universe and God's kingdom. We let go of our individuality and enter the Church.

Falling into the hands of God, entering God's reality, means we must enter the worship of the Church. We become part of the liturgical life of the Church. That life feeds our private prayer. The Church teaches us to pray both publicly and privately. Then as we deepen our life in prayer, we learn to pray constantly, ceaselessly.

Liturgical Prayer

Liturgical prayer, or the prayer of the Church, is given by God and is from all eternity within the blessed Trinity. Within the cosmic creation, everything glorifies God and the angels sing "Holy, holy, holy" before the face of God. The first steps in this liturgical life are none other than *metanoia* or repentance. However, repentance is not just about refraining from an action or thought. The biblical understanding of repentance is a total revolution of one's whole attitude, one's whole approach to life. It is a turning of the mind, the *nous*, towards God. It is a self-conscious action of restructuring one's entire life. We now conform ourselves to the reality of God as our Beloved. Peter's words to the crowd in Jerusalem on Pentecost are important: "You must reform and be baptized, each one of you, in the name of Jesus Christ, that your sins may be forgiven; then you will receive the gift of the Holy Spirit" (Acts 2:38). Repentance and the change of mind are so radical that it is a death in and with Christ, and a rising with him. Then, in the reception and the anointing of the Holy Spirit, there is the fulfilment of the promise: we enter the kingdom of God.

The Divine Liturgy opens with this same affirmation: "Blessed is the Kingdom...." The reality of the Divine Liturgy is the reality of the Church, which is the reality of the kingdom. This is achieved not by something which people do but by the power of God. Sometimes we forget that the Hebrew word *quahal* and the Greek word *ekklesia* share a common image: they are the communities constituted by God. We do not make Church – God makes Church and we join that life. Liturgy is the praise, the prayer of the community, as constituted by Christ. Therefore, when one enters into the Church by repentance, faith and Baptism, one enters into a reality that is already there. It is the reality of the kingdom.

The Personal Rule of Prayer

Liturgy is essential, but it is only a school that fashions us for our ceaseless prayer. Our ceaseless prayer is the fruit, the product of our union with God. In order to come to ceaseless prayer we must sustain our liturgical prayer, sustain our experience of the kingdom by our personal rule of prayer. The teaching of our Tradition is that this rule will be different for every single person. It may be different at different times in people's lives. Usually it has a certain central content built around the Lord's Prayer, which is the paradigmatic Christian prayer. This prayer shows us what we should ask for when we pray, and you will notice in the Lord's Prayer there is no petition for anything earthly. There is no request in the prayer for help, for happiness, for food. There is no request in the Lord's Prayer for anything except "Your Kingdom come, your will be done, your name be holy as it is in heaven on earth, give us the bread of the future age, forgive us our sins as we forgive, let us stand in the tribulation, and let us not fall to the evil one." This should be the centre of everyone's rule. Additional aspects of a rule could be the Trisagion, the "Holy, Holy, Holy"; the Nicene Creed could be added as an affirmation of one's Baptism; the Fifty-first Psalm can serve as a penitential prayer. Of course, one's rule of faith could include the prayer of personal words, intercessions and sitting in silence. A measure of silence is very important. Quoting a Western Christian teacher and saint, Francis de Sales (1567–1622), "Every person, to remain human, should sit at least one half hour a day in total silence." Such a rule of prayer should be brief, regular and frequent. We should not engage in this rule on our own, however. A spiritual guide should lead us: a father, mother, friend, perhaps a pastor. Our Tradition clearly emphasizes that this very dangerous and narrow path should not be undertaken alone. One should have at least one other person to whom we report. That person should know all of our sins, all of our thoughts, all of our feelings, all of our dreams, all of our temptations, and all that happens to us in our daily lives. In monasteries, this opening of one's thoughts is done every night. There must be this other in our lives to whom we are constantly reporting.

Once we have established a consistent rule of prayer, we can begin to develop continuous prayer. Paul appeals to his followers, "never cease praying" (1 Thess. 5:17). This call to ceaseless prayer is taken literally by the pilgrim in the Russian story *The Way of the Pilgrim*.[4] He wanders all over Russia and Ukraine trying to discover the meaning of Paul's words. We also have the example of the Desert Fathers who taught that the best way to remain in the presence of God is to say the Lord's Prayer at certain hours, to have fixed times of prayer, and to have a short verse of prayer connected with bodily activity like breathing and walking and working. They urge their followers to synchronize their thoughts in attentive prayer.

An essential part of ceaseless prayer is attentiveness: making our minds attentive to the words of prayer. The prayer must dominate all aspects of our being. However, we must be realistic and know that the mind loves to wander, so it needs to be disciplined. We need to constantly bring it back to the prayer. We need to do that a hundred times during one fifteen-minute service, so that the short prayer, constantly repeated, can be the focus of our attention. It does not really matter what the words are (although they should be holy words) and they should be repeated rhythmically, very often, with the appropriate breathing. Very early on, this was connected with the name of Jesus because the belief was that the name of Jesus had a very particular power. So "Lord, have mercy" was extended first to "Lord Jesus Christ, have mercy," then extended to "Lord Jesus Christ, Son of God, have mercy," and finally to "Lord Jesus Christ, Son of God, have mercy on me, a sinner." The first part, up to "Son of God" would be done on the in breath and the remainder on the out breath. Nevertheless, we need not get fixed on the method; doing it however one can is important. After one does it verbally for a while, the prayer becomes internalized and descends into the heart. Then the mind is united to the centre of one's existence and one cries out from one's heart. The prayer becomes simply part of a person's actual life. Thus, the body can become a living temple of God. One becomes the temple of God, which is able to facilitate the fullest liturgy; one is constantly praising God in action and in one's heart. Here the Tradition clearly asserts this is not just for monks and nuns; it is not just for priests – it is for everybody. Ceaseless prayer is the goal of all Christians because it is about being in love with God and allowing God to fill one's being with Life.

Prayer thus becomes the action of becoming passive in the heart of God! We can now know that God is active within us and nothing should get in the way of this: no human emotion, no physical necessity, and no career obligation. Short rhythmic prayer of the heart binds us in communion to God and we become the living temples of God. We become continuous prayer, continuous liturgy. Our prayer becomes not something we do, but someone we are! We are prayer!

For Further Reading

Allen, Joseph J. *Inner Way: Toward a Rebirth of Eastern Christian Spiritual Direction.* Grand Rapids, MI.: Eerdmans, 1994.

Archimandrite Sophrony. *On Prayer.* Crestwood, NY: St. Vladimir's, 1998.

Bloom, Anthony. *The Essence of Prayer.* London: Darton, Longman and Todd, 1989.

Doherty, Catherine de Hueck. *Poustinia.* Glasgow: Collins, 1975.

Gillet, Lev [A monk of the Eastern Church]. *Orthodox Spirituality.* London: SPCK, 1974.

Hopko, Thomas. *All the Fulness of God: Essays on Orthodoxy, Ecumenism and Modern Society.* Crestwood, NY: St. Vladimir's, 1982.

Igumen Chariton, ed. *The Art of Prayer.* London: Faber, 1966.

Maloney, George A. *Prayer of the Heart.* Notre Dame: Ave Maria Press, 1981.

Tataryn, Myroslaw. *Praying with Icons.* Ottawa: Novalis, 1988, 1997.

---

[1] The perspective developed from the teachings of Pelagius (fl. 410).

[2] The rule of liturgical prayer.

[3] The volume which codifies the regulations relating to the order of services, seasonal variations, etc.

[4] Also called *The Pilgrim's Tale,* Classics of Western Spirituality 90, ed. Aleksei Pentkovsky, trans. T. Allan Smith (New York: Paulist, 1999).

Chapter 6

Prayer and the Body of Christ – Prayer and the Body of Humanity

ANDRIY CHIROVSKY

Father Chirovsky is founder and director of the Metropolitan Andrey Sheptytsky Institute of Eastern Christian Studies at Saint Paul University, Ottawa. He holds the Peter and Doris Kule Chair of Eastern Christian Theology and Spirituality. Among his extensive publications is most notably Pray for God's Wisdom: The Mystical Sophiology of Metropolitan Andrey Sheptytsky *(1992). He is currently the Editor-in-Chief of* Logos: A Journal of Eastern Christian Studies.

Christian Division

The division of Christ's Church is perhaps the single greatest scandal and obstacle to the evangelization of the human race. Yet, there are many who are not interested in healing the divisions in the Church. Many Christians think that they are actually acting ecumenically when they contentedly accept and respect the divisions among Christians. However, is this ecumenism? Is this even remotely close to what we mean when we pray during the Divine Liturgy for the well-being of God's holy churches and the union of all? Yet, it is important that we recognize that the unity of Christians is something wished and willed by God and essentially something to be received as a gift from God.

It is easy to forget that the Church, the community of faithful, is a gift to the disciples of Christ. An eminent Orthodox theologian says,

The Church is God's gift to men of communion and life with Himself: with the Father through the Son in the Holy Spirit. The Church is the gift of life *within* the Blessed Trinity by means of divine power and grace, the uncreated divine energies which flow essentially and eternally from the three divine persons and are communicated to men always and forever from the person of the Father, through the person of the Son and Word, in the person of the Holy Spirit. Just as the uncreated Trinity is one and holy, so the Church of the Trinity is one and holy.[1]

Father Hopko goes on to say that "the unity and holiness of the Church depend solely on God and can neither be created nor destroyed by any creaturely power."[2] Here we see underlined the essential mystery of the divine dispensation: salvation is uniquely and completely a gift.

In the third century, Cyprian of Carthage uttered the immortal words, *extra ecclesiam nulla salus,* "outside the Church there is no salvation." This phrase of Cyprian's has been used for centuries to condemn those who are not members of the church of the particular speaker. However, is there not a deeper sense to the phrase, in which it expresses a tautology? Saying that outside the Church there is no salvation is really to say that outside of salvation there is no salvation. The Church is a divine gift of community life, which is the kingdom; therefore, there can be no salvation outside this reality.

The Genesis account of the creation of the human race declares that we were made in the image and likeness of God. From the Fathers of the Church up to our own times, many have speculated on the precise content of that divine image. Is it the mind and its intelligence, or the will and its freedom? Alternatively, is it speech, perhaps, the capacity to name and give meaning to things? Alternatively, is it possibly something quite more mysterious and more at the root of things? Could we perhaps say that to be created in God's image is to be created in the image of three persons who live as one? If God is three persons, inter-related, inter-woven, inter-penetrating to such an extent that these three are really, essentially one – three divine persons living one divine life – then to be created in the image of this God is to be created as many human persons who live one human life. There precisely is the problem: we human beings have miserably missed the mark. We have not lived as inter-woven, inter-dependent, inter-penetrated persons in the perpetual *perichoresis*[3] of love and joy. Instead, we have turned in on ourselves. Some Orthodox authors like to talk about the difference between a person involved in deep mutuality and communion and an individual who is self-centred and isolated. If we use this type of language, then the Fall consists of human persons, created in the image of the mutuality of the Holy Triad, becoming egotistical individuals.

The most basic problem of the human race (exhibited in behaviours ranging from the completely self-centred infant to those who greedily and mercilessly exploit the poor and the weak for their own personal gain) is the loss of an understanding of the self as related to and inextricably bound up with others. This fundamental mutuality and inter-wovenness hearkens back to our very creation in the image of the Three who are One. However, how could human beings turn against their very nature and begin the course of mutual destruction? Let us return to the Genesis account of the Fall. There we find that the root of this disharmony among us is not a choice to be against other human beings, but rather the Fall is described as an act of disobedience against God. In fact, human beings are given paradise and told that it belongs to them. They need only recognize one limit: they may not eat of the fruit of the tree of the knowledge of good and evil. The tempter comes into this scene and he says, "God knows well that the moment you eat of it your eyes will be opened and you will be like gods" (Gen. 3:5). According to Genesis, Adam and Eve liked this idea of being like God, of being the centre of the universe. Why submit to another when I can be the centre of it all?

We still have this problem, you and I. Every time we over-schedule our days we think we are God; every time we take on too many things to do we delude ourselves that we are omnipo-tent. We fail to accept the limits that are imposed on us as creatures who are not the source of our own beginning; we do not accept the sovereignty of God and we grasp at equality with God. This is the fundamental act of disobedience at the root of all sin and all evil in the world. It is because of our disobedience to God that an enmity has been sown between our neighbours and us. It is because we break the proper relationship with God, the vertical relationship, that our horizontal relationship cannot work. When our relationship with God is wrong, our relationship with our neighbour or with our very self, for that matter, cannot hope to be right. Thus, when Jesus was asked what the gospels are all about, he answered, "You shall love the Lord your God with your whole heart, with your whole soul, and with all your mind" (Matt. 22:37). Then, if there is something left over after you have given your whole self to God, he added, "You shall love your neighbour as yourself" (Matt. 22:39). This triple love for God, for neighbour and for self is, however, only attainable in the new human race, the Church, the Body of Christ. These new human beings, these Christians, die to their old selves as they drown in the baptismal font and are made Christ's by the anointing of the Spirit and mix their molecules with those of Jesus as they consume his body and his blood; they look like others around them, but they are in fact strangers to the world of self-centred gain. They exist within, but are not co-extensive with, the old human race.

Thus, we see that the very salvation of the human race lies in the undeserved gift of a new life from God, in a new humanity in the one, undivided, unselfish, interdependent, inter-woven, inter-penetrating fellowship of the Holy Spirit, which is the Church. Thus, we see that the single most heinous crime that we have introduced into this new community is the wilful, hateful, ignorant and paranoid division of the one new humanity, the one Body of Christ. Although it remains undivided, as the mystery of God's working among us in our response to God's initiative, the reality is otherwise. We have divided the Body of Christ.

There are times when one must stand for the truth come what may. Countless martyrs have chosen truth over convenience and we cannot watch indifferently. Heresies do arise and they must be put down, because if the Word who is incarnate as Christ, and whose one body we share, is not the word of Truth, then we are not saved; we are simply deluded. In his essay on "Catholicity and Ecumenism," Father Hopko declares:

> In confessing itself to be the one catholic Church of God, the Orthodox Church identifies itself with the one catholic Church in history and claims that there is an absolute identity and continuity of this Church from the time of the apostles to the present day. The Orthodox

Church identifies the catholic Church in history as the apostolic Church which is witnessed to in the canonical New Testament Scriptures, the Church of the seven ecumenical councils, and the Orthodox Church of the East that continues to exist today in separation from the Western churches of Rome and the Reformation. Only in this Church do the Orthodox recognize the absolute identity and completely unbroken continuity of the catholic faith and life of the one Church of Christ.... The Orthodox Church affirms the legitimacy and necessity of its separation from all other Christian confessions on the basis of its inability to identify itself, and so the catholic Church of all ages with these communions.[4]

This defence of the continued separation of the Orthodox Church from all other Christian confessions clarifies that Christian unity is not about convenience or appearance. It is a question of truth. The only thing worse than disunity in the Body of Christ is false unity. The Catholic Church also claims that the one true Church of Christ subsists in the Catholic Church and other Christians are regarded as in less than perfect communion with it. Since the Second Vatican Council, it has permitted some limited sharing in the sacraments with the Orthodox churches on the basis of the real, if yet imperfect, communion in the faith and sacraments between the Orthodox and Catholic churches. No such sacramental sharing is yet envisaged with the Christians who trace their roots to the Reformation. However, it was just over thirty years ago that the Second Vatican Council made this tremendous leap from a very exclusivist soteriology to its present position regarding the Orthodox. Practising *akribeia*, strictness, rather than *oikonomia* or compassion, when it comes to sacramental sharing, the Orthodox Church nevertheless feels compelled, as Father Hopko ably explains,

To recognize these bodies as originally of the catholic Church, possessing, practising, and preaching many things in common with it and so to enter into ecumenical relations with them in the difficult and painful, yet God-inspired and God-willed effort to restore them to the catholic fullness of the Church of the Most Blessed Trinity.[5]

Now a clear paradox stands before us. As an Eastern Catholic I believe that the Catholic and Orthodox claims to each be the truest heirs in an unbroken line of the new humanity, claims that appear mutually exclusive, must be retained and accepted. I believe in my heart of hearts that this paradox is irresolvable, just as the paradox of the God who is three and one and the paradox of Christ who is God and human are irresolvable. In this agonizing antimony I see two poles, seemingly opposed but equally true. I believe that this is the only credible basis for remaining an Eastern Catholic or, as I like to call myself (without permission from either the Latins or the Greeks), an Orthodox Christian in communion with Rome.

Prayer for Unity

The Church is the mystery of our salvation and I stand before this mystery in awe, perplexed, anguished and joyful. A glad sorrow wells up in my soul and I see my brothers and sisters of the Orthodox and Catholic communions pass each other like ships in the night, both bearing the mystical cargo of my desire and both struggling with the question of how to connect. I cry out from my heart, "Lord, have mercy." A million repetitions of these words cannot express the helplessness I feel. I know that both are pleasing to the Lord. I simply do not know how to help them see it in each other. But others' eyes I cannot control, and others' perceptions I cannot ignore, so I call in desperation on the Lord, "Have mercy upon us." I believe in that prayer of fervent supplication. I pray for the impossible because God is the Lord of the impossible. I know the time is not right. I know the people are not yet prepared. The obstacles remaining in the way of Church unity are many. I know that my Catholic brothers and sisters look at me with suspicion, not quite trusting my loyalty. I know that my Orthodox brothers and sisters think that I am up to no good, conspiring to subject them to the Papal throne. I know that both sides view me as a simpleton who has not grasped the complexity of the issues at hand. Yet before my eyes there unfolds the drama of the rapprochement between the Orthodox and the pre-Chalcedonians. For fifteen hundred years, each side anathematized the other as holding a heretical position on the very central doctrine of Christ's divine-humanity. Within the last few decades, both sides have concluded that the other's expression of this central doctrine is "within the orbit of Orthodox teaching," according to Armenian Catholicos Karekin I (1932–).[6] Fifteen hundred years of accusations of Christological heresy seems to be dissolving into nothing. Suddenly, when both sides started speaking English to each other, we see the problem as a terminological misunderstanding. The heavenly King, the Comforter, the Spirit of Truth, has overcome the firmest of accusations and unveiled the churches to each other so that they can see themselves reflected in the heart of the other and take a step toward oneness. This is not compromising the truth.

Taking up an idea expressed by Pope John XXIII (1881–1963) at the opening of the Second Vatican Council, the Decree on Ecumenism mentioned ways of formulating doctrine as one of the elements of a continuing reform. Here it is not a question of altering the deposit of faith, changing the meaning of dogmas, eliminating essential words from them, accommodating truth to the preferences of a particular age or suppressing certain articles of the creed under the false pretext that they are no longer understood today. The unity willed by God can be attained only by the adherence of all to the content of revealed faith in its entirety. In matters of faith, false compromise is in contradiction with God, who is truth, and the Body of Christ, the way, and the truth, and the life. Who could consider legitimate a reconciliation brought about at the expense of truth?[7] The Council's Declaration on Religious Freedom (Dignitatis Humanae) attributes to human dignity the quest for truth especially in what concerns God and his Church, and adherence to truth's demands. A being together which betrayed the truth would thus be opposed both to the nature of God, who offers his communion, and to the need for truth found in the depths of every human heart.[8]

Pope John Paul II in his encyclical Ut Unum Sint (May 25, 1995) goes on to say:

By its nature the content of faith is meant for all humanity; it must be translated into all cultures. Indeed the element that determines communion and truth is the meaning of truth. The expression of truth can take different forms. The renewal of these forms of expression becomes necessary for the sake of transmitting to the people of today the Gospel in its unchanging meaning.[9]

So, what is it that enables human beings to see the same truth in a new way and to discover in the other another valid expression of the same truth? It is prayer that makes this possible. Prayer, when it is heartfelt and true, and accompanied by repentance, humility and obedience to God, changes our relationship with God, which is ever distorted by sin. Prayer restores us to the proper relationship with God, where we no longer consciously or unconsciously see ourselves at the centre of the universe. In addition, once our relationship with God is on the mend, then our love for neighbour and a healthy, proper love for our own selves become possible. Pope John Paul II, again in *Ut Unum Sint,* says:

> Prayer, the community at prayer, enables us always to discover anew the evangelical truth of the words, "You have one Father" (Matt. 23:9), the Father, Abba, invoked by Christ himself, the only-begotten and consubstantial Son. Again, "You have one teacher and you are all brethren" (Matt. 23:8). Ecumenical prayer discloses this fundamental dimension of brotherhood in Christ, who died to gather together the children of God who were scattered, so that in becoming sons and daughters in the Son, we might show forth more fully both the mysterious reality of God's fatherhood and the truth about the human nature shared by each and every individual. (26)

Ecumenical prayer, as the prayer of brothers and sisters, expresses all this. Precisely because they are separated from one another, they meet in Christ with even more hope, entrusting to him the future of their unity and their communion. Here, too, we can appropriately apply the teaching of the Council. The Lord Jesus, when he prayed to the Father that all may be one as we are one (John 17.21-22), opened up vistas closed to human reason for he implied a certain likeness between the union of the divine persons and the union of God's children in truth and charity.

> The change of heart, which is the essential condition for every authentic search for unity, flows from prayer and prayer guides its realization. For it is from newness of attitudes, from self-denial and unstained love, that yearnings for unity take their rise and grow towards maturity. We should therefore pray to the divine Spirit for the grace to be genuinely self-denying, humble, gentle in

the service of others, and to have an attitude of brotherly generosity toward them. (*Ut Unum Sint*, 26)

Now this is nothing new. There is no surprise in any of this. Isaac the Syrian (d.c.700) helps us to see that we need not even be praying specifically for Christian unity. He speaks of the prayer of the humble:

> A humble man does not dare even to pray or petition God about something and does not know what to ask for. He simply keeps all his senses silent and waits only for mercy and for whatever the most worshipful Majesty may be pleased to send him. When he bows down with his face to the earth and the inner eyes of his heart are raised to the gates of the holy of holies where he dwells whose abode is darkness, before whom the Seraphim close their eyes, then the humble man dares only to speak and pray thus, "May thy will be done upon me, O Lord."[10]

Thus, we do not even need to know what exactly to ask for when we pray for Christian unity. I certainly do not know what to ask for exactly. There is an old saying, "Watch out what you pray for because you just might get it." I am afraid that I might pray for the wrong thing. The solutions that my feeble mind can invent to reweave the bonds of love between the Orthodox and Catholic churches are not to be trusted, for my mind has been darkened by sin. However, if I simply pray, "Thy will be done," then I place the cause of Christian unity in the most capable of hands. Gregory of Nyssa explained:

> Now the health of the soul is the accomplishment of the divine will, just as on the other hand the disease of the soul that ends in death is the falling away from this good will, [thus] our nature was conquered by this evil and deadly disease. Then there came the true Physician who cured the evil perfectly by its opposite, as is the law of medicine. For those who had succumbed to the disease because they had separated themselves from the divine will, he frees once more from their sickness by uniting them to the will of God. For the words of the prayer brings the cure of the disease which is in the soul. For he prays as if his soul was immersed in pain saying, "Thy will be done." Now the will of God is the salvation of men.

That was Gregory of Nyssa on the Lord's Prayer. Since the will of God is the salvation of the human race and the salvation of the human race is being reunited in the one Body of Christ, the Church exists so that we can live in the mutuality and love of persons in the image of the holy Three. Thus, praying for God's will to be done is praying for the unity of the Church. It is this mutuality and love that we most earnestly desire.

All sin is a perversion of the need to love and to be loved. Our pride is a desperate cry for love, which turns into a grasping at love, a forcing of others to respect us, when we cannot even love ourselves. Maximus the Confessor speaks of true love. In his *Centuries on Love* he wrote,

> Perfect love does not divide human nature which is one according to men's different characters, but looking always on this nature, it loves all men equally. It loves the good as friends and the wicked as enemies, doing good to them, being long-suffering, enduring things caused by them, never returning evil for evil but even suffering for them if occasion demands in order if possible to make friends even of them. But if this proves impossible, it still retains its good disposition toward them, always showing the fruits of love equally to all. Thus our Lord Jesus Christ, showing his love for us, suffered for the whole of the human race and gave equally to all the hope of resurrection although each one makes himself worthy either of glory or of the torment of hell.[11]

This life of love, this life in the image of the Father, Son, and Holy Spirit in their eternal dance of love, is what God wants for us, for you and me. However, we can reject it. It is, I believe, John Chrysostom who said that there is one thing that God cannot do: to save you against your will.

So praying changes everything, if it is a prayer that is open to God's will, and when it is a prayer together, it is an even more powerful prayer. I quote Pope John Paul II:

> When Christians pray together the goal of unity seems closer. The long history of Christians marked by many divisions seems to converge once more because it tends toward that source of its unity, which is Jesus Christ. He is the same yesterday, today, and forever (Heb 13.8). In the

fellowship of prayer, Christ is truly present. He prays in us, with us, and for us. It is he who leads our prayer in the Spirit Consoler whom he promised and then bestowed on his Church in the upper room in Jerusalem when he established her in her original unity.

Along the ecumenical path to unity, pride of place certainly belongs to common prayer, the prayerful union of those who gather around Christ himself. If Christians, despite their divisions, can grow ever more united in common prayer around Christ, they will grow in the awareness of how little divides them in comparison with what unites them. If they meet more often and more regularly before Christ in prayer, they will be able to gain the courage to face all the painful human reality of their divisions. They will find themselves together once more in that community of this Church which Christ constantly builds up in the Holy Spirit, in spite of all weakness and human limitations. Finally, fellowship in prayer leads people to look at the Church and Christianity in a new way. (*Ut Unum Sint,* 22–23)

Experiencing Other Churches

I have personally experienced looking at the Church and Christianity in a new way. Every summer for ten years now, the Metropolitan Andrey Sheptytsky Institute holds an intensive summer program at Holy Transfiguration Monastery in Northern California and one of the highlights of this program is a visit to the San Francisco Bay area, where we attend liturgies in various Eastern Orthodox, Pre-Chalcedonian and Eastern Catholic churches. In addition, when we return year after year, there is a sense of expectation both on our parts and on the parts of those who host us. We rejoice, seeing each other again and praying together again. We see each other in a new way. The same is true of our day-to-day life at the Sheptytsky Institute at St. Paul University in Ottawa. We have Eastern Catholic and Orthodox professors and students and we share in daily *orthros* – matins and vespers. As one Orthodox Church of America deacon put it succinctly, "Once you have prayed together as deeply as we have, it's hard to go back to the old suspicions and fears that once reigned supreme."

I belong to an unofficial ecumenical dialogue called the Kyivan Church Study Group. It consists of interested individuals: bishops, priests and lay scholars from both the Ukrainian Greco-Catholic Church of Kyiv and our mother Church, the Patriarchate of Constantinople. After one of our sessions, a Greek Orthodox theologian said to us Ukrainian Catholics, "It is obvious that you are Orthodox. That is quite evident from the way you live, the way you pray, and the way you believe. There is no question about that. But what can we do with you? You are in communion with Rome. What can we do with you?" Well, I do not know what the answer is, but I certainly would not want to try to heal one schism by creating another. Perhaps that is another one of those inscrutable questions that the human mind can never fully answer.

Praying and worshipping together can be a painful experience as well as a pleasant one. During our field trip to the San Francisco Bay area churches, we visited a certain parish that belonged to Orthodox jurisdiction. The parish had a vibrant community, a liturgy that was very alive, and a community with absolutely no ethnic ties to Orthodox Christianity. These are former evangelicals of all nations and races who have chosen this Tradition; they were not born into it through the accident of history. Their liturgy is beautiful. We would return there year after year and year after year. My students and my family and I were reduced to weeping because we could not share in the Eucharist. We desire it so much, yet we are refused the cup.

A similar experience happened in Ottawa at our Institute. I took my students to a Divine Liturgy and one of the Orthodox students, a seminarian for the Carpatho-Russian Orthodox Church came up to me and he said, "That was the most painful experience of my life. I was completely one with you in that liturgy and yet I knew that I could not partake of the Eucharist with you because we are divided." He and I had tears in our eyes. I am thankful for that pain because until we have experienced the pain of schism, the pain of the division of the Church, the pain of this separation, we will not be sufficiently motivated to change things. This pain is good. It motivates us to turn to God with this impossible dilemma.

We stand before a mystery, the mystery of salvation, the uniting of a disunited broken humanity in the body of the new Adam, Jesus Christ. It is God's gift. We cannot destroy it, but we can hinder its action through stubborn non-compliance. We cannot forge its unity ourselves, but we can co-operate with the divine *energia*. We can be co-authors with God, and that is the true essence of prayer and the true path to Christian unity.

The Aesthetic and Spirituality

All too often, however, when we speak of prayer we only think of spirit, of a disembodied prayer. Yet, God has created us as psychosomatic beings. God became incarnate and lived as one of us. Christ embraced, he rejoiced at the sight of children. He ate. He even chose as his first public miracle, as is recorded in the Gospel of John, to do something utterly body- and pleasure-oriented. The Lord of the universe, the Creator of the cosmos, the Almighty *Pantocrator*, chose as his first miracle at Cana of Galilee to make wine.

Christianity does not aim at the dematerialization of the human person. It aims at spiritualization, but spiritualization and dematerialization are two different things. Spiritualization is about being filled with the Holy Spirit. It is not becoming any less material than we are. The Incarnation should put us at ease about that particular dilemma. However, we need to learn to live with and properly work with our bodies. Ascetical discipline or religious athletics are prescribed. Many great ascetics are spoken about in the hymnography of the Church as athletes of the faith. They practice a spiritual ascetical discipline; they work very, very hard.

The body is a gift from God. Thus, the important question is how do I use it in a way that brings me closer to God. Prayer is not so much something we do; it is more something that happens to us. As it happens, we are drawn into the love of God, and the more God's love brings us to love God, the more we begin to know God. However, this knowledge is not a function of discursive reason; it is not an analytical linear kind of knowledge. It is rather an epiphanic moment.

Romano Guardini (1885–1968) once noted that sacred art had as its basic function neither the formation of the viewer's character nor the imparting of knowledge, but only the preparation for epiphany.[12] The same may be said of the Divine Liturgy. This notion seems to be a stumbling block for many a Western Christian's understanding of the liturgical tradition of the Christian East. The totality of texts and gestures, sights, sounds and smells are all brought together and made articulate in the divine praise,[13] which is at once doxological and revelatory. It is especially difficult for someone from the rather aliturgical Protestant Tradition to understand how the gestures and sense-phenomena in the liturgy can be revelatory. The scriptural quality of Byzantine worship is more readily accepted as a stream of revelation, but any direct epiphany, especially if it is not explicitly tied to the words of Scripture, seems to some to be out of the question. Even Catholics of the Latin rite, although they proceed from a rich liturgical milieu, do not find it easy sometimes to understand the Byzantine idea of theophany within the liturgy. Somewhat indicative of this problem is the scholastic emphasis on the *essentia* of the mass. In the modern or post-modern secularized state, this difficulty with the Eastern concept of symbolic wording, iconography and gesture as not merely didactic, but also as revelatory, is only heightened.[14] Alexander Schmemann said, "The secularist is constitutionally unable to see in symbols anything but audio-visual aids for communicating ideas."

The entire liturgy is an epiphany, in fact, a theophany, a manifestation of God's presence. We, who mystically represent the cherubim, stand before the throne of the living God. Heaven itself is opened for us at the liturgy. John Chrysostom makes this point clear. He says, "What do I care of heaven when I already am in heaven?" In fact, the Cherubic Hymn is the key for our understanding of the Divine Liturgy of St. John Chrysostom and St. Basil the Great. Let me read that one wonderful sentence to you: "Let us who mystically represent the Cherubim and sing the thrice-holy hymn to the life-giving Trinity, now set aside all earthly cares." Let us reflect on the profound meaning of this prayer.

"Let us who mystically represent the Cherubim...." Who are the cherubim? They are those most-exalted of God's creatures

Christ the Redeemer

Christ the Redeemer is steadfast and strong. The chiton of deep red with gold edge and outer robe of blue with a gold background complete this composition. The right hand of the Saviour is raised in blessing while in his left he holds the Book of the Gospels calling all to him. The Saviour's head is surrounded by a golden halo inscribed with the Greek letters for "The One Who is"; Yahweh's response to Moses' request for the name of God: "I am who am" (Ex. 3:14).

egg tempera on prepared wood panel
1998
20" x 26"
Collection of Welcome House Chapel
Winnipeg, Manitoba

St. John the Theologian (the Evangelist)

The author of the Johannine writings is known as the Beloved Disciple of Jesus. His Gospel is the most commonly read in the Eastern Church and its Prologue is the Gospel read on Easter Sunday. In the icon St. John holds a book symbolizing the Word of God, which he is writing down. One of his ears is shown, symbolizing that he is listening to the prayers of those who stand before the icon and venerate it. This icon is shown on a circular background because it is one of the medallions of the four gospel writers found on the Royal Doors of the iconostasis. It is through the Gospels that we come to the Eucharist and enter into the Kingdom of Heaven.

egg tempera on prepared wood panel
1993
13" round
St. Volodymyr Ukrainian Catholic Church, Iconostasis
Red Deer, Alberta

The Entombment of Christ (Plashchanytsia)

This icon, painted on canvas and used for the veneration of the faithful on Good Friday and Easter Saturday, represents the preparation of Christ's body for burial. The dead Christ lies on his back on the anointing stone, with a winding sheet unfolded upon it. The Mother of God cradles his head in her arms and touches his cheek to hers. John, the Beloved Disciple, who is always presented as a young man with a halo, looks on sorrowfully. Joseph, also with a halo, stands at the foot of the stone. Nicodemus leans on a ladder and looks at Christ. Next to the Mother of God are Mary Magdelene and other weeping women who look on. Behind them is the Cross of Christ.

oil on canvas
1998
5' x 3.5'
Dormition of the Mother of God
Edmonton, Alberta

The Mother of God Hodihitria

This is a classical representation of the Hodihitria form of icons of the Mother of God. Her head is covered with a dark red omophorion; her adoring eyes looking at Christ are full of sadness. With a delicate gesture of her right hand, she points to the Christ Child who lives under the threat of death. Christ, although a youth, is represented as a sage who blesses with his right hand while in the left he holds a scroll representing the Gospel.

egg tempera on prepared wood panel
1995
10" x 12"
Private collection
Edmonton, Alberta

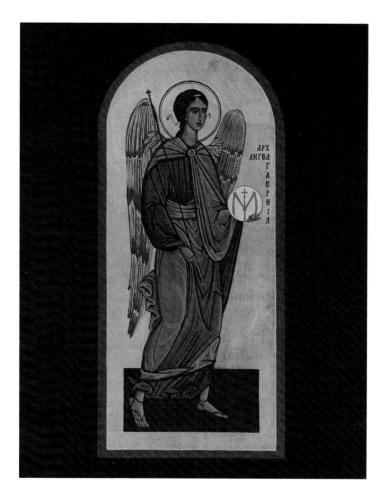

Archangel Gabriel

The Heavenly, Bodiless Powers, or angels, are spirits sent to serve "those who shall inherit salvation" (Heb. 1:14). They are guardians and guides both to individual human beings and to communities and societies. The choirs of angels continually participate in the heavenly liturgy, surrounding the Divine Altar and singing the Thrice Holy Hymn. The Church places special emphasis on two of these Heavenly Powers: Gabriel, meaning "Power of God," and Michael, meaning "Who is like God."

egg tempera on prepared wood panel
1997
8" x 18"
Private collection
Edmonton, Alberta

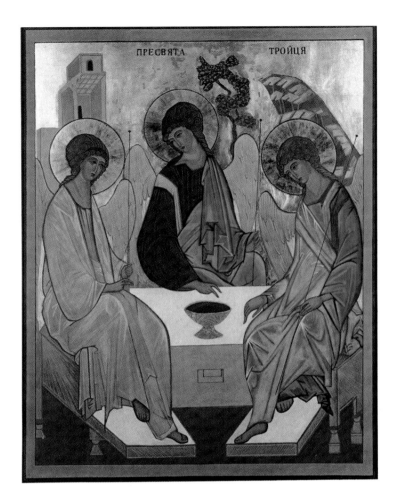

The Most Holy Trinity

The "Old Testament Trinity" as recounted in Gen. 18:2 is the only way in which the Trinity has ever been "seen." The icon represents the three visitors to Abraham and Sarah at Mamre who enjoyed the hospitality of the Patriarch and his wife. In response the visitors bring news of Sarah's soon-to-occur pregnancy. This icon is also, therefore, known as the Hospitality Icon, representing the hospitality offered to the visitors in the Old Testament and now the call of God to all of us to join in the Heavenly Banquet/Eucharistic Meal.

egg tempera on prepared wood panel
1999
22" x 28"
Collection of the Sister Servants of Mary Immaculate
Dauphin, Manitoba

The Annunciation

The angel Gabriel brings the "Good News" to Mary that she will bear the Messiah (Luke 1:35f.). The young virgin immediately responds, saying, "Let it be with me according to your word." The icon represents the wholesale embrace of God's grace by the Most Pure One. It was Mary's 'yes' that opened the doors of salvation for all humanity and the cosmos. As a result this icon is found on the Royal Doors of the Iconostasis, surrounded by the medallions of the four Evangelists. It invites all the faithful to accept the call of God and enter into the Divine Life.

egg tempera on prepared wood panel
1994
8" x 10"
St. Volodymyr Ukrainian Catholic Church, Iconostasis
Red Deer, Alberta

Vyzhorodska – Tenderness Icon of Vladimir

This Byzantine icon brought to Ukraine in the 12th century and kept in a church in the city of Vyzhorod is one of the most popular and well-known icons of the Mother of God. With the fall of Kyivan Rus' to the Tatars in the 13th century, many church objects were pillaged by the princes of the Vladimir-Suzdal' principality to the north (later Muscovy). This icon was taken to Vladimir and is now known in the West as the Vladimir Mother of God.

The icon represents the compassion and love of the Mother of God for her son, the Christ Child. However, her tender embrace is balanced with a longing, somewhat melancholy gaze into the distance. The Mother of God embraces and loves her son yet knows well what awaits him. She wears greenish-blue undergarments, earthly colours representing her humanity, and a cloak of heavenly colours, reddish brown and gold. Although she is haloed, it is only Christ's halo that has the inscription within it. The stars on the Mother of God's shoulders and head represent the three mysteries of her physical, mental and spiritual virginity. The Christ Child returns her embrace with equal warmth. The placement of the hands creates concentric circles, all of which point to "the One who Is," Christ, the Son of God.

egg tempera on prepared wood panel
1992
18" x 12"
Collection of the Sister Servants of Mary Immaculate
Willingdon, Alberta

who stand directly before the throne of God, and for some reason that we do not understand, in some mystical way we have been chosen to be like them. "Let us who mystically represent the Cherubim and sing the thrice-holy hymn to the life-creating Trinity." "What do the Cherubim do," you might ask. What they do is stand before the throne of God and they sing the thrice-holy hymn. They say, "Ho-ly, ho-ly, ho-ly." If you were to put that into colloquial English, it would probably translate best as "Wow!" That is enough: just to stand there, to behold the sublime magnificence of God, and to be at a level where it does not crush you but you can take delight in it. For some unknown reason, God has made us like those cherubim, to stand before the throne of God and to sing, "Holy, holy, holy," the thrice-holy hymn to the life-creating Trinity. Therefore, let us set aside our earthly concerns. Sure, my roof needs repairing, but who cares? Here is God. Sure, I have not finished my taxes, but who cares? This is God! Wow! That is what is happening in the Divine Liturgy. It is not something that we do; it is something that happens to us.

The point, which I should like to examine within the totality of liturgical epiphany, is the role that gesture, posture, sense-perception – in short, the gamut of bodily functions – play in the reception of revelation. My purpose here will be to show that these purely bodily actions can bring "an intuitive grasp of reality through something usually simple and striking," which is precisely what *Webster's Dictionary* terms as "epiphany." In focusing on the notion of epiphanic phenomena at prayer and within the liturgy, it would be wise to examine the three bodily functions of posture, gesture and sense perception, from the point of the layperson. Since the clergy have been specifically educated in liturgical theology and know to a greater degree what to expect from symbolic actions, they are not getting the spontaneous kind of epiphanic moment. The cleric has been prompted in advance on what to expect. Therefore, it is much more interesting to look at the laity, because in most cases they lack that measure of formal liturgical training and are more truly open to what a symbol in essence is: an object or event that conveys more meaning than it itself contains. That added meaning is the epiphanic element that all symbols include. It is this factor that we will be searching for in an examination of the human body within liturgy and within prayer.

First, let us look at posture. Byzantine churches should not have pews in them, but unfortunately, on this continent, many of them do. The absence of pews in a properly appointed Byzantine Church allows for freer movement of the faithful. It is wonderful to watch. I was in Lviv in Ukraine, and I was standing in the choir loft of one of the larger churches, the Holy Transfiguration Church (and also at St. George's Cathedral), watching from there the movement of the people. It is a sea, a moving human sea of people, and as one person makes a gesture – the sign of the cross for example – that movement moves along in waves through the whole crowd. I was there during Great Lent and I watched how, in a Church that was so packed that you could not walk through it, one was still able to perform full prostrations to the ground. They had it worked out; they had a system. They knew precisely at which moment to go up and at which moment to go down. They knew how to go down so that they could make the prostration and touch their forehead to the ground in this solidly packed Church and still allow the next round of people to go down. The whole congregation is one, living organism. One might notice that in an Eastern Church people very often do not conform to one set of rubrics regulating posture during the divine services. Some people are standing, some people are kneeling, somebody is making a prostration, and some are sitting if they are old or infirm. No self-respecting, healthy, young person or youthful person would sit down; it is a sign of weakness to sit down, and so only those who really need it do sit down. However, there is nothing in the liturgical books to indicate the appropriate time to kneel down or stand. The goal is free, spontaneous, respectful movement.

There are in fact very few such stipulations of how exactly one is to be positioned. However, those that do exist are very helpful for an examination of the correlation between bodily position and spiritual disposition within the liturgy. The most basic liturgical posture in the Eastern Churches is standing. It is a fundamental stance of respect and attentiveness. This we do to show respect for an important person who walks into the room. It is what we do in Church, because we are in the presence of God. We also kneel in Church as a repentant, ardent sign of supplication and admission of guilt. Kneeling is not comfortable; it is in fact somewhat humiliating. Kneeling and its symbolism are magnified in another posture, the full prostration. This is a position of alienation, and for precisely that reason it is most evident in the Lenten services of the Eastern Churches. The one who is prostrate can no longer stand aright and gaze into the eyes of Jesus. The Christian who already feels remorse usually assumes the prostrate posture, but it also serves to heighten that feeling. The late Father Alexander Schmemann used to say that the body and soul interact here, and he states, "Prostrations, the psychosomatic sign of repentance and humility, of adoration and obedience, are thus the Lenten rite *par excellence*."[15]

The use of various positions and their effects on the person praying are not known only in the East. Contemporary Roman liturgists are also increasingly examining the possibilities in this realm and they often manifest their indebtedness to the Orthodox churches in this respect. They also say that they got the idea of liturgical dance from the East. For example, the Ethiopian Church has a very clear tradition of liturgical dance performed by the clergy. In fact, a type of liturgical dance is present in the Byzantine liturgy: a priest and a deacon on opposite sides of the altar, incensing (the priest with the censor and the deacon with the candle) and moving harmoniously about. At the wedding ceremony and at Baptism,the triple circumambulation of the tetrapod, the little table in the middle of the Church, is a dance. It is a much formalized, much stylized, very dignified dance, but remember that not so long ago a lot of dancing was very formalized and very dignified. We find that the movement of the clergy and the people is an uplifting thing, much like a dance.

The Byzantine liturgy also abounds in symbolic actions on the part of the celebrant and laity. Upon entering the Church, the individual goes through a whole ritual of greeting. First, one makes the sign of the cross and bows. The bow is an Eastern greeting. Although the slight bowing of the head still occurs in North America, it is less and less common, being replaced by a wave of the hand, which is a very ancient form of greeting. The bow of the head is a way of saying, "I am no threat to you. I submit myself to you. This is obviously your territory." The further you go across the Eurasian continent the deeper the bows get. When we come into the Church and we make these bows, these half *metanias*, we recognize the presence of another, of God.

The next thing the Orthodox Christian does in his greeting ritual is to kiss the icon. The kiss is such a universal act that there would normally be no need to explore its symbolism. It is one of the few rites to which even secular culture can relate. However, I think it would be well worth our while to reflect on the matter briefly. We do not kiss strangers; we kiss only people who are known to us, and in our Tradition this is a triple kiss in honour of the Trinity. I always tell people, one time is pagan, three times is Christian. Kissing requires a previously established proper relationship. It is difficult to kiss the face of Jesus Christ in an icon while fully aware of the ways that we betray and hurt him. Yet this is exactly what the Orthodox often do and, though this very sacred act may often be performed without any real thought in relation to God as well as in relation to loved ones, beneath the action, somewhere deep down, there is the understanding that there has to be love and trust and peace. Father Alexander Schmemann commented on this ritual in a most interesting manner. He said, "Most of us hearing the exhortation, 'Let us love one another,' take it as a pious exhortation but the Church is not inviting us to love one another. The exhortation really means, 'Let us kiss one another.' Here we are led to something physical, a sacramental act that is most important. There will be a transformation of the one who stands next to me into what the Church is, namely, a true brotherhood, a unity of persons."[16] There is a grassroots movement to return to the kiss of peace amongst the laity.

The most common, the most basic, the most important of all ritual gestures in the Eastern Tradition is the sign of the cross. A visitor to a Byzantine Church will be always struck by the number of times the faithful make the sign of the cross. In fact, this action becomes semi-automatic for most people and at this level it can enter into the discussion at hand. At this level, it is the seal of a covenant. One hermit once told me that the faithful cross themselves when they feel that the Spirit has shown them something within the liturgy. This is the way to receive it, to make the sign of the cross. At first, the sign of the cross is merely an accepted convention, much like the nod of the head. Subsequently the individual will come to the realization that this word, which the Spirit has given, was accepted with a cross and was made possible through the cross in Jesus Christ and yet at the same time in the wholeness of the Trinity. These two insights –

the first into the nature of revelation and the second into the full participation of the Trinity in the redemptive act, because the cross and the Trinity are inseparable – these are received simply and strikingly, sparked by simple gesture, the sign of the cross. Granted, this full realization does not occur nearly as often as it should simply because that spark is not attended to, but still it is there at a level that is perhaps not fully conscious. Sometimes making the sign of the cross is like yawning; one person makes the sign of the cross, and the people next to them make the sign of the cross and it passes through the Church. One person yawns; everybody will start yawning. They cannot help themselves. Is that necessarily bad? I think it is a good thing when we can spark other people unconsciously to make the sign of the cross, the most beautiful sign of Christ's love and action – the salvific action of the Trinity upon ourselves.

All the senses are involved in Byzantine worship. The eyes feast on the icons and on the gold brocade of the vestments, on the metal work on the Gospel book, and on the chalice and all of the visual beauty surrounding us. The ears feast on the singing and on the little bells. We actually attach little bells to our thuribles (censers) so that the act of incensing sometimes has a sound to it as well. The ringing of the Church bells – especially when they are rung during the hymns of the Theotokos after the epiclesis and at Pascha as *"Christos Voskres!* Christ is risen!"* is sung out loud – marks a moment of joy. During those moments the ears worship God through listening to these beautiful sounds.

Taste is also involved. We eat in Church. We bless various foods, and this is not just the Eucharist. The Eucharist is the summit of it all, but we bless fruits, we bless boiled trail mix concoctions, we bless bread and wine and oil, and we eat in Church. There is a Eucharistic ecclesiology in the East, but I think that we could go further and develop a theology of eating together, because when we eat together we establish a bond. When we share with each other the *antidoron*, the bread from which the eucharistic Lamb has been cut, which is shared at the end of the liturgy, that eating together brings us closer and that perhaps is something that needs to be explored more. The olfactory senses participate as well. The nose deserves to worship God. That is why we have beeswax candles and a lot of incense. It is why we use rose oil for anointing. The touch, the kissing of the icon, is the most intimate way of using one's sense of touch.

165

Touching the Eucharist with our lips is the touch that heals, that takes away our iniquities and heals our senses. Every sense is involved – in fact, there is sensory overload.

I have been told, "You know there is too much going on in your Church. You should really limit the number of icons that you have because it is very distracting. In addition, you have too much motion; there is too much singing; and everything is happening at the same time. There is just too much." Moreover, I say, "Now you've got it. That is exactly what we are after." What we want is sensory overload. When one's senses are overloaded, and the rational mind cannot process information anymore, that is when the gates of the subconscious open, the floodgates of the subconscious, and God can finally get inside of us. We keep our barriers up pretty well against God and sometimes God has to exhaust us with long liturgies and a lot of singing. We have to be exhausted before we will let down our barriers so that God can invade us.

The point of all of this is that there really is a world of the liturgy for all of reality, spiritual and material; it is present there in a transfigured, sanctified state. It is all there. Each Church is a microcosm and each liturgy is a micro-history. This is the last great revelation that the liturgy has to make after one has experienced epiphany through the body and the universal symbols, through poetry, prose and song: that God is all in all. Even in our sickly, overweight, underdeveloped, balding, wrinkling bodies, God is all in all.

For Further Reading

Archimandrite Sophrony. *His Life is Mine.* London: Mowbrays, 1977.

Chirovsky, Andriy. "Anathema 'Sit': Some Reflections on Pews in Eastern Christian Churches and their Effects on Worshippers." *Diakonia* 15 (1980): 167-173.

Chirovsky, Andriy. "Falling Into the Eyes of an Icon: A Theological Postscript." In *The Icon in Canada: Recent Findings from the Canadian Museum of Civilization,* edited by Robert Klymasz, 157-167. Hull: Canadian Museum of Civilization, 1998.

Doherty, Catherine de Hueck. *Poustinia.* Glasgow: Collins, 1977.

Hausherr, Irénée, S.J. *Spiritual Direction in the Christian East.* Trans. A. Gythiel. Kalamazoo, MI: Cistercian, 1990.

John Paul II. *Ut Unum Sint* (May 25, 1995).

Taft, Robert. *Beyond East and West: Problems in Liturgical Understanding.* Washington, DC: Pastoral Press, 1984.

Schmemann, Alexander. *Liturgy and Tradition: Theological Reflections of Alexander Schmemann.* Ed. Thomas Fisch. Crestwood, NY: St. Vladimir's, 1990.

Winkler, Gabriele. *Prayer Attitude in the Eastern Church.* Minneapolis, MN: Light and Life Publishing, 1978.

---

[1] Thomas Hopko, *All the Fulness of God* (Crestwood, NY: St. Vladimir's, 1982), 91–2.

[2] Hopko, *All the Fulness of God,* 92.

[3] The Patristic understanding of the mutual indwelling of the three members of the Most Holy Trinity. For a discussion of this view see G.L. Prestige, *God in Patristic Thought,* 2d ed. (London: SPCK, 1952).

[4] Hopko, *All the Fulness of God,* 99.

[5] Hopko, *All the Fulness of God,* 101.

[6] These words were spoken by the Catholicos at Metropolitan Andrey Sheptytsky Institute in Ottawa, a few days prior to Fr. Chirovsky's address in Saskatoon.

[7] See *Unitatis Redintegratio* 912, in vol. 2 of *The Decrees of the Ecumenical Councils,* 2 vols., ed. Norman P. Tanner (London: Sheed & Ward; Washington, DC: Georgetown University Press, 1990).

[8] *Dignitatis Humanae,* 1 & 2. See vol. 2 of *The Decrees of the Ecumenical Councils.*

[9] *Ut Unum Sint,* 19. www.vatican.va/holy_father/john_paul_ii/encyclicals/documents/hf_jp-ii_enc_25051955_ut-unum-sint_en.html

[10] Consult Isaac of Nineveh (Isaac the Syrian), *The Second Part: Chapters IV-XLI,* ed. Sebastian Brock (Louvain: Peeters, 1995).

[11] Century 1.71 in *Maximus the Confessor: The Ascetic Life, The Four Centuries on Charity,* Ancient Christian Writers 21, trans. Polycarp Sherwood (Westminster, MO: Newman, 1955).

[12] Romano Guardini, "Sacred Images and the Invisible God," *Cross Currents* 10 (1960): 215.

[13] Matthew Gervase, *Byzantine Aesthetics* (London: 1964), cited in A.M. Allchin, *Sacrament and Image: Essays in the Understanding of Man* (London: Fellowship of Sts. Alban and Sergius, 1967), 8.

[14] Many of the issues addressed in this chapter I have dealt with in my "Revelation and Liturgy: The Epiphanic Function of the Human Body in Byzantine Worship," *Diakonia* 13 (1978): 111-117.

[15] Alexander Schmemann, *Great Lent* (Crestwood, N.Y.: St. Vladimir's Seminary Press, 1974), 39.

[16] Alexander Schmemann, "Liturgical Spirituality of the Sacraments," in F. Wilcock, ed., *1966 Byzantine Christian Heritage,* vol. 2, *John XXIII Lectures* (Bronx: John XXIII Center for Eastern Christian Studies, 1969), 30.

V. Holy Trinity:

Exemplary Paradigm of Community, Evangelism and Ecumenical Relations

(1997)

Chapter 7

Holy Trinity,
Holy Community and Evangelism

THEODORE STYLIANOPOULOS

Father Stylianopoulos is Professor of New Testament at Hellenic College and Holy Cross Greek Orthodox School of Theology (Boston). He is widely engaged in ecumenical activities on many levels. Among his publications are The New Testament: An Orthodox Perspective *(1997) and* The Good News of Christ *(1991). He is a senior editor of the* Orthodox Study Bible.

As a scholar of the New Testament, I would like to approach the topic of the Most Holy Trinity, not only as a teaching, but also by viewing the Trinity as a paradigm, the living God, who is the ground of the Gospel and the source of our salvation.

Commission and Mission

Let us begin with the great commission in Matthew:

The eleven disciples made their way to Galilee, to the mountain to which Jesus had summoned them. At the sight of him, those who had entertained doubts fell down in homage. Jesus came forward and addressed them in these words: "Full authority has been given to me both in heaven and on earth; go, therefore, and make disciples of all nations. Baptize them in the name of the Father, and of the Son, and of the Holy Spirit. Teach them to carry out everything I have commanded you. And know that I am with you always, until the end of the world." (Matt 28:16-20)

In our Eastern Churches, this passage is read at the time of Baptism. It is truly a magnificent passage. It is a crowning conclusion to the Gospel of Matthew, which sums up the central teachings or themes of that Gospel. It sets down in the name of the risen Christ both the mission of the Church and the means by which to fulfil it.

We have here a Christological assertion: "Full authority has been given to me." As earlier in the Gospel in the prayer to the Father, Jesus said, "Everything has been given over to me" (11:27). Here we have a proclamation of the divine authority of the risen Christ before the disciples who fall prostrate to worship him. Indeed, in his promise to be with them, he is Emmanuel: God with us. He not only commands them, but also empowers them to carry out this mission until the end of all things. Therefore, this passage is pregnant with Christology – a great theme of the Gospel of Matthew.

This statement also includes missiology and ecclesiology. Sometimes this particular passage is presented as the charter to evangelism, to mission, to preaching the Gospel. Nevertheless, it is also a charter for the Church: an ecclesial charter. Mission and Church are inseparable. In fact, if you look closely at the passage, the main verb is not "go"; the Greek there is only a participle. The main verb is [matheteusate], "make disciples" or "disciple." A literal translation would read, "going forth, disciple all the nations, to join them into *one Church*," which earlier in the pericope (16:18) Jesus calls "*my Church*," against which the gates of hell, the powers of death, shall not prevail. Discipling is not merely announcing the Gospel and moving on, but baptizing and teaching, initiating the nations, and raising them up in the life of the Church. This is an ecclesial mission charter.

There is another great theme in this passage: triadology, a trinitarian understanding of God. This is somewhat startling, but nonetheless the precise and full reference declares the requirement to baptize in the name of the Father, and of the Son, and of the Holy Spirit. The three Divine Persons are enumerated together, as equals, bearing the same authority, the same saving power, and the same glory.

Another theme in this passage is liturgiology, the sacramental life of the Church. Baptizing is a priority. Given Matthew's silence on Baptism earlier in the Gospel, this reference is rather abrupt. However, it is clearly very significant to the process of making disciples. This reference suggests discipleship involves participation in the liturgical, sacramental life of the Church. This life, together with the reference to the Holy Trinity, signifies a foundational aspect of the life and faith of the Church.

This final instruction includes a concern with righteousness, or right conduct. Disciples are "made" by baptizing and "teaching them to observe all that I have commanded you." In the context of the Gospel of Matthew, surely this "teaching" includes the great discourse of Jesus on the Sermon of the Mount (5:1-12) and the mission discourse (10:5-33). These are calls to the followers of Jesus to righteousness: "you must be perfect as your heavenly Father is perfect" (5:48). Finally, in this passage we have eschatology, the looking to the future consummation of the Lord's kingdom with his word, "Behold, I am with you always, to the close of the age." As I prepared for this presentation, I recognized more than ever before what a crowning declaration this was as an expression of the ecclesial, Church, dimension of Christian life.

The Trinity in Scripture

However, let us now turn to the Holy Trinity and its presentation in Holy Scripture. This has been a clear teaching of the Church from the days of the apostles. It was a fundamental teaching of that Church which came to see itself as the one, holy, catholic, and apostolic Church. It took some three hundred years to work out the intellectual contour, the understanding of God as Trinity, and its articulation. Of course, the Trinity and its eternal reality does not of itself change, but surely the understanding of it, the articulation of it, took many generations to be completed. This was a difficult struggle. Some Christians in the second century, as they tried to interpret and understand all those things in the Old Testament, went off the deep end, as it were. I have in mind here the great heresiarch Marcion (c.85–160), who was the son of a bishop. His father actually kicked him out of the house, so Marcion went off to Rome and established his own churches. He taught that the God of the Old Testament was not the Father of Jesus Christ, that another God was the high God. There were even others who taught there were many gods: nine gods, twenty-five gods, three hundred and sixty-five gods. The religious movement known as Gnosticism enunciated a very broad set of positions.

Over against all this, the Church insisted, "No, God is one and he is the Creator!" This fundamental teaching eventually came into our creed: "We believe in one God, Creator...." The same problems arose in the process of coming to explain the Holy Trinity: the Father, the Son and the Holy Spirit. Gregory the Theologian described the Holy Trinity – God as revealed as Trinity in the history of salvation – as three great quakes, three great times that God shook the earth. He takes this imagery apparently from the book of Hebrews (12:26-27) where the text speaks of the two quakes of the two covenants at Sinai and Calvary. To this Gregory adds the shaking of the outpouring of the Holy Spirit on the day of Pentecost. The articulation of the doctrine of the Trinity was a hard-won struggle. Gregory the Theologian mentions how bishops of good faith in his generation in the second half of the fourth century were not entirely sure how to regard the Holy Spirit. It was not an assured intellectual position: they had to pray, they had to think through, they had to discuss together towards a final solution to the question. Even his friend Basil (c.330–379) had some hesitations about clearly supporting the position that the Holy Spirit is a distinct being, equal with the Father and the Son, although he eventually did. Clearly, the Church took an interpretive, what we theologians call a hermeneutical position, as to how these great Fathers, saints and teachers of the Church viewed and interpreted Scripture. Finally, they agreed that the Christian God is a God in Trinity: Father, Son and Holy Spirit. This became the most important doctrinal teaching of classical Christianity, of those who identify with the one, holy, catholic and apostolic Church.

Objecting to a Trinitarian God?

Two objections have been raised against this classic view of God as Trinity: one on a popular level, the other on a sophisticated level, equally superficial, equally false, and equally dangerous. I begin with the popular one, the view that all the gods we speak of are just forms of the real god. In ancient documents, the idea was expressed that there are many gods, with many names, but all refer to the same thing. There may be the name Zeus or Mars or Moloch or Baal, just as today you hear people saying there are many religions, but all seek to climb the same mountaintop from different sides of the mountain. This sort of popular teaching must be opposed as being unbiblical. It must be juxtaposed to the biblical teaching about the only true and living God of Abraham, Isaac and Jacob. The understanding of the Hebrew prophets' God and the biblical expression and confession of faith in the one true and living God make precisely the point that this confession of faith is offered over against the many gods of paganism, the false gods of paganism and the dead gods of the idols of paganism. That is precisely the force of those adjectives attached to God: the one, true and living God in Holy Scripture. Our view of God makes a great deal of difference. Our view of God and our view of life go together. It makes a difference whether one worships the somewhat morose and unpredictable Zeus, especially when he has difficulties with his wife, or Baal the fertility god of Canaan, or Mars the war god, or Moloch, to whom children were offered as sacrifice. Heaven forbid that the name of the holy one of Israel and the father of Jesus Christ should be mentioned in the same breath with such gods! They are whom Scripture and Tradition view as idols, in fact, demons. Recall 1 Corinthians 10:20-21: "The Gentiles sacrifice to demons and not to God, and I do not want you to become sharers with demons. You cannot drink the cup of the Lord and the cup of demons. You cannot partake of the table of the Lord and likewise the table of demons." The God of Scripture is a personal and moral being, a holy God. The God of Scripture is clothed in mystery and transcendence, yet is revealed. The living God is the One who sanctifies all creation. The Creator is the source of life, yet remains distinct from creation. This God is a loving and compassionate Father who forgives and heals, but who also demands justice and righteousness, who judges sin and disobedience and will not be manipulated by gifts and sacrifices.

This biblical faith and our faith in and understanding of God is expressed by Paul, in 1 Corinthians 8:5-6:

> Even though there are so-called gods in the heavens and on earth – there are, to be sure, many such "gods" and "lords" – for us there is one God, the Father, from whom all things come and for whom we live: and one Lord, Jesus Christ through whom everything was made and through whom we live.

The second and more modern and sophisticated objection to a trinitarian God is traced back to late nineteenth-century German theologians. It is suggested that the doctrine of the Trinity, the trinitarian dogma, is a philosophical doctrine, one that derives more from Greek metaphysical thought and much less from the Bible. According to this view, the Bible speaks of the saving activities of God, not ontological relations. Dogma is founded on philosophical abstractions and not living faith. The Church Fathers were allegedly lured by Greek philosophy to depart from the true Jewish monotheism and move into the realm of pagan thought and religion, and thus developed a tritheism. All this is unfounded and simply masked by an intellectual veneer. One of the strongest exponents of this was Adolf von Harnack (1851–1930), who early this century argued that dogma manifested the Hellenization of Christianity. For him and others, this process of Hellenization was paralleled by another alleged great evil perpetrated by the Church Fathers, namely, to make the Christian faith catholic – to catholicize the New Testament Church. It is humorous that (or so it seemed to me when I attended graduate school a couple of decades ago and studied other German professors) the heirs of that tradition were now coming around saying, "No, the catholicizing of the Church begins in the New Testament itself. And as far as Hellenization, that began even two hundred years, three hundred years, before Christ." The fact is that, although the Church Fathers used several philosophical terms,[1] the content of the terms is certainly biblical, and deals with the biblical texts and the biblical descriptions of God and the activities of God in the history of salvation.

Replies to the Objections

Now pertaining to this argument that the Trinity is something of an abstract, metaphysical or philosophical theory I would like to say the following. When I was growing up as a boy in the Church and reciting the creed, I never thought of it as something abstract or distant. It was part of the liturgy, like the Lord's Prayer. We recited it often. I thought of it as a prayer, a hymn, a song of faith, and to this day, I recite it and hear it in the congregation in the same way. It told me and helped me proclaim what I heard in the Bible. Later, as a student of theology, reading the Church Fathers, Justin (c.100–c.65) and Irenaeus, Athanasius, and the Cappadocians, I wondered whether the detractors of the trinitarian doctrine had read the same Fathers I was reading. These Fathers were students of the Bible, biblical theologians, especially Athanasius and the Cappadocians, and yet they were very sensitive to philosophical considerations. Granted, not all the positions were explicit from the outset; nonetheless, when one reads Basil's "On the Holy Spirit" or Athanasius' "Letters to Serapion," the fundamental arguments demonstrate the divinity of the Son in the one case, the divinity of the Spirit in the other. This is done on the basis of the activities of the Son as described in Scripture: if he exhibits and acts with divine attributes and divine powers, then we draw the conclusion that he is God, as is the Holy Spirit.

I may say here that the simplest explanation is to think that the whole understanding of God as Trinity hinges on the incarnation of the eternal Word, on the historical revelation of the person and work of Jesus Christ. Given that the Prologue of John states that the eternal word existed eternally with the Father and was God (John 1:1), and given the apostle Thomas' confession of Jesus as "My Lord and my God!" (John 20:28), which are divine titles, and many other such passages, one has to deal then with the relationship of this Jesus to God the Father. Therefore, the incarnation itself becomes the pivot and the anchor of understanding God as Trinity. The incarnation is the actual revelation of the eternal Word in the person and the ministry of Jesus Christ. According to the teachings of the Church Fathers, the three Persons of the Trinity share all things. They dwell in each other; they share the glory and the kingdom of heaven. The only variation is that the Father is not the Son, nor the Son the

Father, nor is the Holy Spirit the Son or the Father. They are all distinct. Therefore, in these eternal modes of existence, they are distinct. Paul and others have encountered the full, divine presence in the work of the Son, in the risen Christ, as they discovered the full, divine presence in the gift of the Holy Spirit and thus came to this affirmation. These were the data of experience. These were the data that were taken up in prayer and worship and doxology, out of which the early Christians came to understand this dynamic view of the one, living God – of Abraham, Isaac and Jacob – as Father, Son and Holy Spirit.

In our own generation a number of books have been written which recognize that the Holy Trinity and the relevant teachings of the Church Fathers are indeed rooted in Holy Scripture, and are of the greatest magnitude and importance for the life, preaching and teaching of the Church. First, I have in mind the works by Jaroslav Pelikan, his great books on the Christian Tradition. In his book *The Christian Tradition* (Vol. 2), he makes the point that the teaching regarding the Holy Trinity pertains to the historical revelation and not philosophical metaphysics.[2] He argues that the Fathers approached the understanding of God as the mystery of God, presented in majesty and holiness just as Holy Scripture describes it. One particular element of continuity between the patristic understanding of God as Trinity and the understanding found in Holy Scripture is especially the view, and the clear teaching of Scripture, that the Father is the primary source of deity, of divinity – that the Father is the fountainhead from whom both the Son and the Spirit derive. We see this already in the passage cited earlier (Matt. 28:18) when Jesus says, "All authority has been given to me." By whom? By the Father! A similar relationship is presented when speaking of Jesus' resurrection: "He has been raised" (Matt. 28:6) By whom? By the Father. He was given all authority. By whom? The Father. As is made clear earlier in Jesus' prayer to the Father: "Everything has been given over to me by my Father" (Matt. 11:27). In the Lord's Prayer, Jesus directs the disciples to pray to the Father. In the Gospel of John, the Father sends the Son and from the Father issues the Holy Spirit. In John 1:1, the article is missing from the attribute *Theos* (God). It is missing primarily because in that context *ho Theos* (the God) is a reference to God the Father. So in all of Scripture, including the New Testament, the primary subject, initiator, actor of the drama of salvation is the Father, who works through the Son and in the power of the Holy Spirit. Now, if you go and read the great prayer of the anaphora in the Liturgy of St. John Chrysostom, you will see that is exactly what happens. The Father is the main subject: the prayer is addressed to the Father, already in the prayer of the preparation of the gifts (*proskomidia*) which reads, "Lord God Almighty." I looked this up in my Greek concordance and I was amazed that it was directly taken from the book of Revelation that has six or seven such references to "*Kyrie ho Theos ho Pantocrator.*" In addition, later on, the Father is addressed with these words: "We thank you, we bless you, we worship you in your dominion. We entreat you send down your Holy Spirit upon us and upon these gifts" and so on. There is an amazing coherence between Scripture, the teaching of the Church Fathers, and this language of worship in the Eastern Tradition. We see how the Holy Trinity is presented here in a biblical perspective with the Father as the fountainhead, the primary subject, actor and initiator behind the whole drama of salvation.

Patrick Miller of Princeton recently published an excellent book entitled *They Cried to the Lord* (now touted as a definitive book on prayer in Holy Scripture) in which we find a brief section on the trinitarian character of New Testament prayer.[3] He notes that Christ directed his disciples to pray to the Father. In fact, there are few direct prayers to Jesus. Miller argues that it is the sonship of Jesus, his unique sonship, which defines the particular nuance of the address to God the Father. That inter-trinitarian relationship defines the relationship of Christians as followers, brothers and sisters, and heirs with Christ, who now relate to God and pray to him in union with Christ and through the mediation of Christ, in the power of the Spirit. Thus, the believer's entire relationship to God the Father is determined by the believer's relationship to Christ in the Holy Spirit. The baptismal formula found in Matthew 28:19 is not a mere formula, but the essence of the matter. This confession of faith occurs at a crucial juncture of a believer's life: baptism/conversion presents the first rule of faith, the relationship of the Father and the Son. In the book of Romans, chapter 6, there is a significant section on Baptism that tells us that to be baptized means to participate in the death and resurrection of Christ, to be in union with Christ and to arise out of those waters to a new life in the Spirit. If one reflects on chapter 8 of Romans, the first half of which is devoted to the Holy Spirit, one recognizes that it is through the gift of the Holy Spirit, and the inner testimony that we have in our hearts, that we are sons and daughters of God. We have the Spirit of adoption and in this Spirit we cry, "Abba, Father." All this has to do with the core of the Gospel. Therefore, the good news is not merely an announcement to believe and be saved by faith, our subjective faith response, as important as that is. The content of the Gospel itself has to do with the incarnation, with the saving person and work of Christ, who is the embodiment of God. His saving work is also the work of the Spirit, through whom the redemptive blessings are imparted to the Church and to each individual believer.

The reform theologian Thomas Torrance recognizes the value of this trinitarian and biblical thought.[4] He remarks that a characteristic of the Orthodox Tradition is respect for the mystery of truth and fidelity to that truth. Our fundamental Orthodox truth asserts that God comes to us as the living God, as a numinous being, revealed to us as Father, Son and Holy Spirit. This is evident in worship. At the same time, this fidelity to truth demanded that the Church Fathers develop this insight, interpret and explain it. Torrance defends the consistency of Scripture, early Church teaching and the Orthodox trinitarian doctrine. Torrance's assertion underlines that the very Gospel that we preach concerning the saving work of Christ is a Gospel of the love and forgiveness of God, which we receive through the divine trinitarian nature. God works on the world and on us not singularly but as Trinity. The incarnation is an embrace of humanity. The Gospel of John tells us that believing in the Son gives us the authority to become children of God, not by our will, but by the will of God. The Spirit, through whom the love of God is poured into our hearts, is the one who makes this so.

I will go further than Torrance here, to also assert that the trinitarian understanding of God binds us to the sacramental life of the Church, particularly Baptism and the Eucharist. Christian Baptism is different from that of John the Baptist. It brings a person into existence in a relationship to Christ, united with him and becoming a new creation. In that existence, the believer is fundamentally ruled by the Father, the Son and the Holy Spirit.

Finally, we recognize the Holy Trinity as the plenitude of life, of light and love. The Trinity is the inexhaustible source of light and life. This is the source of radiance and salvation which we receive through prayer and worship and Christian living. In patristic theology and the hymnology of the Church, the Virgin Mary is described as that burning bush in whom the Lord God dwelled as a Son and radiated from her without consuming her; this is also an image of the Church. The living God comes to us through his Son and the Spirit. This is true because the Son promised us that he would come and dwell in us with the Father, and make a home in us. That God – as Father, Son and Holy Spirit – comes to be in us as a holy fire, God in our midst, Emmanuel, and makes the Church a vibrant and radiant spiritual community, to witness to divine majesty and glory.

Community and Covenant

This very personal disclosure of the living God as Father, Son and Holy Spirit creates community. An existence under this God, the true and living God implies, by its very nature, a corporate character. I remind you of the notable passages in Genesis 12 and 17, the call of Abraham.

The Lord said to Abram, "Go forth from the land of your kinsfolk and from your father's house to a land that I will show you. I will make of you a great nation and I will bless you; I will make your name great, so that you will be a blessing." (Gen. 12:1-2)

Later in Genesis 17:1-7 we read:

"I am the God Almighty. Walk in my presence and be blameless. Between you and me I will establish my covenant, and I will multiply you exceedingly." When Abram prostrated himself, God continued to speak to him. "My covenant with you is this: you are to become the father of a host of nations. No longer shall you be called Abram; your name shall be Abraham, for I am making you the father of a host of nations.... I will maintain my covenant with you and your descendants after you throughout the ages as an everlasting pact, to be your God and the God of your descendants after you."

God's personal self-disclosure creates relationship, not only singly with Abraham, but also with his whole clan, the community. Here we find those basic truths and themes of the Hebrew Scriptures, of covenant and election of God's people based on divine love. "Why do you choose us? We are the weakest of all nations." "I chose you because of my love for you and that through you my purposes might be accomplished, that you might be a light unto the nations." So here, we have this very fundamental truth of what the Scriptures call *ho laos* – the people of God – as an identifiable group, as an identity, a unity that belongs to God. "I am your God and you are my people, my elect people, my holy people. You are a holy people to the Lord your God." Remember when God called Moses to go to Egypt and Moses said, "Who am I that I should go to Pharaoh and lead the Israelites out of Egypt" (Exod. 3:11). The Lord also said, "I have witnessed the affliction of my people in Egypt and have heard their cry of complaint against their slave drivers, so I know well what they are suffering" (Exod. 3:7), and then, "Come now! I will send you to Pharaoh to lead my people, the Israelites, out of Egypt" (Exod. 3:10). The Lord expressed concern for "my people." This is not a dispassionate or distant God, but a God of love, caring and compassion. Yahweh is a God who is involved.

When God brought up the prophets as critics of Israel's way, their concern was not so much to criticize, to judge this or that sin in particular. It was a deeper critique, a judgment and accusation upon them for breaking this connectedness, this relationship, this intimate love, and this bond of the covenant. The people did not understand the mutual love and fidelity that bound God and the people. Thus is pre-shadowed the need for a new covenant. "It will not be like the covenant I made with their Fathers the day I took them by the hand to lead them forth from the land of Egypt; for they broke my covenant, and I had to show myself their master, says the Lord" (Jer. 31:32). What a provocative image we have here describing the relationship of the living God with his people, as husband and wife. In pagan religions, the gods sometimes came in pairs, husband and wife; not the God of Abraham, the holy God! However, his wife, his bride, was Israel. In that new covenant, "I will place my law within them, and write it upon their hearts; I will be their God, and they shall be my people" (Jer. 31:33). Do you remember the forbidding vision of Ezekiel when he saw the holy presence of

God, the *shekinah* of God, departing from the temple, leaving – a warning that the people would be left defenceless before the nations? Ezekiel also foresaw that God someday would give a new heart to the people:

> I will make with them a covenant of peace; it shall be an everlasting covenant with them, and I will multiply them, and put my sanctuary among them forever. My dwelling shall be with them; I will be their God, and they shall be my people. Thus, the nations shall know that it is I, the Lord, who makes Israel holy, when my sanctuary shall be set up among them forever. (Ezek. 37:26-28)

In the New Testament, this same basic relationship is the fundamental and constituent bond between Holy Trinity and holy community and we find here a deepening of that relationship between God and the people. In the New Testament Scriptures the term *laos* is not frequently applied to the people of God. Rather we see a new term: the Church, *ekklesia*, the *ekklesia* of God, the *quahal*, or the assembly of God whom God has gathered. The relationship and the intimacy of God and his people are deepened with the image of the Church as the temple of the Holy Spirit, no longer the physical temple but the living temple of the believers and the Body of Christ.

The Last Supper

But let us think first of the renewal of the covenant that we find in the Lord Jesus himself, on the night when he was betrayed, or rather, when he gave his life voluntarily for the life of the world. In the parallel texts of Matthew 26:26f. and Mark 14:22f. (Luke 22:14f.), on the night of the Last Supper through certain solemn words and actions Jesus not only announces, but institutes the renewal of the covenant. "This is my body," he says, breaking the bread. "This is my blood, the blood of the covenant, to be poured out in behalf of many for the forgiveness of sins" (Matt. 26:28). Through these solemn words and actions, he institutes the renewal of the covenant sealed by his own blood on the cross. We find this tradition of the Last Supper serves as the sacramental basis for the deepening of the renewal of the covenant written in the hearts of men and women as the Tradition of the Church. Just twenty years after the Last Supper, Paul is writing the Epistle to the Corinthians and he assumes and takes for granted that the Lord's Supper is a continuation of that Last Supper. Paul now cites the Tradition of the Church that he attributed to Jesus himself:

> I received from the Lord what I handed on to you, namely, that the Lord Jesus on the night in which he was betrayed, took bread, and after he had given thanks, broke it and said, "This is my body, which is for you. Do this in remembrance of me." In the same way, after the supper, he took the cup, saying, "This cup is the new covenant in my blood. Do this, whenever you drink it, in remembrance of me." Every time, then, you eat this bread and drink this cup, you proclaim the death of the Lord until he comes. (1 Cor. 11:23-26)

The Church has continued to celebrate this supper of the Lord, which eventually came to be known as the Eucharist. The Eucharist, or thanksgiving, is the constitutive and definitive way of expressing the church's intimate connection and relationship with the Holy Trinity.

This same reality of the new covenant not only has a sacramental basis in the prayers, liturgy and worship of the Church, but in the apostolic ministry of preaching and teaching anchored in the spiritual reality of the new covenant (as a fulfilment of the prophetic texts). Surely the Lord Jesus and the apostle Paul, quoting and referring to the new covenant, had in mind those texts from Ezekiel and Jeremiah. So we find Paul writing to the Corinthians and saying, "Clearly you are a letter from Christ which I have delivered, a letter written not with ink but by the Spirit of the living God, not on tablets of stone, but on tablets of flesh in the heart" (2 Cor. 3:3). Again, "Our sole credit is from God, who has made us qualified ministers of a new covenant, a covenant not of a written law but of spirit. The written law kills, but the Spirit gives life" (2 Cor. 3:5-6). Thus in these statements of Scripture concerning the Spirit of God writing the new covenant we have the return of the *shekinah*, the holy presence of God, in the power of the Spirit. The living temple composed of men and women who believe in the Lord Jesus replaces the physical temple. In 2 Corinthians 6:16ff., Paul says,

Tell me what agreement there is between the temple of God and idols. You are the temple of the living God, just as God said, "I will dwell with them and walk among them. I will be their God and they shall be my people." Therefore, "Come out from among them and separate yourselves from them," says the Lord; "and touch nothing unclean. I will welcome you and be a father to you and you will be my sons and daughters."

These statements concerning the indwelling of God through the Spirit are realistic and transformative realities.

The image of the Church as the Body of Christ is first found in 1 Corinthians 12. One might think that this image of the body, known in the ancient world and deriving from the sociological and political sphere, might appear to be only a figure of speech, a metaphor for the unity of any community. However, when one looks at the texts closely one will see that Paul very much has both a spiritual and sacramental view of the body as the Body of Christ, as the body which the living Spirit of God indwells. In verse 13 he writes, "It was in one Spirit that all of us, whether Jew or Greek, slaves or free, were baptized into one body. All of us have been given to drink of the one Spirit." In addition, in verse 27 he writes, "You, then, are the Body of Christ." Earlier in chapter 10, he connected this unity of the Church in terms of the body with the partaking of the one bread. Again, we recognize the sacramental basis: participation in the Blood and Body of Christ. Because there is one bread, we who are many are one body, "for we all partake of the one bread." A relationship through the revelation of the Trinity is defined in these fundamental ways. In fact, in 1 Corinthians 12:12, there is a remarkable statement that, "The body is one and has many members, but all the members, many though they are, are one body; and so it is with Christ." Now Paul should have said, "with you." Just as the body is one and has many members and all the members though many are one body, so it is with you the community. However, what he does say is, "so it is with Christ." With Christ! As if he could use the terms Christ and community interchangeably! It is a remarkable statement.

Holiness and Catholicity

This teaching of the relationship of holy community and Holy Trinity has tremendous implications for the character, the qualities and the manifestations of the life of the Church. I merely mention two: one is the holiness of the Church, and the other is the universality or catholicity of the Church. The holiness of the Church derives from its very relationship with the holy God. The One who reveals Himself in this numinous and mysterious being, distinct and separate from creation, but disclosed personally with a spiritual and moral integrity, confers Being upon the Church. Holiness of being is shared by the people of God as the Spirit indwells and the Lord indwells in the community. Thus, Paul describes Christ as the new Passover Lamb, the Lamb that is sacrificed for the community. He says, "Let us celebrate the festival not with the old yeast, that of corruption and wickedness, but the unleavened bread of sincerity and truth" (1 Cor. 5:6). Paul is led in an uncompromising way to preserve the holiness of the Church by saying, "Expel the wicked man from your midst" (1 Cor. 5:13). Elsewhere we see in his ethical instructions (1 Thess. 4:1ff.) a reminder of his earlier instructions. He places all the instructions in the category of sanctification (becoming holy). The people of God are called not for uncleanness, but for holiness by God, who has conferred upon them the Holy Spirit.

Secondly, the distinctive and definitive feature of universalism is catholicity: all nations, all classes and all people, called into one body through faith in Christ and through Baptism. Galatians 3:27-28 states that "All are sons and daughters of God through faith in Christ. For as many of you as were baptized into Christ have put on Christ, neither Jew nor Greek, neither slave nor free, neither male nor female, all, you all are one in Christ." The book of Ephesians in a magnificent way lays out this vision of God gathering the people by the eternal plan, recapitulating, and renewing all of creation. In Christ we have this incredible miracle: all peoples are now called to come to be people of God, breaking down the dividing wall, reconciling Jews and Gentiles into one body. Through Christ, we have access in one spirit to the Father; we become fellow citizens with the saints in the household of God, built on the foundation of the apostles and the prophets.

Christ is the cornerstone of the whole structure in which are joined together all people who grow into a holy temple for a dwelling place of God in the Spirit. The testimony of the Scriptures demonstrates this great truth: how the living God through Christ and the Spirit brings the people, the community, into intimate and abiding relationship with God. The purpose of all this is to draw all people into the kingdom, so that the Church might be a light unto the nations: in order to fulfil the prayer of the elder Simeon who beheld Christ in his arms and glorified God, saying that this child will be a light to the Gentiles and the glory of Israel, something that is fulfilled through the life and the work and the mission of the Church.

For Further Reading

Bobrinskoy, Boris. *The Mystery of the Trinity: Trinitarian Experience and Vision in the Biblical and Patristic Tradition.* Translated by Anthony Gythiel. Crestwood, NY: St. Vladimir's, 1999.

Kelly, J.N.D. *Early Christian Doctrines.* [Chapters 4, 5, 9, 10]. Rev. ed. New York: Harper San Francisco, 1978.

Lossky, Vladimir. *The Mystical Theology of the Eastern Church.* [Chapters 3, 7, 8]. Crestwood, NY: St. Vladimir's, 1976.

---

[1] Such as the term *ousia* (essence), *hypostasis* (person) and *homoousios* (of the same essence, consubstantial).

[2] The volume is sub-titled *The Spirit of Eastern Christendom* (600–1700) in Jaroslav Pelikan, *The Christian Tradition: A History of the Development of Doctrine,* 5 vols. (Chicago: Chicago, 1971–1989).

[3] Patrick D. Miller, *They Cried to the Lord: The Form and Theology of Biblical Prayer* (Minneapolis: Fortress, 1994).

[4] For example, see his *The Trinitarian Faith: The Evangelical Theology of the Ancient Catholic Church* (Edinburgh: T. & T. Clark, 1988).

Chapter 8

Community of Being:
A Trinitarian Imperative

MYROSLAW TATARYN

Father Tataryn is Associate Professor of Religious Studies at St. Thomas More College, University of Saskatchewan. Among his publications are Praying with Icons *(1998) and* St. Augustine and Russian Orthodoxy *(2000). Father Tataryn is also co-editor of this volume, associate editor of* Religious Studies and Theology *and book review editor of* Logos: A Journal of Eastern Christian Studies.

Contemporary theological discourse has once more turned its attention to the status of trinitarian theology as "a summary label for doing theology that affects all aspects of the enterprise of doing theology in its various disciplines."[1] This all-informing characteristic of trinitarian theology is perhaps clearest in the Eastern Orthodox Tradition where the very substance of human relationships is a manifestation of humanity's (and all creation's) divine giftedness and an emulation of divinity itself. The social impulse historically actualized by humanity is a clue not only to human rootedness in God, but also to the very nature of God as community.

One God as Trinity

A number of years ago Karl Rahner (1904–84), one of the great theologians of the twentieth century, wrote in his work *The Trinity* that,

> Despite our orthodox confession of the Trinity, Christians are, in their practical life, almost mere "monotheists." We must be willing to admit that, should the doctrine of the Trinity have to be dropped as false, the major part of religious literature could well remain virtually unchanged.... Nowadays when we speak of God's Incarnation, the theological and religious emphasis lies only on the fact that "God" became man, that "one" of the divine persons (of the Trinity) took on the flesh, and not on the fact that this person is precisely the person of the Logos.[2]

Rahner's comments lament the lack of integration which many Christians manifest in regard to the meaning and implications of positing that their God is both one and three simultaneously. These words present a particular challenge to those Christians who purport to place trinitarian teaching at the very centre of their thought, reflection, life and worship. The Christians of the East are rediscovering the social implications of their trinitarian doctrine. This results in particularly practical applications of what at times have seemed as the most esoteric of Christian teachings. This article will argue that this contemporary reappropriation of trinitarian doctrine also presents a new understanding of the very image (*kat'eikon*) of God in humanity.

In the past decades, much has been written about models of Church, notions of Christian community – and some attention has again turned towards the doctrine of the Trinity. Within Orthodoxy, these two concerns have been consistently and integrally linked, and in the past few years other Christian theologians have made the necessary connection between the doctrine of the Trinity and the nature of the Church.[3] Christoph Schwöbel has asserted in his recent volume, *Trinitarian Theology Today,* a very simple truth:

> The doctrine of the Trinity matters. It is not a topic reserved for austere theological speculation or the

language and practice of worship. The conceptual form in which the doctrine of the Trinity is expressed will affect not only the content and emphases of the doctrinal scheme of theology but also the forms of community organization in the Church and its life of worship.[4]

Why this assertion of an intrinsic and essential connection between our trinitarian doctrine and our understanding of community? The answer lies in the Cappadocians (Basil the Great, c.330–79; Gregory of Nyssa, c.330–95; Gregory of Nazianzus, 329–89; and Macrina, c.327–79)[5] and in the work of Gregory Palamas (c.1296–1359).[6] It is to the latter that I first turn. Palamas asserted, in Chapter 134 of his *The One Hundred and Fifty Chapters,* "God is a transcendent substance in which there are observed only relation and creation, which do not produce within it any composition or alteration."[7] In effect, Palamas was asserting that the very being of God is substantial Trinity: God is Father, Son and Holy Spirit and thus God. The essence of God does not precede the relations of God – foundationally God is community of being. The unity of God is the interrelationship of the Trinity not the precursor of the Trinity![8] Palamas' assertion is profound: God is fundamentally relation and creation.[9] Let us set aside creation for a moment because creation, as we shall see, is an elaboration and specification of relation.

The Trinity as Relation

What does it mean to assert that God is substantially relation? Simply put, it means that at the very centre of what is true and what is real is not simple singularity, but rather relation.[10] Maximus the Confessor asserted that *diaphora* (difference) is at the core of all being, and that it is good. Maximus made this point in a number of places; I will refer only to one. In *The Mystagogia,* he reflected upon the nature of the universe. He stated:

> The universe too is one, not split between its visible and invisible parts; on the contrary, by the force of their reference to its own unity and indivisibility, it circumscribes their difference in character. It shows itself to be the same, in the visible and invisible mutually

joined without confusion with each other. Each is wholly fixed in the whole of the other.[11]

In other words, the perceived differences, be they Father, Son, Holy Spirit, or visible and invisible universe, are only parts which must be perceived together in order to know the fullness of reality. It is this insight which allowed Basil the Great to defend the divinity of the Holy Spirit. Basil argued simply: that which is said of the Father, is said of the Son and the Holy Spirit and thus they are all one God.[12] Here Basil demonstrated the significance of worship or liturgy in the development of trinitarian doctrine because his source for this language about the Trinity is both Scripture and Liturgy.

The classic formulation of trinitarian doctrine is given by Prestige in *God in Patristic Thought:*

> If the community of *ousia* is taken as implying an antecedent matter, divided up into the three Persons, says Basil (*Contra Eunomius* 1.19), that is as great a blasphemy as saying that the Persons are unequal ... the right way of understanding the community of *ousia* is by the recognition that the same account must be given of one Person as of another.[13]

However, if the same thing can be said of all three persons – perhaps there is just one God and not three persons. Aware of the inherent danger Basil quickly responded. In his letter *On the Holy Spirit,* he identified the uniqueness of the persons with their interrelatedness. "There is one God and Father, one Only-Begotten Son,"[14] and a bit later "the Holy Spirit is one, and we speak of him as unique, since through the one Son he is joined to the Father."[15] What makes the Father, Father, is then the *monarchia* – being the origin (not in time, nor logically, but by relation). The Son is Son, because begotten (again a relation) and finally the Spirit proceeds from the Father who is *monarchia* – the sole origin. This Eastern perception of the foundational nature of the trinitarian relations means that when Charlemagne had the *filioque* (that the Holy Spirit proceeds from the Father *and the Son*) added to the Creed he was tampering with the very internal relations of the Trinity.[16] To the ear of Eastern Christians familiar with their Tradition, speaking of the Holy Spirit as proceeding from two origins (Father and Son) questions the very nature of God! In addition, Basil uses very specific language to describe the oneness of God; he describes it as "communion" or in Greek *koinonia*. Basil specifically identifies the communion of the blessed Trinity with the communion of the saints (2 Cor. 13:13), that is, with the communion of the Church. This interpretation of the Cappadocian Tradition clearly identifies the nature of God as Trinity with the nature of the Church – the Trinity is the model for the Church! Gennadios Limouris says:

> The Church as a whole is an *icon* of God the Trinity, reproducing on earth the mystery of the unity in diversity. In the Holy Trinity the three Persons are one God, yet each is fully personal; in the Church a multitude of human beings are united in one, yet each preserves his/her personal diversity unimpaired.[17]

This also means that the Church cannot be reduced to simple uniformity. The model which has often been repeated "One God, One Church, One Baptism, One Pope," suggesting there is only one way the Church can be, is fundamentally anti-trinitarian. The Church is necessarily a unity in diversity.

So, what insights do the Cappadocians offer for our reflections on Christian community? Firstly, they make an essential declaration about humanity. If God is essentially Trinity (in relation) and humanity is created in the image and likeness of God, then the Tradition asserts humanity is essentially "being as communion" or, in the words of John Zizioulas, "being is *constituted* as communion."[18] Human relatedness constitutes the very essence of what it is to be a human being. However, what is this relatedness? It is a relatedness that originates in the Trinity and concurrently emulates the Trinity. The Father begets the Son and spirates the Holy Spirit. The Son enters the world and grants the Holy Spirit who rests upon the believer. Why is it the Son who enters the world? One of the reasons is because whoever sees the Son sees the Father. In other words, the very purpose of the incarnation is to give witness to the very relatedness to the Father of the Son and of all believers. The response of humanity to this fundamental relatedness is a response in prayer and worship: the believer, being in the Holy Spirit, prays through the Son to the Father. This movement establishes the first relation for all humans, for all time – it is the same for all. There is no other way of coming to the Father; there are no shortcuts, no privileged approaches, and no higher states that move you ahead in the line.

This movement is internal to what humans are as created by God. The Fall is in fact the very denial of this relatedness.[19] The Fall is a denial of humanity's dependence upon the Trinity and rootedness in the trinitarian relations. In the Fall, Adam mistakenly asserted an independence from God and an ability to know the truth without this fundamental relation. This assertion thus finds its end in death: the denial of relatedness denies life itself! Death, as a universal and cosmic experience, is the product of sin and the ultimate challenge to humanity's inter-connectedness and rootedness in the Trinity.[20] Sartre's "hell is the other'" is a vivid reflection of the faith of the post-Fall human being. The Trinity asserts that "the other" is a call to being! A human being cannot be truly human without "an-other"! Relatedness and relationships are the very core existential affir-mation of being God-like.

The second implication of this trinitarian insight is that this relatedness, rooted in the Trinity, is without beginning and without end; it is eternal. Although originating in the Father, it is constantly moving among the three persons; and when destined through creation to humanity, it is eternal because humanity can never exhaust the depth and implications of this relatedness. The trinitarian model places within humanity an eternal impulse of motion. True humanity, that is the Christian life, is one of constant motion. There is no room for the satisfaction of the "elect" who have "arrived." True humanity is always in *Pascha* – a passage from being other than God to being called by God to enter into the mystery of the divine. Gregory of Nyssa spoke about this process as eternal, never ending:

> Rather let us change in such a way that we may constantly evolve towards what is better, being *transformed from glory to glory* (2 Cor. 3:18), and thus always improving and ever becoming more perfect by daily growth, and never arriving at any limit of perfection. For that perfection consists in our never stopping in our growth in good, never circumscribing our perfection by any limitation.[21]

This eternal movement, eternal action and relation of God is defined by one quality and that is love. The dynamic of love within the human existence is one of constant change, constant perfecting and re-creating. The Romanian theologian, Dumitru

Staniloae, wrote, "from all eternity God is a common act of love according to the measure of his absolute character and pure subjectivity."[22] This efficacious love, which in fact originates in the Father, constitutes in existence the Son from all existence. This love reaches out to touch nothingness and creates the world. This love is so powerful and so efficacious that it creates the universe from absolute nothingness! Palamas' original observation about the Trinity as relation and creation suggests that the love of the Holy Trinity that creates is at the very nature of the Trinity. In other words, there had to be a creation because of the nature of the Trinity! However, how is this love to be characterized? Once more the Tradition uses two powerful words repeatedly: *ekstasis* and *kenosis*. The love of the Father is always directed at the other persons of the Trinity; it is ecstatic – going beyond itself. Similarly, the love of the Son and the Holy Spirit is never self-centred. Again, Staniloae is insightful:

> Each divine "I" puts a "Thou" in place of himself. Each sees himself only in relation to the other. The Father sees himself only as the subject of the Son's love, forgetting himself in every other aspect. He sees himself only in relation with the Son. But the "I" of the Father is not lost because of this, for it is affirmed by the Son who in his turn knows himself only as he who loves the Father, forgetting himself. He affirms himself only implicitly in so far as he affirms the Father. This is the circular movement (*perichoresis* = *circuminsessio*) of each divine "I" around the other as centre. They are three, yet each regards only the others and experiences only the others.... The Trinity is the culmination of the humility and sacrifice of love. It represents the continual mortification of each "I."[23]

When that trinitarian love is aimed at creation it results in the incarnation: the divine *kenosis*, or self-emptying (Phil. 2:6-7). The Son empties Himself of his own will, to do the will of the Father and empties Himself of his place "at the right hand" in order to enter his own creation "taking the form of a servant" (Phil. 2:7).

The Church as Communion

This kenotic and ecstatic love of the Trinity is the model for all human life. The centrality of sacraments/mysteries in the Churches of the Christian East is a clear affirmation of this fact. Christian life is not and cannot be constituted in isolation. It demands *koinonia* and the sacraments are the ultimate affirmation of this. Even the solitary (*monarchos*) is enjoined to occasionally leave the *poustinia* and join the community for the Eucharist. The practical call to relationship is manifested in the liturgical centrality of the Eucharistic assembly that constitutes the Church. Zizioulas remarks:

> This is the heart of the Church, where communion and otherness are realized *par excellence.* If the Eucharist is not celebrated properly, the Church ceases to be the Church.[24]

The trinitarian paradigm thus provides a model for true community. Firstly, it is clearly rooted in a consciousness of being *koinonia*, a communion of persons who in their very essence are in communion. Thus to be in communion necessitates an intentionality by the members to get to know each other. The Church, as *koinonia*, cannot be simply perceived as a sociological construct or temporal historical association of believers; in other words, it is not an optional element in the life of a Christian. This ecclesial *koinonia* in the scriptural and theological sense is the very living out of what we are as human beings in relationship! It is for this reason that all Christians affirm that there is only One Church, regardless of how they then go on to define that one Church. However, the One Church, the true *koinonia*, is not a parish, or a denomination, it is the life that is given to us by the Trinity in our very essence. Secondly, just as in the Trinity, the *koinonia* is an expression of the relations of the Trinity; the Church must be an expression of the *koinonia* of all believers. The Church constitutes the believers as children of God. It is not intended to constrain or eliminate the uniqueness of those who have been created as unique by God. Notions of authority and discipline in the Church should be radically different from those in society; they must be based on service, kenotic love, rather then power and oppression. It is for this reason that Christians affirm that true freedom lies in the *koinonia* of the Church, which is in a proper relation with God and our brothers and sisters. It is for this reason that Eastern Christians are called to "set aside all earthly cares"[25] outside the Church. This does not mean they become purely angelic, but rather that they leave their anger, their pride, their vanity outside of the *koinonia*. If believers are not reconciled with each other, if they do not even know each other, they cannot be *koinonia*.

The primary characteristic of this ecclesial *koinonia* is a responsiveness to what I have called initial relatedness: a response to having been created, and loved, by the Father. The primary task of the *koinonia* is to offer *leitourgia*, or true worship and *eucharistia*, or thanksgiving. The community primarily comes together as a worshipping community. Christians are called together to praise and proclaim the greatness of the Trinity! This is done in many ways: the various services of the Church, the sacramental rites, but primarily in and through the Eucharist. Boris Bobrinskoy calls the Eucharist

> ...the central cultic moment offered by the Church to the Holy Trinity; it manifests the fullness of the Church... it is the strongest and most central location of the spiritual identity of the Church. It is here that the Church prays that she (and humanity) manifests its true identity in a relationship of communion with the eternal Trinity.[26]

However, this communion with the Trinity, most concretely expressed in the partaking of the Eucharistic gifts, is also manifested through the Eucharistic assembly's breaking down of the barriers created by a life focused on sin and death. Zizioulas explains:

> [Eucharist] is the place where difference ceases to be divisive and becomes good.... Whenever this does not happen, the Eucharist is distorted – more than that, it can be invalidated, even if all the other requirements for a "valid" Eucharist are met and satisfied. Thus, a Eucharist which excludes in one way or another those of a different race or sex or age or profession is a false Eucharist. A Eucharist celebrated specially for children or young people or blacks or whites or students is a false one. The Eucharist must include all these; for it is there that the otherness of a natural or social kind can be transcended.

A Church that does not celebrate the Eucharist in this inclusive way risks losing her catholicity.[27]

Thus, a Eucharistic *koinonia*, which actively emulates the Trinity, perpetually challenges the community to be engaged in building inclusive communities. Those communities that justify their existence by defending historic, cultural or social values, although perhaps valuable, nonetheless perpetuate division and should not be regarded as true *koinonia*. Trinitarian communities clearly nurture a *koinonia* respectful of difference.

The context for the Eucharistic assembly is to be one of openness and hospitality towards the stranger in the world. N. Fedoroff (1828–1903) stated, "the Trinity is the social program of humanity."[28] Nikos Nissiotis clearly stated the integral connection between the sacramental life and a working in the world:

Witness as solidarity with the world is of the essence of the sacramental communion within the *ekklesia*, which does not allow either a separation from the world or an absence from all sincere struggles to recover a fully human existence. The human struggles "outside" of the Church for justice, peace and liberation are not foreign elements in the one creation of God, elements outside of his love. There is no opposition between the two concentric realities, Church and world, but rather continuity. The constructive character of the Church's action in the world makes our solidarity even more pressing and urgent.[29]

He even offers a caution that when one is not attentive to expressing this solidarity with the struggles of humanity one can lose an essential aspect of the Christian *koinonia*:

Orthodoxy today is tempted to fall into an introverted ecclesial life. There, where hostile Church authorities prevent the Church from acting as a witnessing community in the world, the renewal issue is hindered by the survival problem, but unfortunately there where full freedom for this is allowed, a sclerotic conservatism negates the practicing of the renewal process as a witnessing diaconal *martyria* in the secular realm. The dynamic process of uniting all things into the oneness of

God by *diakonia* and witness can be then negated by an illusory self-sufficiency in God and a confidence in "our" unchanged Church structures and scholastic dogmatism.[30]

Thus, the only way to guarantee the life of the Church is to live this trinitarian love both internally and externally and, once more emulating the Trinity, to do so without ceasing! Once the *koinonia* ceases to live love fully, ecstatically – ever moving outward and kenotically – always emptying itself, it ceases to be *koinonia*. In the same way, love not shared, not open to others, ceases to be love. The Trinity thus presents an imperative: Christians are to be agents of social change by realizing fully the love of God in all aspects of their lives. Being any less is to accept the barrier imposed by sin.

Communion and Creation

This ecstatic love of God is also the manner by which the creative nature of the Trinity is expressed. Thus far, I have discussed how that creative nature took nothing and made the universe; however, the Eastern Tradition does not posit that the creativity of the Trinity ceased on the sixth day. Rather, it is in the very nature of the Trinity. Thus, the Trinity is always creating, or perhaps better, re-creating. In humanity, this is clearly the power of love, which constantly moves the person unceasingly deeper and deeper into relation with God and with others. An important aspect of this creative nature of God, increasingly valued by Orthodox theology, is the Trinity's relatedness to the world. The very act of creation does not create an unbridgeable chasm between divinity and creation, as many have historically posited, but rather the act of creation establishes a relation! Trinity creates out of nothing and that which is created is ultimately related for its very existence to God. Thus, even creation has as its paradigm the Most Holy Trinity! There is nothing that escapes being related to God! As a result, humanity must relate to creation not simply as some inert matter that is a tool to be manipulated and maligned as is seen fit, but rather as something integrally expressive of the divine life. Creation is then valued not because by its nature it is divine, but because it is an expression of the trinitarian life. Zizioulas states,

> Nature is the "other" that Man is called to bring into communion with himself, affirming it as "very good" through personal creativity. This is what happens in Eucharist where the natural elements of bread and wine are so affirmed that they acquire personal qualities (the Body and Blood of Christ) in the event of the communion of the Spirit. Similarly, in a para-eucharistic way, all forms of true culture and art are ways of treating nature as otherness in communion.[31]

Elsewhere he adds that the "Christian regards the world as sacred because it stands in dialectical relationship with God."[32]

This perspective is deeply rooted in the orthodox teaching of Maximus the Confessor, who on numerous occasions eloquently defended the cosmic significance of the incarnation. In other words, Christ brings salvation not solely to humanity but to all creation because every created thing finds its life and truth in the Trinity. Maximus states unambiguously that "the unique reason for the birth of the Word according to the flesh is the salvation of nature."[33] It is the task of humanity then not only to utilize creation in an appropriate manner, as Zizioulas says, but also to be aware of the manner in which creation serves our relatedness to God. Again, Maximus is instructive:

> It is impossible for the mind to cross over to intelligible realities, despite their connatural relation, without contemplating intermediary sensible things, but it is also absolutely impossible for contemplation to take place without sense (which is naturally akin to sensible things) being joined with the mind.[34]

In other words, creation is needed in order to come to knowledge of God. Creation, therefore, in Maximus' view, has a very positive role to play in our ascent to God, when it is perceived in its true and fundamental relation to the Trinity. As a result, the divine action of creation and redemption is not solely for humanity. Maximus affirms,

> The entire plan of God contained in the Divine pre-existent will, concerning the creation of the humanity

and the world, concerning providence, salvation and the recapitulation of the Universe in God is clearly manifested and explained exclusively and solely in the final divinization of human nature and creation.[35]

The Divine Life then, is not simply the goal of all humanity but also the goal of all creation.

This perspective clearly presents a challenge to humanity, not solely as persons but as community. How do communities, Christian *koinonia*, relate to the created world? Are the issues of water quality, of global warming, of deforestation only of concern to the "eco-fringe" or are these fundamentally Christian issues? Is not the rape of our world a global and fundamental denial of its having been created by God and of its being an essential element in salvation? Ten years ago a gathering of theologians from the Eastern Orthodox and Oriental Orthodox Church discussed these very issues and concluded:

> Humanity can no longer ignore its responsibility to protect [the environment] and preserve it. In order to do this, however, humanity must learn to treat the creation as a sacred offering to God, an oblation, a vehicle of grace, an incarnation of our most noble aspirations and prayers .... We call upon individuals, nations and churches to give effect to a vision of the rightful harmony between the human dimension and the mineral, plant and animal dimensions of the creation. In spirit and in body, we are called to offer the whole of God's creation back to him as a sacrament and as an offering cleansed, purified, restored for his sanctification of it.... [And they conclude:] "O God, the things that are Yours, we offer them to You according to all things and for all things. Amen." [36]

There is then no way around the conclusion that in the Tradition of the Christian East, the doctrine of the Trinity is not simply a philosophical construct, but entails a practical social imperative for Christians and for all humanity. This practical imperative is, however, not simply the product of a logical connection made between the life of the Divine and our social exigencies. Rather, the strength of the argument made above, and generally in much of contemporary Orthodox reflection, lies in its implication for theological anthropology. The central assertion made by John Zizioulas that "being is constituted as communion"[37] and the very clear recognition of the divine life as being fundamentally a life of relationship means that we need to address the question of just what constitutes the *imago Dei* (image of God) in humanity. The traditional exposition of the image of God in humanity has focused attention on rationality, free will, or the possibility of eternal life. Today I suggest we need to add to this list the capacity for relationship. If divine life is eternally kenotic and ecstatic then so must human life also be if it is a reflection of the divine. If divine life is fundamentally communion, so must human life also be if it is to be *kat'eikon.*

Recognition of the essential relatedness of the human person underlies the analysis of many contemporary Orthodox thinkers. Christos Yannaras, for example, sees in the West a breakdown of true Christian values in favour of a perverse individualism that reduces human life to the demands of technological efficiency.[38] Human life is no longer valued *per se*; it is simply an isolated unit within the workings of a vast, impersonal social machine. The perceived nihilism and atomism of today's age is a natural outgrowth for Yannaras of erroneous Western Christian thought. The lack of integration of the communitarian implications of Christian trinitarian thinking manifests itself in the rationalism of the West, which extols the virtues of the individual inquirer, explorer, discoverer, or scientist. The "I" not only dominates the "we," but also in fact is in constant conflict with the "we." Community comes to be perceived as evil, constraining and suffocating. Western thought, in Yannaras' view, artificially juxtaposes the particular and the universal Church. However, Yannaras, Zizioulas, Bobrinskoy and other Orthodox theologians emphasize the need to reject this opposition: the person (their preferred term) constitutes community, not in opposition to the community, but in fact, as person in relationship.

This assertion is an ontological one. Person, being in communion, is the definition of being human, as created by God. One cannot define human nature without reference to God, other humans, and the entire created order. Further, this capacity for relationship is not even limited by temporality. It is an eternal capacity. It is for this reason that original sin, the empowering of death as an ultimate reality governing all realities, is a denial of the Trinity and the communitarian basis of human being. Original sin creates individuals by denying the image of the trinitarian God in the human. Reasserting this aspect of the *imago Dei* is one of the single most important aspects of contemporary Orthodox reflection. It is important not only for its implications for liturgy, ecclesiology and social critique, but because it addresses the concerns of many who have been until now on the margins of societal and theological reflections. It clearly can serve as a basis for an Orthodox eco-theology.

Asserting the capacity for communion as a primary manifestation of the image of God in humanity is to empower many who have been marginalized by earlier reflections. I think here primarily of those persons whom society has labelled as "handicapped," or more accurately, persons who have intellectual disabilities. Slowly, the need for Christian Churches and theologians to embrace the voices of these persons in the theological enterprise is being recognized.[39] Theologies, which are rooted in an anthropology based in rationality as "the image of God" in humanity, immediately preclude the full participation of those with intellectual impairments in their purview. By definition, the intellectually limited human being is somehow deficient in "God-likeness" and so is treated as the object of Christian charity. Such a person is to be pitied rather than considered an active participant in the task of theological reflection. These persons are extensively scrutinized in order to test their "capacity" for reception of sacraments – lest they not "understand" (intellectually is implied here) what is happening. Recognizing the trinitarian basis of human life and that being in communion is the very image of God in humanity allows the Christian to embrace the person with disability as equal: they too develop and engage in communion/relationship. It is the quality of relationship, of communion, which then becomes the test of Christian faith, not an intellectual capacity or incapacity. Zizioulas's approach needs repetition: neither doctrinal definitions nor liturgical standards can as effectively attest the depth of Christian life as can the lived reality of communion.[40] It is the life of the community which emulates (albeit imperfectly) the trinitarian life; doctrine, liturgy, ecclesiology are simply products of the reflections upon that life.

Conclusion

In the end, the contemporary revisiting of trinitarian theology, especially in Orthodoxy, necessitates a revisiting of many of our traditional theological categories. However, in a most acute manner it demands the inclusion of capacity for relationship in the traditional theology of image and likeness of God in humanity. The recognition of this call to communion as fundamental to defining humanity allows our theologies to be more inclusive of those historically marginalized, and especially those defined by society as having some form of intellectual disability. Recognizing the trinitarian communion as the paradigm for humanity allows theological anthropology to be more inclusive and to expand the notions of created humanity beyond the categories of rationality and intellectual ability. The people of God can thus be recognized by how they live this trinitarian life, rather than by how they define it. The Church is then the living witness to the Trinity and the Christian is the embodiment of that witness. Trinitarian life is entered into not exclusively in some future, heavenly kingdom, but here and now!

For Further Reading

Thunberg, Lars. *Microcosm and Mediator: The Theological Anthropology of Maximus the Confessor.* Chicago: Open Court, 1995.

Yannaras, Christos. *The Freedom of Morality.* Trans. Elizabeth Briere. Crestwood, NY: St. Vladimir's, 1996.

Zizioulas, John. *Being as Communion: Studies in Personhood and the Church.* Crestwood, NY: St. Vladimir's, 1985.

---

[1] Christoph Schwöbel, ed. *Trinitarian Theology Today: Essays on Divine Being and Act* (London: T&T Clark, 1995), 1.

[2] Karl Rahner, *The Trinity* (London: Burns & Oates, 1986), 10-11.

[3] Metropolitan John (Zizioulas) (1931–) is in many ways the pre-eminent voice today associating the doctrine of the Holy Trinity with an Orthodox ecclesiology (or teaching on the *ekklesia*/Church community). His voice, however, is not a solitary one. In this century alone such important figures as Dumitru Staniloae (1903–1993), Vladimir Lossky (1903–1958), Sergei Bulgakov (1871–1944), Nikos Nissiotis (1925–1986), Christos Yannaras (1935–), and Boris Bobrinskoy (1925–) have all helped remind us of the Patristic insight that the Holy Trinity is the foundation of all Christian reflection and particularly the norm for Christian community. Two prominent Protestant theologians developing this approach are Jürgen Moltmann and Miroslav Volf.

[4] Schwöbel, *Trinitarian Theology Today,* 4.

[5] An excellent guide to the Cappadocians is provided by Jaroslav Pelikan, *Christianity and Classical Culture: The Metamorphosis of Natural Theology in the Christian Encounter with Hellenism* (Grand Rapids: Yale, 1993).

[6] The standard English language introductory text to the thought of Gregory Palamas is John Meyendorff, *A Study of Gregory Palamas* (Crestwood, NY: St. Vladimir's, 1974).

[7] St. Gregory Palamas, *Saint Gregory Palamas: The One Hundred and Fifty Chapters,* trans. Robert E. Sinkewicz (Toronto: PIMS, 1988), 239.

[8] One should also recognize that this classical position is shared by many Christians of the Protestant Tradition. See Thomas F. Torrance, *The Christian Doctrine of God: One Being, Three Persons* (Edinburgh: T&T Clark, 1996).

[9] These are clearly Aristotelian categories, but their implication for the development of Eastern Christian trinitarian theology goes far beyond the philosophy of Aristotle.

[10] In an interesting development and marriage of Eastern and Western insights Catherine Mowry LaCugna attempted to develop an "ontology of relation." See her *God for Us: The Trinity and Christian Life* (New York: HarperSanFrancisco, 1991).

[11] St. Maximus the Confessor, *The Church, the Liturgy and the Soul of Man: The Mystagogia of St. Maximus the Confessor,* trans. Dom Julian Stead, O.S.B. (Still River, MA: St. Bede's, 1982), 69.

[12] St. Basil the Great, *On the Holy Spirit,* 19.48, trans. David Anderson (Crestwood, NY: St. Vladimir's, 1980).

[13] Prestige, *God in Patristic Thought,* 243.

[14] Basil, *On the Holy Spirit,* 18.44.

[15] Basil, *On the Holy Spirit,* 18.45.

[16] Various approaches to this pivotal debate in the history of Christianity are well summarized in Lukas Vischer, ed., *La Théologie du Saint-Esprit dans le dialogue oecuménique,* Document Foi et Constitution 103 (Paris: Le Centurion, 1981). Also see the contributions in the *Greek Orthodox Theological Review* 31:3–4 (1986).

[17] Gennadios Limouris, "The Church as Mystery and Sign in Relation to the Holy Trinity in Ecclesiological Perspectives," in *Church, Kingdom, World: The Church as Mystery and Prophetic Sign,* Faith and Order Paper 130, ed. Gennadios Limouris (Geneva: WCC, 1986).

[18] John D. Zizioulas, *Being as Communion* (Crestwood, NY: St. Vladimir's, 1985), 101.

[19] See the work of Christos Yannaras on this point, especially his *De L'Absence et de l'Inconnaissance de Dieu* (Paris: Cerf, 1971) and *The Freedom of Morality,* trans. Elizabeth Briere (Crestwood, NY: St. Vladimir's, 1984).

[20] Boris Bobrinskoy, "The Adamic Heritage According to Fr. John Meyendorff," *St. Vladimir's Theological Quarterly* 42/1(1998): 35.

[21] Gregory of Nyssa, *On Perfection,* [PG 46.285 A–D]. This translation is from *From Glory to Glory: Texts from Gregory of Nyssa's Mystical Writings,* trans. and ed. Herbert Musurillo (Crestwood, NY: St. Vladimir's, 1979), 84.

[22] Dumitru Staniloae, *Theology and the Church,* trans. Robert Barringer (Crestwood, NY: St. Vladimir's, 1980), 78.

[23] Ibid., 88-89.

[24] Zizioulas, "Communion and Otherness," *Sobornost* 16 (1994): 15.

[25] From the Cherubic Hymn of the Divine Liturgy of St. John Chrysostom.

[26] Boris Bobrinskoy, *Le mystère de la Trinité* (Cerf: Paris, 1986), 167.

[27] Zizioulas, "Communion and Otherness," 15.

[28] Bobrinskoy, *Le mystère de la Trinité,* 168.

[29] Nikos A. Nissiotis, "The Church as a Sacramental Vision and the Challenge of Christian Witness," in *Church, Kingdom, World,* Faith and Order Paper 130, ed. Gennadios Limouris (Geneva: WCC, 1986), 112.

[30] Nissiotis, "The Church as a Sacramental Vision," 126.

[31] Zizioulas, "Communion and Otherness," 18.

[32] John D. Zizioulas, "Preserving God's Creation," *King's Theological Review* 13 (1990), 5.

[33] Maximus the Confessor, *Book of Ambiguities* 3 [PG. 91.1040B].

[34] Questions to Thalassius 58. From Paul M. Blowers, *Exegesis and Spiritual Pedagogy in Maximus the Confessor: An Investigation of the Quaestiones ad Thalassium* (Notre Dame: Notre Dame, 1991), 137.

[35] Artemije Radoslavljevic, "Le Probleme du 'presuppose' ou du 'non-presuppose' de l'Incarnation de Dieu le Verbe, " in *Maximus Confessor: Actes du Symposium sur Maxime le Confesseur, Fribourg, 2–5 septembre 1980,* ed. Felix Heinzer and Christoph Schönborn (Fribourg: Èditions Universitaires, 1982), 200.

[36] "Orthodox Perspectives on Creation," in *Justice, Peace and the Integrity of Creation: Insights from Orthodoxy,* ed. Gennadios Limouris (Geneva: WCC, 1990), 15.

[37] Zizioulas, *Being as Communion,* op. cit., 101.

[38] See his *The Freedom of Morality,* trans. Elizabeth Briere (Crestwood, NY: St. Vladimir's, 1984).

[39] See Nancy L. Eiesland, *The Disabled God: Toward a Liberatory Theology of Disability* (Nashville: Abingdon, 1994).

[40] For example, see his chapters on "Personhood and Being" and "Truth and Communion," in *Being as Communion.*

VI. Mary: The Model for Christian Life and Ministry (1998)

Chapter 9

Mary: Model for Christian Life and Community

FRANCES COLIE

Dr. Colie has advanced degrees in school administration and a degree in Eastern Christian studies from John XXIII Institute, Fordham University. She served as associate director of Educational Services for the Melkite Catholic Church of the United States.

The Theotokos, the Mother of God, her role in the incarnation, the salvation of the world, and her role in Christian life are central to the experience of Eastern Christianity.

Joachim and Anna

Mary was born into a fallen world, where the peace and harmony that God had intended for creation was broken. Moreover, mankind was in darkness due to the fall of Adam and Eve. Humanity obeyed the Law, prayed and hoped; yet, God was known as transcendent – beyond human experience. However, through the incarnation, because of Mary's "yes," she comes to be the Mother of a new humanity, a new creation. Mary was born to a Jewish couple, Joachim and Anna, who were elderly and childless. Now a barren couple in those days suffered a two-fold humiliation. Childless parents were seen as cursed by God and a second curse resulting from this state was that parents without children would have no one to comfort them in old age. One of the most beautiful icons, and the only one of a man and a woman embracing in iconography, is that of Joachim and Anna at the gates of Jerusalem: a wonderful icon reflecting an apocryphal story of Anna running to Joachim, who happens to be in the temple at prayer, wanting to tell him of her good news. In the meantime, he has received the message from God and is on his way to tell Anna. They meet each other at the gates of Jerusalem and embrace. This is a perfect icon for married couples.

Mary's conception in the womb was a feast of joy, not only for Joachim and Anna, but also for the entire cosmos. It was the dawn of the world's salvation and fulfilment of the whole history of the Old Testament. Her nativity was also a feast of joy in the eyes of God. God had prepared her from all eternity. Humanity could now see, with the eyes of the heart, the extent of God's love. Barrenness was no longer a shame, no longer a curse, because barren as they were, Joachim and Anna produced the source of the life, which would produce the Giver of Life, Christ our God. The pure happiness expressed at Mary's conception in the womb of Anna becomes at her birth an overflowing river of joy, encompassing the whole universe. This is a constant theme in Eastern Tradition. Everything that is good in creation rushes forward to develop itself into divine beauty. Mary, the new light, comes into the darkness and darkness recognizes her radiance and is illumined by it. Joy is here again. In the Eastern Church, we speak constantly of joy: a joy for humanity, for the parents Joachim and Anna, and for the whole universe. At Vespers we sing:

> Today glad tidings go forth through the whole world. Today sweet fragrance is wafted forth by the proclamation of salvation. Today is the end of barrenness of our nature, because the barren one becomes a mother. Mary, the daughter of Anna, will become the mother of the one who by his nature is the Creator and God. He it is who took flesh by which he brought salvation to the lost.[1]

The joy of the nativity belongs first to Joachim and Anna, who, after long years of expectation, disappointment and social rejection because of their barrenness, can now enjoy the fruits of their long, faithful and enduring love of each other. So also,

Through your holy nativity, O Immaculate One, Joachim and Anna were delivered from the shame of childlessness, and Adam and Eve from the corruption of death; your people redeemed from the debt of their sins cry out to you to honour your birth: "The barren one gives birth to the mother of God, the sustainer of our life."

As to the name of Mary, in the Old Law a name was officially given a boy on the eighth day after his birth, at his circumcision. Therefore, our Lord was given a name on the eighth day when he was circumcised. A girl was given a name on the very day of her birth. Now, a name is not simply a convenient label to distinguish one person from another. Rather, the name represents the whole person. The name enshrines within itself the qualities and the attributes of the person. According to the *Proto-evangelium of James*, the angel of the Lord who announced to Joachim and Anna gave the order to call her Miriam, Mary. This name was rarely used in the Old Testament. It appears only one other time. It was the name of the sister of Moses and Aaron (Exod. 15:20-21). The Jewish people seemed to have avoided giving this name to their children due to the pious reverence they had for these great heroes. In a similar sentiment, this same idea prevented early Christians from calling their children Jesus. The name Mary means "hope" because Miriam, the sister of Moses, was the hope of the liberation, which was the promise of God to his people. Miriam saved Moses, who would become a saviour of Israel.

So, the name Mary/Miriam is already attached in Jewish Tradition with the saving action of God. But this second Mary does not just help the one who saves (Moses) but rather she gives birth to the one who saves (Christ) and she becomes his faithful disciple. Mary, the Mother of God, becomes the first of the saints, the best exemplar of a divinized human being.

The Annunciation

The best example of Mary's status as exemplar of all humanity is in the story of the Annunciation (Luke 1:26-38). According to legend, when Mary was a young girl of fifteen, the messenger of God, the angel Gabriel, appeared to her in the temple. This was a supremely positive event. He said to Mary, "You shall conceive and bear a son." She questioned the angel. Hers was not a blind obedience. However, once she understood that it was the will of God, she accepted. Consider how intense her relationship with God already was at that point, for her to have said, "Yes." She freely agreed to co-operate with God, and became an unwed mother in spite of the social stigma, which could lead to death. Mary was totally and freely co-operating with God in this event. She expressed a sublime act of love. God actively called her and, out of her relationship with him, she responded, "I am the servant of the Lord. Let it be done to me as you say." Now God speaks to all of us from the moment of creation. If we are not God-centred, we do not recognize who is talking to us. Mary's "yes" was an act of self-determination. The angel closed the conversation by telling her, "The Holy Spirit will come upon you and the power of the Most High will overshadow you" (Luke 1:35). From this action of the Spirit, the Word and Son of God became flesh. However, flesh does not simply mean a body, but a real human being. The Word not only became a human body but a real human being with will, freedom, thought and speech; he accepts the whole of life and human sensibility, except sin. Meanwhile, Mary will become a mother while remaining a virgin and the power of her fecundity will be exclusively the work of God. Thus, Mary's is a very special type of motherhood. Mary's "Yes" was the objective human condition that made the incarnation possible. In that "Yes," she said "Yes" for all humanity, for all of us. She freely accepted to have God born in her. Thus through the incarnation, we have the potential to say "Yes" to God, who may then be born in us.

Why did the incarnation happen? Irenaeus of Lyons speaks of the incarnation as the necessary means to bring about salvation, something that we human beings would never have attained by our own power. The Word of God became human in order that we might become God through God's graceful, divine life. The Son came to restore in us the likeness of God that was lost by the fall of Adam and Eve. He came to restore humanity now born bankrupt in a bankrupt world. Because of Adam's refusal to live according to God's image and likeness, we live in a cosmic condition that the early Fathers called corruption and death, a process of disintegration resulting from sin. Death then is understood in the sense of a life that is not going anywhere; it is not producing anything. Athanasius of Alexandria (c.295–373) described this state of human beings losing the divine life of eschatological incorruptibility within them, and becoming mortal, corruptible, and deprived of divine life or grace. Life according to the image and likeness of God is diminished not only in the individual, but also through us, in the sub-human cosmos, which now is no longer harmoniously moving back to God.

The incarnation, God's becoming fully human, has three purposes. The incarnation demonstrates the divine will to identify with creation. God took on humanity in order to identify fully with humanity. Secondly, the incarnation is the restoration of the corrupted creation: it is the means of salvation. Thirdly, through the divine condescension humanity and the whole universe are divinized – made like God. The whole universe is restored along with humanity. The incarnation is as much about the world as it is about us humans.

Mary's role in the incarnation is to demonstrate our human co-operation with God. Her "Yes!" is about our "Yes!" to God. This "Yes" is our means of participation in the incarnation and co-operation in God's divine plan to divinize us. In the Eastern Church, we call this *synergeia* (synergy). God loves us so much that we are the recipients of the constant offer of divine assistance. We prepare ourselves and God comes and picks us up. This is the fundamental dialogue between God and humanity. We do not save ourselves. In Mary, God touches humanity to raise it to the divine. She is the bridge. Heaven and earth have united. She is the prototype of all Christians, the model of what we are to become in Christ. The Dormition demonstrates the reality of her deification or divinization. Mary is thus the first of the new creation, the first of the saints. Her "Yes" means that, as she bore Christ the Word physically in her womb, all Christians now have the privilege of bearing God within them spiritually. God now is not only transcendent but also immanent! God is here, within us.

Let us summarize Mary's role: she stands as the archetype for humanity, the epitome of what every human being can become and is becoming by participation in the incarnation. She is the first redeemed of new creation, and she is our role model for humanity, brought to the likeness of God by freely co-operating with God. She is the mother of the new humanity. She guides the way for us to participate in the incarnation in a like manner. This theme is beautifully shown in iconography. Mary is rarely ever seen without the Incarnate Son of God, since the human nature of the Lord is inseparable from that of his mother. For example, in the Smolensk icon of the Mother of God, the Theotokos is the one who with the child points the way, guides us. She does not point to herself, but to her Son, always pointing the way.

Recognizing and valuing Mary, then, is nothing less than asserting the meaning of the incarnation and our potential for salvation. Our Eastern Church emphasizes the words of 2 Peter 1:3-4:

> That divine power of his has freely bestowed on us everything necessary for a life of genuine piety, through knowledge of him who called us by his own glory and power. By virtue of them, he has bestowed on us the great and precious things he promised, so that through these you who have fled a world corrupted by lust might become sharers of the divine nature.

Theosis

In the East, salvation is about sharing the divine nature, deification or *theosis*. The goal of our life is to be like the Theotokos and live the life of *theosis*. However, how do we do that? How do we become like God? How is it possible for us to be divinized? Who are we that we may participate in divinity? In the writings of the early Fathers, starting with Irenaeus and later with Athanasius and others, the incarnation meant God became one of us so that we might become like God. To Athanasius this statement meant that God and only those worthy of God have one and the same energy. They do not share the divine essence; no one can penetrate the essence of God. We know God through the divine energies as we know human beings through their energy. What we know of God is Love and Life. These are the divine energies. This does not mean that as we get close to God that we lose our free will, but that our energies and the divine energies become synchronized – they come together – so that we are in fact activating that synergy in the entire cosmos.

Thus, we remain creatures while becoming God by grace. The early Fathers in formulating doctrine on the incarnation went back to the Old Testament. They looked at Genesis 1:26-27 in which the creation of Adam is described: in the passage, "Let us make man in our image, after our likeness," they found a theological anthropology of humanity formed according to the image and likeness of God. In addition, they said it explained our true nature as consisting of the image, which is the seed of divine life that can never be taken away. It is the imprint of God's love and it will never be withdrawn for all eternity. If it could be taken away, it would be like God turning his back on his own creation, and this will never be. Thus we sing at funerals, in the odes, "O mortal man, no matter how you have sinned you still bear the imprint of love, the image of God within you." This image speaks to that relationship between the Creator and the creature. There is a bond. The bond between us will always exist.

The likeness of God is understood as the capacity for our growth in divinity or deification. It is an area where we exercise our free will. This is the basis of a process theology, a dynamic movement of becoming like God, a movement of the created back to the Creator by our free choice. In one of the greatest feasts, the Transfiguration, we see the blessing of grapes and their distribution. This ritual is a reminder that the little seed that was planted has now become a glorious fruit. That is exactly what we are to become: glorious, divinized people. We see that God's love is constant in the image, and as we freely respond, God transforms us into the likeness. To be holy is to be human. We are not fully human until we find God. The more we grow in God, the more we are human. Mary taught Jesus how to be human. Now she is our role model to teach us how to be divine.

The fundamental truth, which this doctrine gives us, is that our fullness and perfection reside in assimilation into the likeness of Christ. It is not just Christ as a moral example living outside of us, but Christ dynamically and ontologically living in us and working in us through his energy, which we call grace. So grace for the early Fathers is not a thing, it is an encounter with the living God, a moment of love with the beloved.

Christians of the East have always honoured Mary in a special way. Her irreplaceable significance in the scheme of salvation was asserted at the Council of Ephesus in the year 431. Early in its concern to crystallize and formalize its statement of faith regarding Mary, the Church emphasized her ever-virginity. The concern with the virginity of Mary was not a statement on the alleged impurity of sexuality. Insistence on the virginity of Mary was a patristic defence against early scepticism, which disputed the reality of the humanity of Christ. Paradoxically, the ever-virginity of Mary is a guarantor that the incarnation was a unique action of God for humanity's salvation. Mary conceived the Lord in a virginal way, which means without human intervention, a unique action of God. She gave him birth, yet remained a virgin. The one who in the beginning established the laws of human conception alters them now for this unique conception and birth, combining in his mother the two most splendid glories of womanhood: virginity and motherhood. Virginity then means giving life: it refers to the capacity for union with God. It is perfect freedom because it liberates and frees all the forces of the human person, leaving them open and receptive to the perfect lover.

In honour of her virginity, Mary is always depicted in iconography displaying three golden stars. They symbolize the eternal presence of this seal of virginity in her. On her forehead, there is the star declaring the virginity of her body, which combines the freshness of virginity and motherhood – she is virgin and mother. On her right shoulder, the star symbolizes the virginity of her soul – Mary was virgin before motherhood. On her left shoulder, the star symbolizes her virginity after motherhood – Mary is a virgin in spirit. To refute the views of some heretics denying the real humanity of Christ, the early Church included the clause about virginity in the Nicene Creed. John of Damascus makes the connection between virginity and incarnation in his exposition of the orthodox faith. He says, "The Son of God incarnate therefore was born of her, not a divinely inspired man, but God incarnate.... But just as he who was conceived kept her who conceived still virgin, in like manner also he who was born preserved her virginity intact."[2] Thus in the Church's teaching, Mary is ever virgin because she was a virgin before, during, and after the divine birth.

The second important affirmation of Eastern Christians regarding Mary is her title as Theotokos, a title literally translated as "Birth-giver of God" or "Bearer of God." Frequently in liturgical use the term is translated as "Mother of God." The precise time when the expression was first applied to Mary has been difficult to establish. The title was affixed to Mary already by Alexander of Alexandria (d.328) around 325, by the Council of Antioch in 341, and by Fathers of the fourth century, Athanasius, Cyril of Jerusalem, and the three Cappadocians. It was formally established as the most appropriate title for Mary at the Council of Ephesus in the year 431. The council was convened not to propose a dogma about Mary, as some might think, but to define and explain that the human nature of Christ taken from her was completely and hypostatically, meaning substantially and totally, with the divine person of the Son of God. Thus, Christ is one person with two natures; he is fully human and he is fully divine. Christ is true God and true man united in the person of Jesus, thereby guaranteeing for humanity complete salvation. Because of this union, the council decreed that the holy virgin is Theotokos, Bearer of God. Now the heresy that was refuted at that council was the Nestorian heresy, which said that divinity did not really unite with humanity and that there were really two distinct persons in Christ: one was God the Word and the other Jesus-man; and Mary was simply the mother of the man Jesus. Consequently, according to Nestorius, we cannot say that God really became flesh in Mary; we cannot say that divinity was born in humanity. What was at stake here was true and full incarnation that permits the true and full salvation of mankind. If Christ was not human, he could not stand with us and bring us to divinity. In one of many powerful statements by the early Fathers of the Church, Gregory Nazianzus says, "He who would interpret the incarnation in any other way, denying that Jesus Christ was at once divinely and humanly formed in her, is in like manner godless." He concluded by saying, "Let them not begrudge us our complete salvation."

The third rubric of the orthodox doctrine of the Theotokos is that of Mary's sanctity and purity. She is called *Panagia* – all holy. The confidence concerning the natural and acquired goodness, purity and humility of the Virgin Mary, who has been elevated to Theotokos, was established by the fourth century. Orthodoxy has never accepted the doctrine of the Immaculate Conception, according to which Mary was born without stain of original sin. This doctrine, in Orthodox eyes, threatened all that was gained and all that was preserved in the term Theotokos. The Eastern Christian Tradition speaks of original sin as the root of all our other personalized sins. Above all original sin is an inherited death, mortality. Humanity stands condemned in the face of death: bound by original sin. This mortality, the consequence of Adam's sin, was transmitted by natural generation. Mortality and corruption were transmitted to every being except Jesus Christ. If Christ had come from a human sperm, he would not have been born a new person. However, he was born into the human race, not yet totally under the bondage of corruption or mortality. He was of eternity and destined for eternity. The teaching of the Western Church on the Immaculate Conception removes Mary the Mother of God from that which is inherited by every human being in birth. The Eastern Church seeks constantly to preserve the humanity of Mary so as to preserve our complete salvation in Jesus Christ.

Nevertheless, it is the Eastern Church's opinion that the sanctity of the Virgin was real before and after the birth of Christ. The Theotokos is sinless, in the sense of an absence of personal sin before the descent of the Holy Spirit upon her in the Annunciation, and afterwards, because of it. In the view of John of Damascus, it was an act of divine grace, which led to her birth. Her sinlessness is a manifestation of the Holy Spirit who dwells within her. *Panagia* stands as proof of the reality of the profound consequences of life in the Holy Spirit and membership in the Body of Christ, the Church. She is not a goddess; she is one of us who has become what each of us is destined by our Creator and Saviour to become. In the Liturgy of St. John Chrysostom, the Church expresses its honour, not worship (worship is reserved for God alone), and we sing:

> It is very meet to bless thee, Theotokos, the ever-blessed and most-pure virgin and mother of our God. More honourable than the Cherubim and more glorious than the Seraphim, who without sin did bear God the word. You are truly the mother of God. We magnify you.

This meditation on the Most Holy Theotokos leads us to recognize that we can and must learn from her about our own lives.

Mary and Prayer

Mary is primarily our exemplar for prayer. Prayer is not regarded as a recitation of words; rather it is a state of a being. It is a being in communion, just as Mary was in communion with God. Prayer is the path to our growth in the likeness of God. Eastern Christians have always embraced contemplative prayer. Our style of prayer is moving inward, allowing God to transform us, and then moving out. The movement is always inward first, and that is why we are contemplatives. Contemplative prayer is the experience of prayer in the incarnation of our lives. The mother of our God is an example of the perfect model of contemplative prayer. The writings of the Fathers of the Church give us some principles regarding prayer that reflect the reality of the incarnation in our lives. We can glean from looking at the *Philokalia*[3] and *The Art of Prayer*[4] several things: prayer transforms; prayer is inward; it is a stillness, moving away from the hustle and bustle of life; it is dynamic, renewing, recreating; and it is growth. Prayer is our response to God in us. True prayer is not magic; it is not praying for things; it is not the repetition of words; nor is it an obligation. There is no ledger up in heaven and God is not an accountant. Prayer is an encounter with God within us. The early Fathers were true charismatics; they were so experientially in touch with God in their lives, praying constantly. This is what we mean when we talk about the relationship developing in prayer. The Theotokos is the true model of that inward prayer, prayer of the heart. Throughout her public life Mary kept in the background; her Son was primary. Our calling is to enter, as the Theotokos did, into God's primal silence and hear the divine words of love. We are called to answer in the shared silence of the word as we repeat our constant "Yes" in total silence. This silence of the divine presence moves us from chronological time – *chronos* – into divine time, the time of revelation – *kairos.* So in that moment, that intense now, there is stillness, there is silence, and there is love.

Mary is also a model for us in the proper use of freedom. Jesus Christ has come to liberate us from our false selves. He has come to bring us true freedom as children of God. As Paul says in Romans, we are carnally minded and we are held down by the law (Rom. 1:18-32), but the Spirit liberates us to be children of

God (Rom. 8:14-17). God did not force Mary into submission; instead he awoke her to freedom and asked her to consent. When humans offer themselves to God, they do not enrich God. God does not need anything from us; rather, when we offer ourselves, we open our emptiness to receive the divine gift that perfects us through the work of divinization.

Freedom involves choice and freedom involves risk. Each choice can put us at odds with our true nature or lead us to greater co-operation with God's divine plan. Our freedom does not consist primarily in choosing between good and evil, between purity and fornication, between love and hatred. Rather, it consists in our ability to determine ourselves in an ever-increasing total consciousness to be more perfectly the person God, the Creator, intends us to be. We are called to listen, to understand, and to believe in God's intimate communication with us through the Word made flesh, in and through the Spirit. We are obligated in our freedom to answer God's call. In our answer, we alone either fulfil or deflect God's purpose in creating us. The Fathers call this freedom *eleutheria*, which is harmony: bringing our nature that sometimes is a little bit dissonant, into integration.

The Theotokos is the model for us of such harmony and freedom. Mary is the model of full human authenticity and integration. Her whole being reacts to the powers that God has given her for the fulfilment of the divine plan. In her, we do not find someone who is constantly engaged in an internal war with themselves. In Mary, we have a fully integrated human nature, always acting with freedom but not against its nature, not against growth in the divine likeness but always moving toward the goal of *theosis*. According to the Fathers, there are two parts of human will. The first is self-possession, whereby we are determined by ourselves and thus are completely autonomous. The other dimension of our free will is what we call integrated nature. Integrated nature signals acting and reacting according to our true nature, which finds fulfilment in God. The integrated nature is one that acts with a singular orientation to God, towards perfect harmony and unity within ourselves. In being restored to Christ, we find true freedom always acting toward our best nature, toward the divine likeness.

Mary as the New Eve

Mary is also spoken of as the new Eve. The "Yes" of the Theotokos was the beginning of a new humanity, a humanity that has the potential to allow God to transform them, make them new men and women, and lovers of humanity. Today there is a danger in Christian devotion of forgetting Mary's historic, even cosmic role as a paradigm for humanity. The early Fathers of the Church developed the concept of Mary as the new Eve, the mother of the living and of the new creation. She is the mother of the new creation because she is the first of post-resurrection humanity. She undoes the error of Eve. The Fathers of the Church frequently refer and compare her with Eve, and present her as the mother of life, in contrast to Eve as the cause of death. Epiphanius (c.315–403) wrote, "Mary became the occasion of life, through whom life itself was born for us." John Chrysostom wrote, "A virgin cast us out of paradise and...through a virgin we have found life eternal."

As the new Eve, as *Panagia*, and Theotokos, Mary stands at the head of the new community of saints. She is the first of the saints and so she is "mother" of the Church. However, it is the confidence of the Church in her intercessory concern that most of all emphasizes the bond of unity among Christians. The deeper meaning of intercession is mutual concern, which binds the faithful to the saints in a tight bond of coexistence and communion. The sense of community, of interpersonal concern for the welfare of others, is an inevitable corollary for the Christian lifestyle, in as much as the person of the Theotokos inspires that lifestyle. Christ's transforming activities through the powers of the Holy Spirit continue through the Church. In the Church, the living word is preached, and through the sacraments, Christ is encountered in his resurrectional life by the Christian faithful. The early Fathers linked Mary with the Church and saw both of them as the source of universal mediation with Christ, the Head. The Church is humanity saved, but it is also that which saves humanity. Mary is placed in the centre of the Church, whose essence is to receive as Virgin Spouse the fruits of Christ, and to give birth as mother to the people of God. The building of the Church is not the gathering together of an elect group of the human race, while the rest of creation is destined for destruction. It is the resurrected body of God's creation, evolving through history, and brought to its completion with our help. The only obstacles that hold back the process are those moral evils that we suffer: selfishness, fear, and pride. Christ, as at the tomb of Lazarus, still stands at the tomb, not only of us individually but of the whole world; the whole world is in that tomb, groaning in travail (Rom. 8:22). He is continually saying, "I am the resurrection and the life.... Come to life" (John 11:25-26). We are granted an immense dignity allowing us to co-operate with the creative powers of God to bring this universe to its fulfilment. The Eastern Church's ecclesiology is a manifestation of the eternal moment, of that *kairos,* which brings us the new kingdom in its final consummation, rather than a historic and earthly journey toward heaven. It is a celebration of the risen Christ, the Resurrection. It is a celebration made possible by the Most Holy Theotokos.

Conclusion

For Eastern Christianity Mary is clearly archetypal and exemplary of what we must become by imitating her faith, hope and love. She is also actively interceding for all of us that we may actually become what she is. She is praying with us. Only in the Holy Spirit will we grow in an understanding of the dynamics of the process of God sending his Spirit, not only upon the virgin of Nazareth, but upon all of us and upon God's created world. The heavenly Father is continually sending the Spirit of Love upon us who, with Mary and all the saints, are impregnated by the divine Word. Through the same Spirit, with Mary, we are to become the mother of Christ as we bring the Spirit forth and give it to the world. Mary has done what each of us must do. Through her, and because of her, we know that it can be done!

For Further Reading

Cyril of Alexandria. *On the Unity of Christ.* Trans. John A. McGuckin. Crestwood, NY: St. Vladimir's, 1995.

Maloney, George. *Mary: The Womb of God.* Denville, NJ: Dimension, 1976.

Pelikan, Jaroslav. *Mary Through the Centuries: Her Place in the History of Culture.* New Haven: Yale, 1996.

---

[1] English translations of Eastern liturgies are not commonly available. However, a limited number of texts are available in *The Festal Mendion,* trans. Mother Mary and Archimandrite Kallistos Ware (London: Faber and Faber, 1977), and *Lenten Triodon,* trans. Mother Mary and Archimandrite Kallistos Ware (London: Faber and Faber), 1978

[2] John of Damascus. *On the Orthodox Faith.* Bk. 4, ch. 14. *A Select Library of the Post-Nicene Fathers. Second Series.* Volume IX (Grand Rapids, MI: Eerdmans, 1974–1983).

[3] The English text is available in three volumes: *Early Fathers from the Philokalia,* trans. E. Kadloubovsky and G.E.H. Palmer (London: Faber and Faber, 1978); *The Philokalia: The Complete Text,* Vol. 1 & 2, trans. G.E.H. Palmer, P. Sherrad and K. Ware (London: Faber and Faber, 1979–).

[4] *The Art of Prayer: An Orthodox Anthology,* comp. Chariton of Valamo, trans. E. Kadloubovsky and E.M. Palmer (London: Faber and Faber, 1966).

Chapter 10

Mary: Model for the Diaconate

ELAINE HANNA

Khouriye Elaine Hanna did her doctoral studies in Historical Theology at Fordham University. She has participated as a representative of the Greek Orthodox Archdiocese of North and South America on a number of bilateral dialogues, including the Eastern Orthodox–Roman Catholic, the Eastern Orthodox–Lutheran and the Eastern Orthodox–Anglican dialogues. Khouriye Hanna has also been a presenter at international Orthodox consultations on women in the Orthodox Church.

This overview of the history of the ministry of the order of women deacons in the Eastern Church will be introduced by offering some images of Mary the Theotokos that might pertain to deaconesses. I will concentrate this introductory material on four roles assumed by the Theotokos: Mary as Handmaid of the Lord, Mary as Spiritual Mother, Mary as Disciple, and Mary as Spirit-Bearer.

Mary as Handmaid of the Lord

Mary as Handmaid of the Lord: the word handmaid or servant is from the Greek *doulos*, which can even be rendered more strongly as slave. However, a secular handmaid or slave under the control of a master simply obeys, perhaps blindly, perhaps in fear, perhaps harbouring resentment, or perhaps even seething in anger. There is certainly no merit found in that relationship. The account of the Annunciation in Luke 1:26-38 presents a much different kind of handmaid. The angel tells Mary that she will conceive and bear the Son of God. The young virgin freely and boldly engages the angel with her question: "How shall this be since I do not know man?" When Gabriel answers her question, that the Holy Spirit will overshadow her, Mary responds wholeheartedly, "I am the servant of the Lord. Let it be to me as you say." As handmaid of the Lord, Mary exercises human freedom, not bondage as a slave. She makes, in essence, an informed choice. Mary as handmaid of the Lord demonstrates that there is only one real choice, and that is to freely, with love, joy and humility, assent to the will of God. She demonstrates the ultimate human response to God, to say, "Yes" without reservation, with complete surrender of self to God, no matter how strange, or unbelievable, or difficult this may seem. God chooses Mary to be his mother, but she also chooses freely and consciously to be his mother. She is not simply a conduit for him to pass through, but becomes a partner and spouse for God. She could have refused. In that case, the Incarnation would not have taken place. However, she acted courageously and received her Lord in her womb, in submission to the will of God. At the Vespers of Christmas Eve we sing:

> What shall we offer thee, O Christ, who for our sakes appeared on earth as a man? Every creature made by thee offers thee thanks: the angels offer thee a hymn, the heavens a star, the magi gifts, the shepherds their wonder, the earth its cave, the wilderness the manger, and we offer thee a virgin mother.[1]

She is the greatest gift we could offer God, and she freely consents to be our gift to God. Therefore, with her courageous assent the Incarnation can take place. The handmaid of the Lord becomes the Theotokos, the new Eve, and gives birth to Christ, the new Adam.

Mary as Spiritual Mother

The Incarnation is the great mystery of the Church. The pre-eternal God becomes a little babe, the Son of Mary. Through her biological motherhood, the Theotokos also becomes a spiritual mother to us. Because Christ makes us children of his Father, heirs of the promise, what he is by nature, as Son of God, he makes us by grace. While on the cross, Christ gave his mother into John's care. She extended her love for her Son to his disciples. She thus became spiritual mother to all the disciples from that point on and to all of us who become the Lord's disciples. By becoming children of God by grace and disciples of Christ, we also become spiritual children of the Theotokos and she becomes our spiritual mother. Nor does her motherhood end with the death of her Son on the cross, but it extends into the midst of the Church and continues to the second coming. Because women are also life-bearers who have the gifts to give biological and spiritual life, they can approach Christ on behalf of others with the same motherly boldness that Mary assumed. In addition to being the model for all of humanity, Mary can be viewed also particularly as a model for women in the Church.

Mary as Model of Discipleship

By freely obeying and surrendering to God, Mary becomes a disciple of Christ. In Matthew 12:46-50, and parallel passages in Mark and Luke, Christ brings her beyond her biological maternity and includes his mother in discipleship as one who hears the will of his Father in heaven and does it. She becomes his disciple because she surrenders herself fully, in humility and obedience, to God's will. She co-operates fully with God. This synergy means she becomes a fellow-worker with him and an active participant in the mystery of salvation.

Mary as Spirit-Bearer

Mary is the Spirit-Bearer because, in the Incarnation, the divine and human are co-mingled. Pneumatology and Mariology are integrally connected: in an active synergy with her Creator, Mary becomes the Spirit-bearing Theotokos. The Spirit enters into a personal relationship with her, fulfils her as a person, makes her whole, vivifies her, and exalts her. The Holy Spirit creates and is ever creating. The integral relation of Mary to the Spirit then enables God to bring something totally new through her into the world. Two things then naturally flow from this union of Mary and the Spirit. The first is that the Spirit leads her out of solitude into the midst of the Church. The Holy Spirit reveals Mary to us and she is uniquely the revelation in the Church of the Holy Spirit. The second thing that happens is that she stretches out her arms in prayer. She symbolizes the soul in prayer, the praying ministry of the Church, and her charism is that of intercession. Mary is at the heart of the Church both as one who prays, continually gazing on her Lord, and as the basis for her role as intercessor in the Church. Her love for her Son extends to his followers and in this spirit-filled loving prayer, she brings us to joy which prompts us to cry out, "Rejoice, O virgin Theotokos, Mary full of grace, the Lord is with thee." Then together with her, we too, filled with the Holy Spirit, continually say "Yes" to God, bend to him, and submit to him freely and joyfully.

Deaconesses in the Early Church

Bearing in mind these images of Mary as Handmaid of the Lord, Spiritual Mother, Disciple, and Spirit-Bearer, let us look at a history of the order of deaconesses and outline the ministry that the order fulfilled, considering that deaconesses also bear these charisms. Two New Testament passages are worth noting before we examine the history of the order of deaconesses. The first is Romans 16:1-2, in which Paul commends Phoebe, whom he calls a deacon of the Church at Cenchreae. Now, whether or not we understand this *diakonos* (deacon) as a technical term at this point or not, what we do see is that certainly Paul is acknowledging the services rendered by Phoebe as a ministry. The second passage here that is of interest to us is 1 Timothy 3:11, in which Paul talks of "the women" within the context of describing the qualifications for the male deacons. The women whom he speaks about were probably women who belonged to a specific category of female ministry bearing some relation to the ministry of deacons.

Now following the New Testament period, there are initially very few references to women deacons. However, in the third century and beyond, we find substantial documentation concerning the order of deaconesses.[2] I will use four documents here in the study of the early development of the institution of deaconesses: the *Didascalia Apostolorum*,[3] and the *Ethiopic Didascalia*[4] from the mid-third century, the *Apostolic Constitutions*[5] from the late fourth century, and the *Testament of Our Lord Jesus Christ*[6] from the early fifth. These documents tell us that the deaconess was chosen and ordained by the bishop and subsequently came within his jurisdiction. The *Didascalia Apostolorum* (3.12) here says:

> Wherefore, O bishop, appoint thee workers of righteousness as helpers who may co-operate with thee unto salvation. Those that please thee out of all the people thou shalt choose and appoint a woman for the ministry of women, for there are houses whither thou canst not send a deacon to the women, on account of the heathen, but may send a deaconess. And also because in many other matters the office of a woman deacon is required.

The deaconess also enjoyed a close relationship to the bishop and the male deacon in a sort of trinity of ministries. After comparing the bishop to the Father, and the deacon to Christ, the *Apostolic Constitutions* (2.4.26) says:

> Let also the deaconess be honoured by you in the place of the Holy Spirit. And not to do or say anything without the deacon, as neither does the Comforter say or do anything of himself, but gives glory to Christ by waiting for his pleasure. And as we cannot believe in Christ without the teaching of the Spirit, so let not any woman address herself to the deacon or bishop without the deaconess.

The work done by the female deacon was as varied as it was necessary. She was encouraged to be diligent in her ministry to women for the sake of modesty and propriety. A primary task for the deaconess was to visit Christian women in heathen households because male deacons could not go there without creating scandal. Another crucial function of the deaconess was to assist the bishop or presbyter in baptizing women, specifically, to anoint the neophyte's body, to go down into the water with her, to instruct her, to be a liaison for her with the bishop, and to care for her spiritual upbringing as a whole. The *Didascalia Apostolorum* (3.12) describes this and says:

> When women go down into the water, those who go down into the water ought to be anointed by a deaconess with the oil of anointing. And where there is no woman at hand and especially no deaconess, he who baptizes must of necessity anoint her who is baptized. But where there is a woman and especially a deaconess, it is not fitting that woman should be seen by men. And when she is being baptized and has come up from the water let the deaconess receive her and teach her and instruct her how the seal of Baptism ought to be kept unbroken in purity and holiness. For this cause we say that the ministry of a woman deacon is especially needful and important.

Deaconesses also acted as keepers of the doors of the church, particularly in charge of the women's entrance to, and section of, the church. She kept order in the women's section and escorted visiting women to their places. The deaconess was devoted to works of charity toward other women as well. Her work corresponded to the same work done by deacons on behalf of the men of the community. She visited and ministered to the sick, she brought communion to those who were unable to attend the liturgy, and she attended to the poor, the widows, the orphans, and any who had need among the women. She distributed the charity given by the Church to those whom she recognized as needy. In many respects, the deaconess functioned as the female counterpart to the deacon; she carried out the diaconal ministry toward women precisely as he did it toward men. The *Apostolic Constitutions* (3.2.19) tell us:

> The deacon is exhorted to ministry to the infirm as workmen that are not ashamed. And let the deaconess be diligent in taking care of the women. But both of them, deacon and deaconess, let them be ready to carry messages, to travel about, to minister, and to serve.

They were both collaborators of the bishop, freely chosen by him from among the people, and appointed to assist him in his pastoral duties. However, the ministry of deaconesses was only exercised for women and did not include the same liturgical function as male deacons.

According to the documents we have, bishops, presbyters, deacons, deaconesses, subdeacons and readers were to be ordained, unlike confessors, virgins, widows and exorcists who were appointed to their ministries. The ordination rite of deaconesses followed that of deacons and preceded that of subdeacons. The *Apostolic Constitutions* offers the first known rite of ordination of deaconesses. It was clearly a clerical ordination and not simply a blessing. The deaconess was included among the clergy, unlike the widows and virgins. She received communion after the male clergy in the altar, before the other female orders, followed by the children and the rest of the people.

The Fourth to Sixth Centuries

From the fourth century through the sixth century, there were very many references to deaconesses in both the legislation of the empire, the Church canons, patristic writings and histories.[7] I would like to mention just some of these to give you a flavour of the ministry of the order of deaconesses in this period, which was probably the heyday of the order.

The code of the Emperor Justinian reflects extensive thought about the order of deaconesses for his time. In order to restrict the number of clergy serving the great Church of Constantinople, and thus control the expenses for such from the imperial treasury, Justinian decreed that there should be 415 clergy for Hagia Sophia: 60 priests, 100 male deacons, 40 female deacons, 90 subdeacons, 100 readers, and 25 chanters. In addition, there were to be 100 gatekeepers. Justinian declared that all regulations that apply to the male clergy apply equally to the women deacons as well. He declared that the deaconesses should be about 50 years old, neither too old nor too young to do the things that are necessary; they should be virgins or once-married widows; a woman whose lifestyle was suspect in any way would not be admitted to the diaconate. She might be ordained younger than 50, if she was ordained within a monastery and remained there.

She might live alone if she was older, if she did not share her home with any men, even as brothers, but it was preferable for her to live with her parents, children, or blood relations. A woman deacon would be excommunicated or even executed if she either committed an immoral act with a man or married, and her property would go to the monastery or church with which she had been associated. Likewise, the men who thus defiled a deaconess of the Church or entered into marriage with her would be punished by imperial legislation, suffering property confiscation and even death by the sword.

Several Church canons also addressed some of the issues relating to deaconesses. Canon 15 of Chalcedon (451) prescribed an age and marital status for deaconesses.

> A woman shall not receive the laying on of hands as a deaconess under forty years of age. And then only after searching examination and if, after she has had hands laid on her and has continued for a time to minister, she shall despise the grace of God and give herself in marriage, she shall be anathematised and the man united to her.[8]

Two canons of the Trullo Quinnesext Council (692) also confirm the age of deaconesses to be 40, which is different from the age of 60 prescribed for widows by Paul and of 50 by the Emperor Justinian in his code. The council gives a rationale for changing the age limitation: the 'apostolic' edict that a widow should be elected in the Church at 60 years old. But the sacred canons had decreed that a deaconess should be ordained at 40 since they saw that the Church by divine grace had gone forth more powerful and robust and was advancing still further and they saw the firmness and stability of the faithful in observing the divine commandments.

In other words, they needed deaconesses who were young and strong enough to do the work. A third canon of this same council allows the wife of a man who is ordained bishop to become deaconess if she is worthy. When her husband becomes a bishop, she must separate from him and reside in a distant monastery where he will provide for her.

Canon 24 and 44 of *Letter* 199 by Basil the Great associates deaconesses with widows and forbids their remarriage.[9] Epiphanius speaks of deaconesses several times, emphasizing that their role is not one of priestly function but of diaconal service to women, particularly in Baptism. He said,

> Deaconesses are instituted solely for service to women, to preserve decency as required, whether in connection with their Baptism or in connection with any other examination of their bodies. Deaconesses can only have been married once, and they must lead continent lives, or else be the widow of a single marriage or else have remained perpetual virgins.[10]

Gregory of Nazianzus wrote to Gregory of Nyssa to console his friend on the death of his wife, Theosophia, who was a deaconess. He writes to his friend:

> But what we must now feel in presence of a long-prevailing law of God which has now taken my Theosophia, for I call her mine because she lived a godly life, for spiritual kindred is better than bodily. Theosophia, the glory of the Church, the adornment of Christ, the helper of our generation, the hope of women. Theosophia, the most beautiful and glorious among all the beauty of the brethren. Theosophia, truly sacred, truly consort of a priest, and of equal honour and worthy of the great sacrament.[11]

This reference to the great sacrament refers to her office as a deaconess, as does the description of her attributes. It appears that the deaconess, Theosophia, continued living with her husband, Gregory of Nyssa, in spite of the norm to the contrary.

Now the most extensive references to deaconesses by a patristic writer comes from John Chrysostom, who had a staff of 46 deaconesses at the great Church of Hagia Sophia in Constantinople. Some of these numbered among his closest associates. One of these in particular, the deaconess Olympias, was considered his close friend. Seventeen of his extant letters are addressed to her from his exile from 404 to 407.[12] The historians Sozemnos (early fifth century) and Palladios wrote about Olympias in their histories. They tell us that she was of most illustrious birth but that when she was young she was orphaned, then later given in marriage at the age of 18. Within a short time, she was widowed and Palladios claimed that the marriage went unconsummated. Now when the Emperor Theodosius heard of her widowhood, he tried to convince her to marry one of his relatives. She refused though and said,

> If my King had desired me to live with a male, he would not have taken away my first husband. But he knew that I cannot make a man happy, so he liberated him from the bond and me likewise from the burdensome yoke and he freed me from subjection to a man while he laid on me the gentle yoke of chastity.[13]

Therefore, Theodosius ordered that her property be taken away from her and held in trust until she turned 30. She in turn thanked him for relieving her of the burden of possessions and suggested that he distribute it to the poor in the churches. Since he had done her no harm by his action, he returned her property to her.

Archbishop Nectarios of Constantinople (d.397) ordained Olympias as deaconess while she was in her twenties, which was well under the canonical age of 40. With her property that had been restored, she provided for him and she took care of him to such an extent that she even advised him on ecclesiastical policy. John Chrysostom, who succeeded Nectarios, became her dearest friend. Perceiving that she bestowed her goods very liberally on anyone who asked her for them, and that she despised everything but the service of God, he advised her to bestow her wealth on others more prudently and economically. Palladios also tells us that Olympias prepared for the holy John, meaning Chrysostom, his daily provisions, and sent them to the bishop and continued to do so through the end of his life. When Chrysostom was leaving Constantinople to go into exile, Palladios tells us:

> He went into the baptistery and called Olympias along with the deaconesses Pentavia and Procla and Sylvinia and he addressed them: "Come here, my daughters, and listen to me. I see that the things concerning me have come to an end. This is what I ask of you."[14]

Then in very flowery language, to convince them, he said, "Please accept my legitimate successor." Further, we learn that Olympias was accused of setting fire to the Church in protest of the exile of John. When brought before the prefect to answer the charges she replied, "My past life ought to avert all suspicion from me for I have devoted my large property to the restoration of the temples of God." Palladios wrote extensively of her in reply to his deacon. His deacon asked him, "What kind of woman is she?" Moreover, the bishop replied, "Do not say woman, but rather manly creature for she is a man in everything but body, in her way of life, her works, in knowledge, and courage in misfortunes."[15] The bishop explained that Patriarch Theophilus of Alexandria had persecuted Olympias because she took in monks whom he had expelled. Palladios claims that in her actions she thus imitated her Lord. He also hinted that Theophilus' wrath against her had more to do with her refusal to give him money than to her sheltering the monks. The bishop claimed that "It is to the shame of men that a manly woman should take them in and it is to the accusation of bishops that a deaconess should befriend them." In other words, the priests and bishop should have taken care of these monks and not left it up to the deaconess to do it. "Her fame is enrolled in all the churches for many reasons. She imitated that Samaritan," he continues.

Theodoret, another historian from the early sixth century, tells us an enchanting story of the relationship between a young man and the deaconess-friend of his mother. He says,

> A young man who was a pagan priest's son, and brought up in impiety about this time, went over to the true religion, for a lady remarkable for her devotion and admitted to the order of deaconesses was an intimate friend of his mother. When he came to visit her, she used to welcome him with affection and urge him to the true religion. On the death of his mother, the young man used to visit her and enjoyed the advantage of her teaching. Deeply impressed by her counsels, he inquired of his teacher by what means he might both escape the superstition of his father, and have part and lot in the truth which she preached.[16]

Then in a very lengthy and flowery way, Theodoret tells how she taught him and hid him from his father. His father found him, caught him and tortured him but the young man escaped. "And back," he says, "I ran to my instructress."

Before the end of the fourth century, the term for ordination of deaconesses varied. The different documents tell us different things. Some use the word *hierotonia*, which means ordination, and other documents use various terms such as *heirothesia* or *kathisthesa*, which mean appointment or giving a ministry as a blessing. This indicates the fluidity of the nature and perception of the order up until that time. However, by the end of the fourth century, the term used virtually exclusively was *hierotonia*, to ordain rather than to appoint to an office. By this time, the practise of ordaining deaconesses was widespread in the East. Later in the sixth century, when Severus was going into exile, he stated, "The practice of devout women being ordained deaconesses is very usual and if I may say so, over the whole world" [the world that he knew].

We also have at least 75 funeral inscriptions of the fourth through sixth centuries that mention deaconesses. Some of these mention the particular attributes or functions of deaconesses. Several tell us of women who were both deaconess and *higoumenia*, which means that they were both deaconesses and heads of monastic communities. One called Sophia was "a second Phoebe." Another was "a deaconess of this hospital," meaning that she had a hospital ministry. There was a Mary who "raised children, practised hospitality, washed the feet of saints, and distributed her bread to those in need."[17] Several were mentioned as being deaconesses of the great Church of Constantinople. A number were mothers, daughters, sisters, or wives of clergy, so ministry was certainly a family affair. There was an Athanasia who was most pious, who led an irreproachable life. An Aiaria lived her life as a deaconess of the saints. There was an Evian who erected a place of worship to Saint Andrew. Moreover, fulfilling her vow, it was Matrona, the most pious deaconess, who had the mosaic of the Exedra built.

The Seventh to Tenth Centuries

Now we come to some documentation of the seventh through tenth centuries. In the late seventh century, Jacob of Edessa defined the role of deaconesses in his Church in response to questions from one of his disciples.[18] The disciples asked, "Does the deaconess like the deacon have the power to put a portion of the sacred gifts into the consecrated chalice?" Jacob answers, "In no way can she do this. The deaconess did not become a deaconess in order to serve at the altar but rather for the sake of women who are ill." The disciple then asks, "Well then, what are the powers of the deaconess in the Church?" And Jacob answers,

> These are her sole powers: to sweep the sanctuary and to light the lamps. If she is in a convent of women, she can remove the sacred gifts from the tabernacle only because there is no priest or deacon present. She may give them to the other sisters and to any children who may be present. She anoints adult women when they are baptized and she visits women who are ill and cares for them.

At about the same time, the synod of Mar-George I defined the function of a deaconess of that Church who came from the ranks of the virgins living in monasteries: "The most virtuous of these sisters should be set apart to carry out the ecclesiastical ministry. She should be ordained as a deaconess. Her task is to anoint those women being baptised with the holy oil. She must always carry out this task, the ceremony of Baptism, in the way that modesty requires." It is in the eighth century that we find the first complete text of the ordination service, which was being used for deaconesses in the Byzantine Church. The *Euchologion* of the Barbarini Greek manuscript 336, which is in the Vatican Library, includes successively the ordination rites for bishops, priests, deacons, deaconesses and subdeacons. The appointments of lectors, psalmists and hegoumens follow this. We also have about eight or nine other manuscripts, dating from the tenth through fourteenth centuries, that include an ordination service for the deaconess.

The text for the ordination includes the following: after the holy anaphora (eucharistic prayer) has been completed, and the doors have been opened, the deaconess who is to be ordained is presented to the bishop.[19] The bishop recites aloud the formula, the grace divine, while the candidate herself bows her head. Making three signs of the cross, he prays,

> Holy and all-powerful God, you who sanctified the female sex by the birth according to the flesh of your only Son and our God from a virgin and who granted the gift of your grace and the coming of the Holy Spirit not only to men but also to women, you, Lord, look kindly on this maidservant now before you. Call her to the work of the deaconate and cause to descend upon her the precious gift of the Holy Spirit. Preserve her in the Orthodox faith

and in conduct that is irreproachable according to what is pleasing to you, while in all things she continually fulfils her ministry. For to you is due all glory and honour.

After the "Amen" one of the deacons prays, "In peace let us pray to the Lord, for the peace that comes from above, for the peace of the whole world." Then he says, "For our bishop, his priesthood, his responsibility, his long life, his health, and also the for work of his hands" and then, "For this deaconess who is now being set apart and for her salvation, may the Lord who loves mankind give her the grace to fulfil her diaconate without either spot or stain. For all these things, let us pray to the Lord." Then he continues the litany. While this is being said by the deacon, the bishop once again with his hand on the head of the deaconess who is being ordained, prays,

> You, Lord, our Master, you who do not reject women who are consecrated to you, in order to serve in your holy places with a fitting holy desire, but who accept them into the ranks of your ministers, grant also to your servant here present who has wished to consecrate herself to you, perfectly to fulfil the gift of the deaconate. Grant the grace of your Holy Spirit, just as you gave the gift of your deaconate to Phoebe, whom you called to the work of ministry. Grant her the grace to persevere without reproach in your holy temple, O God. May she apply herself to household government. May she especially be temperate in all things. May she be your perfect servant in order that presenting herself before the judgement seat of your Christ, she may receive the worthy reward of her just stewardship through the mercy and love of mankind of your only Son.

After the "Amen" he places around her neck the diaconal *orarion* under the *omophorion*, bringing its two ends out in front. Then the bishop gives her the chalice and she takes it and puts it down on the sacred table.

The similarity between the ordinations of a deacon and that of a deaconess is striking in all of the manuscripts. It is clear that the rites for the ordination of deacons and deaconesses were meant to be as symmetrical as possible. Both ordinations took place during the eucharistic liturgy within the sanctuary. At this point, the candidate advanced toward the bishop who was standing within the royal doors, and the ordination began with the grace divine. It continued with two prayers by the bishops, separated by a diaconal litany, through which the deacon held his *omophorion* under his hand on the head of the one being ordained. In both cases, the bishop conferred the diaconal *orarion* and communicated the new deacon or deaconess within the sanctuary after the priests, and presented the chalice to the new deacon or deaconess. The prayers were altered slightly, with the protomartyr deacon Stephen as the model for deacons, and the deaconess Phoebe as the model for the deaconess.

Now there were three differences in the ritual. These included that the deaconess did not kneel on one knee, as did the deacon, because it would have been considered immodest or improper for her to do so. Her *orarion* was placed around her neck with the two ends brought in front instead of over the shoulder as for the deacon. This was probably to differentiate their two ministries. Finally, she did not distribute communion as did the deacon, but when the bishop presented the chalice to her after the people had communed, she placed it directly on the altar.

During the ninth and tenth centuries respectively, we also find Armenian and Georgian rituals for the ordination of deaconesses, which differ considerably from the Byzantine rites. These rituals were not accompanied by a description of rubrics, so they cannot be compared with what they were doing at that time for the ordination of the deacons.

The Eleventh to Fourteenth Centuries

Now we come to the documentation of the eleventh through fourteenth centuries. Unfortunately, we do not have a wealth of information. By this time, the order of deaconesses in some parts of the Eastern Church had already declined to the point of being non-existent while the order was declining further in the places where it was in existence. We still have in the eleventh and early twelfth centuries the comment from Anna Comnenna (1083–c.1156) in her *Alexiad,* that her father, the Emperor Alexius I (1048–1118), had restored and enlarged a large orphanage located next to the sanctuary dedicated to Paul, partly for the purpose of accommodating the work of the deaconess. Therefore, we know that at least in the late eleventh and early twelve centuries we still have some deaconesses in the Byzantine Church. The Chaldean Nestorian Church of the eleventh century also gives us an indication that deaconesses are still there, albeit declining. The documents from the Syriac Church, though, tell us only of the memory of the deaconess. They say:

> This ordination was formerly carried out for deaconesses and it is for this reason that a ritual for this was always transcribed in the ancient books. But we see plainly that this practice has now ceased in the Church. But if a bishop acting under the spur of a passing necessity finds it necessary to ordain a deaconess, then he should ordain a woman of proven chastity who is getting along in years. For the holy apostles and Fathers decreed that these were the requisite qualities for ordination.

By the end of the twelfth century, we find that the order of deaconess has disappeared in the Byzantine Church. The extant reports are made with great scepticism, fundamentally questioning whether the order had actually existed. "How could it have been possible for deaconesses to have existed in the early Church when we know that women are unclean, so how could they have existed?"

These seem to be the last references to deaconesses up to the nineteenth century, except for a couple of references in the seventeenth century, where we find that the wives and widows of priests in Greece are being given the title of deaconess. Their primary function was to oversee the women's section of the Church. It appears that these women were highly revered in the Greek Church.

Deaconesses in Modern Times

Throughout the mid-nineteenth and early twentieth centuries, a number of prominent clergy and laity in Russia sought to establish the order of deaconesses for the Russian Church. While the order had been a solid presence in the Georgian Church, deaconesses had never been a presence in the Russian Church. This is probably a function of the fact that Christianity did not become established in Russia until after the order of deaconesses in the Byzantine, Syriac, Georgian, Armenian and Chaldean churches had already declined. Nonetheless, the Russian Church had a great interest in the order. Although none of their efforts resulted in the restoration of the order, the Synod of Russia accepted a significant proposal for the order of deaconesses on the eve of the revolution. In 1906, the pre-Sobor commission[20] approved the guidelines for the deaconesses and by 1911 the Church was ready to establish the first community of deaconesses in Moscow. However, protests from several members of the hierarchy, who opposed the provision that allowed the deaconesses to make a temporary rather than life-long commitment to the order, stifled the project.

In Greece, similar efforts were taking place. On Pentecost Sunday in 1911, St. Nectarios, Bishop of Angina (1846–1920) ordained a nun to the diaconate. Subsequently the nun-deacon admitted to her convent another nun whom St. Nectarios also ordained to the diaconate. They wore a *sticharion* to the waist, but not reaching their feet, and wore the diaconal *orarion* and cuffs. Soon after St. Nectarios ordained deaconesses, Archbishop Chrysostomos of Athens appointed what were called monastic deaconesses, who in fact were sub-deaconesses. They had the following rights: to wear the orarion, to cense, to decorate the holy sanctuary, to read the gospels during the services when an ordained clergyman was not present, and to bring the pre-sanctified holy gifts to the nuns who were ill. In the mid-fifties, the Greek theologian Theodorus states that there were a few monasteries in Greece where certain nuns had been ordained as deaconesses. In 1952, the Church of Greece, through the Society of the Apostolic Diakonia, established a school for deaconesses in Athens. The women were required to hold degrees in theology, to receive instruction in social work at the college, and to do field work in parishes, hospitals, orphanages, homes for the aged and schools for the blind. Currently, graduates of this program are not ordained, though it is hoped by some that there will be a move in that direction soon. They act primarily as social workers assisting priests in parishes.

In 1976, under the auspices of the World Council of Churches, Orthodox women from around the world met in Agapia, Romania, to discuss the role of women in the Church. Part of their report included a discussion of the diaconate and I would like to read that section of the report:

> It is recommended that the office of deaconess be studied and considered for reactivation in the churches where the needs of society could be met more effectively by such a service. The content of this diaconal service is similar to that mentioned above [i.e. another section of the report] dealing with the Church service. The service of deaconess however differs in that it is a service consecrated by the Church with the blessing of the bishop and is a life-time commitment to full vocational service in the Church as presently dictated by the canons of the Church. Necessary adjustments or recommendations concerning the office of deaconess are subject to change by any future councils of the Church to meet present day conditions and needs. It must be noted that the role of the deaconess is that of a *diakonia* and it is not a priestly function; its form and content is that of service and does not have the character of a liturgical, sacramental function though the very nature of its service is an extension of the sacramental life of the Church into the life of society. The office of deaconess is distinct and is not new, nor can it be considered as a first step to the ordained priesthood.[21]

Then in 1988 the Ecumenical Patriarch Demetrius I called an international conference in Rhodes, Greece, in which I also participated, to discuss the role of women in the Church and the question of the ordination of women was raised. The proceedings of this consultation produced the following recommendations for the restoration of the order of deaconesses:

> The Apostolic order of deaconesses should be revived. It was never altogether abandoned in the Orthodox Church though it has tended to fall into disuse. There is ample evidence from apostolic times, from the patristic, canonical and liturgical tradition well into the Byzantine period and even into our own day, that this order was held in high honour. The deaconess was ordained within the sanctuary during the liturgy with two prayers. She

received the *orarion*, [the deacon's stole], and received holy communion at the altar. The revival of this ancient order should be envisioned on the basis of the ancient proto-types testified to in many sources and with the prayers found in the Apostolic Constitutions and the ancient Byzantine liturgical books. Such a revival would present a positive response to the many needs and demands of the contemporary world in many spheres. This would be all the more true if the diaconate in general, male as well as female, were restored in all places in its original manifold services with extension in the social sphere, in the spirit of ancient tradition, and in response to the increasing specific needs of our time. It should not be solely restricted to a purely liturgical role or considered to be a mere step on the way to higher ranks of clergy. The revival of women deacons in the Orthodox Church would emphasize in a special way the dignity of women and give recognition to their contribution to the work of the Church as a whole. Further would it not be possible and desirable to allow women to enter into the lower orders through a blessing of the Church, sub-deacon, reader, chanter, teacher, without excluding new orders that the Church might consider to be necessary. This matter deserves further study since there is no definite tradition of this sort.[22]

Some bishops have already acted on these recommendations. They have given blessings or tonsure for women in certain parishes to be readers or chanters. In some areas girls and women serve in the sanctuary as acolytes, particularly in small parishes or during weekday services when few people are present, or at women's retreats when there are no men present. The Greek Orthodox Diocese of San Francisco has been developing guidelines for an order of myrrh bearers that would provide a ministry for girls in parishes. These are significant developments.[23]

The Crete Consultation

In 1990, again under the auspices of the World Council of Churches, Orthodox women from throughout the world met in Crete, Greece, for a consultation. The discussions and report focused on three areas: ministry, human sexuality, and participation in decision-making in the Church. The section on ministry, which I chaired and co-authored, focused almost exclusively on a framework for rejuvenating the order of deaconesses in the Church, coupled with a recommendation to likewise renew the order of male deacons. This report will be the basis of the present discussion on what the women's diaconate might look like today.

According to the deliberations in Crete, the first function of a deaconess would be engaging in the full breadth of catechetical work. This would include teaching the faith to children, youth, and adults; instructing those preparing to become godparents; training catechumens and prospective converts; preparing couples for marriage; and developing the curricula for these educational programs. Such catechetical work is a ministry of the Church and to be undertaken with sufficient preparation and understanding of the faith. Included in this ministry would be the establishment and directorship of quality parochial or religious-based schools from pre-school through college. Our children need to be spiritually and theologically nurtured and grounded. Even our own Church school programs, which often meet for much less than one hour a week, are pitiful attempts to educate our children in the faith. A deaconess or even a battalion of deaconesses, with responsibility for the education of the entire parish, especially the young, would certainly be able to improve matters.

A second function outlined in Crete would be to open closed parishes. Churches closed because of a lack of clerics could be opened for non-eucharistic liturgies. The priestly ministry, based on the high priesthood of Christ, is primarily one of leadership in the liturgical and sacramental ministry of the Church. It is the norm, the ideal, and desirable for the head of the eucharistic assembly to be a bishop or presbyter. The diaconal ministry, based upon the understanding of Christ as the servant, is primarily one of service to the community, which does not include, as a major responsibility, the leadership of the eucharistic community. We see this distinction being made in the book of Acts, where deacons are appointed to relieve the apostles of serving tables, so that the apostles can be devoted to what is proper to the apostolic ministry. When this norm cannot be met, when for any number of reasons a bishop or presbyter is not the head of a eucharistic community, then it is appropriate, though not ideal, for a deacon or deaconess to fulfil this function within certain parameters.

This second recommendation of Crete responds to an actual experiential need. There are many small parishes, mission parishes, rural parishes, isolated parishes, and scattered groups of Orthodox families throughout the US and Canada, which have little or no contact with a presbyter for either liturgical or pastoral needs. Sent by a bishop, the deaconess could help to fulfil those needs by leading the community in liturgical prayer, including distributing the Pre-sanctified Eucharist to the faithful. The form of this liturgical service could either be determined by the bishop case-by-case, or established as a rite in the service books, perhaps something akin to the long-standing reader's service. By her regular participation in the life of such a parish, the deaconess would also establish an essential relationship with the parishioners, in order to meet their pastoral needs as far as the diaconal ministry would allow. She would, of course, consult with the bishop about those things which would not be within her sphere of ministry, especially those things which relate to the sacramental ministry.

Crete foresaw deaconesses serving the same needs for monastic communities as for those communities without a presbyter. This same ministry, as seen in recommendation two, could be served by deaconess nuns in women's monasteries where a full-time presbyter is not present. Candidates for ordination to the order of deaconesses would be determined by the monastic community itself in consultation with the bishop. Since monastic communities have a fuller liturgical life than most parishes, it would be appropriate for the monastic deaconess to order a fuller liturgical ministry than her counterpart in the parish.

Reading prayers of blessings for special occasions is a fourth function of deaconesses envisioned in Crete. We Orthodox love to bless everything: we bless people, we bless homes, we bless cars, bicycles, businesses, animals, grapes, eggs, palms, paska baskets, water, and all kinds of objects. We also offer a blessing at every occasion: before childbirth, after childbirth, the eighth day naming of the child, the churching of a child, the prayer for a child beginning school, prayer before a journey, prayer at the founding of a house, blessing a cornerstone, a blessing for adoption, and many other occasions. Many of these prayers or blessings could fall within the ministry of the deaconess.

A fifth function proposed at Crete was performing social work, in connection with the Church, as part of pastoral care. This is a major component of the diaconal ministry. Ministry to women and families would be her primary, though not exclusive task. The list of possibilities is endless: ministry both within and outside our Church communities to poor women, sick women or women with disabilities, single mothers, mothers of troubled or troublesome children, alcohol and drug dependent women, victims of domestic violence, victims of rape, pregnant women for whom abortion seems the only viable option, new mothers who need assistance, elderly women who need assistance, emotionally troubled women, prostitutes, sexually active girls, victims of child abuse, victims of pornography, women who neglect or abuse their children, lesbian women, runaway girls and women, troubled adolescents, women with AIDS, immigrant families, institutionalized women, women with burdens too great for them to bear alone, divorced or abandoned women, girls caught in gangs, women in any dysfunctional situation, and homeless women with or without children.

The diaconal ministry of the Church has been sorely neglected, though many of us have done some things to be sure, but largely we have lost the sense of service within and outside the parish, and have relinquished our responsibility to the government, to other churches, and to social service or charitable agencies. We have concentrated our focus on the liturgical and sacramental life of the Church, and perhaps, the social ministry of the Church, to the neglect of this vital diaconal ministry. We can certainly recover it both in the male and female diaconate and in the ministry of the royal priesthood. It is especially in this latter ministry that the deaconess would exercise her role as spiritual mother.

Our Cretan consultations proposed a sixth function: engaging in youth and college ministry, including developing fellowship

246

among Orthodox youth and developing leadership training. We send our youth off to university or jobs, hoping that they are sufficiently prepared educationally and emotionally to meet the challenge. However, what also concerns us is whether they are spiritually, theologically, morally and ethically prepared to face the doubts, temptations and troubles they are bound to encounter. This ministry would involve teaching, counselling and guiding our youth through these years, providing them a support group of other Orthodox Christian youth (who may eventually marry one another, we hope), and training them to take on the adult responsibilities of the Church.

Encouraging and co-ordinating the lay ministry of the Church, and training persons for it, could be a seventh function of a renewed female diaconate. One of the functions of the deaconess would be to help the laity discover its ministry in the Church and to help organize the work of the royal priesthood, training and encouraging persons for it. The report of Crete in addressing this issue said:

> Our conviction is that creative restoration of the diaconate for women, which we hope will lead in turn to a renewal of the diaconate for men, will encourage and enhance the ministry of the royal priesthood, strengthening the faithful to engage in lay ministry, and will provide an essential link between the bishop who sends the deacon or deaconess and the local parish. Because of this it is hoped that such a ministry will help to bridge the gap which sometimes exists between clergy and laity in their common ministry in the life of the Church.

The proposed eighth function would be counselling the faithful in spiritually related matters. The deaconess would minister to the spiritual needs of the people she serves, guiding them through their crises of faith, their doubts, those troubling thoughts and times which debilitate a person spiritually. Girded with the strength of her own life of prayer, fasting, service, discernment, and her experience as a woman in the Church and society, the deaconess would offer an invaluable ministry to the Church in this area.

At Crete, we concluded that deaconesses could anoint the infirm. Visitations to hospitals, nursing homes, hospices, various other institutions and homes would necessarily be part of a deaconess's ministry. The most common reason for these visits would be to visit someone who is ill, handicapped, or confined. Since the Church's response to those who are infirm includes anointing them, this would naturally fall within the ministry of the visiting deaconess.

A tenth function would be to carry out missionary work within the communities in which they live, drawing people to the Church through the proclamation of the Gospel. This recommendation calls for the deaconess to look close to home, yet beyond the confines of the walls of the Church building, to seek out those who have not heard of or have not responded to the Gospel proclamation. This includes entering those deteriorating neighbourhoods populated with immigrants, minorities and the poor. All too often, an inner city parish seeks to move to the upper and middle-class suburbs, to where the "better" people live. The deaconess would instead remain where they are, and knock on the doors of our Church neighbours, inviting them to our churches, providing programs for their youth, offering food pantries, working perhaps through a parish ministry team, and proclaiming the Gospel faith to them. Her neighbourhood would be any place, any corner, where the Gospel needs to be heard.

I would like to give you a small example of this, just a beginning of this, at our parish of St. George in Indianapolis. Our parish is located in one of the worst sections of town; the area is run down. Last year alone, three murders took place behind the church property. On one occasion, there were twenty police cars in our church parking lot, combing our church property looking for the murderer; they even entered the church and told my husband to leave and go home because they were afraid for him. We have to have a security cop in our parking lot at all times; otherwise all of our cars will be vandalized and stolen.

How do you respond to a situation like this? We have started in a small way. Granted it is not a grand movement at this time, but we have developed what we call a charity ministry team and through this team we are providing for our neighbours. Within our church, we provide a food pantry, which includes food, clothing, diapers and baby food for anyone in the neighbourhood who needs something to tide them over before the next cheque comes in. Therefore, they know that they are free to come to our church at any time for these items. Additionally, my husband has a Good Samaritan fund that he administers when it is necessary to give money, rather than food or clothing. At Christmas time, we choose families for whom we do something special. This year we were able to provide food, clothing and toys for the children of a dozen families. It is a small step and I am not sure that our parish is quite ready to invite these people to come to our church yet. I am not sure that they are ready for that, but that time will come and it should come. This is one of the activities of a deaconess that could move the lay people to be good neighbours to those outside the confines of the walls of the Church.

The Cretan consultation also proposed that deaconesses could minister to the sick, imprisoned and confined and bring them Communion when needed. As anointing is one of the Church's responses to the infirm, so is offering the Eucharist to those unable to gather with the eucharistic community. Within the context of visiting these members of the Church, the deaconess would be able to offer the pre-sanctified gifts for them.

A final function would be that of assisting the bishop or presbyter in the liturgical services. This recommendation calls for the deaconess to assist in the liturgical services in whatever way is deemed necessary and appropriate. This ministry could range anywhere from simply keeping order in the sanctuary during services, to performing those functions considered proper to acolytes, to serving in the same manner as the deacon does. This would be totally up to the discretion of the bishop.

Besides this list of functions, the consultation also proposed a list of qualifications for deaconesses. The report stated:

> The qualifications for a deaconess would certainly include a training in theology and other related fields, practical experience, maturity, involvement in Church life, dedication to ministry, moral integrity, spiritual depth, and a call to this vocation, taking into consideration the issues raised by canons which described the qualifications of clergy in general. These are virtually identical with the necessary qualifications for bishops, presbyters, and deacons. It is crucial that this ministry be recognized and sanctioned by the Church through ordination of the deaconess. The form of this

ordination, the questions of marital status, age, appropriate dress, and other specific matters might best be worked out according to the needs and requirements of each local church. Decisions on this subject should be taken in the context of a conciliar process and dialogue between bishops, presbyters, and laity, both male and female.

Comment on three of these issues would be advisable. The first is theological training. We were very careful not to specify seminary education, because a number of the women who were in Crete with us were from countries and cultures that do not permit women to attend seminary. Nevertheless, I believe that here in Canada or in the USA no such cultural impediment exists, and a seminary education geared to preparation for the diaconal ministry would be essential. This means that the seminaries have to develop such a program.

The second issue is the age for a deaconess. Canonical and imperial legislation specified a minimum age of at least 40. But just as canons which specify age limits for bishops, presbyters and deacons were meant to ensure maturity in the candidates, I think we can ascribe such a spiritual sense to the age limits for the ordination of deaconesses and ordain mature women younger than 40.

The third issue is that of marital status. Virtually all deaconesses in the early Church had been once-married widows, virgins, or the wives of bishops who, following the ordination of their husbands, retired to monasteries. Very few married deaconesses who remained with their husbands are referred to in the documentation. Though advocating the use of the earlier centuries as a model for the modern order, the international consultations in Agapia, Rhodes and Crete preferred to leave a decision about married deaconesses to the local churches rather than to dictate a universal law. It is important to remember why the Church required virginity or widowhood from deaconesses when it did not require this from the deacons. Historically, the culture of the day regarded a married woman's primary task to be the raising of her children and the management of her household. Activity outside the home, even Church work, would detract from her primary duty. The rise of the ascetic ideal predominated in certain periods of Church history, and especially the period when deaconesses were popular, thus providing the impetus for women to choose monastic living in droves. Hence, the Church had a ready-made, strictly regulated, and confined community from which to draw its workers. Thus, the requirement of single women as deaconesses was probably based on practical or disciplinary foundations rather than theological ones. One must ask whether these concerns remain significant today. I have concluded that, despite the validity of certain of these arguments, it would be appropriate in the Canadian or American churches to offer the same option for marriage or celibacy to a deaconess as to a deacon.

The Crete consultation strongly affirmed that the fullness of ministry is present in the Church when men and women serve our Lord together, offering whatever charisms he has given them. The consultation expressed its confidence in the ability of the local churches to renew creatively the diaconate for men and women, adapting the historical diaconate to the present needs of the Church as well as the societies and cultures within which we live.

For Further Reading

Behr-Sigel, Elisabeth. *The Ministry of Women in the Church.* Trans. Steven Bigham. Redondo Beach, CA: Oakwood Publications, 1991.

Bradshaw, Paul F. *Ordination Rites in the Ancient Churches of East and West.* New York: Pueblo, 1990.

Kyriaki Karidoyanes FitzGerald, ed., *Orthodox Women Speak: Discerning the Signs of the Times.* Brookline: Holy Cross and Geneva: WCC Publications, 1999.

Tarasar, Constance and Irina Kirillova, eds., *Orthodox Women: Their Role and Participation in the Orthodox Church.* Geneva: WCC Publications, 1976.

[1] *The Festal Mendion,* 254.

[2] For additional commentary and analysis, see Ellen Gvosdev, *The Female Diaconate: An Historical Perspective* (Minneapolis: Light and Life, 1991) and Thomas Hopko, ed., *Women and the Priesthood* (Crestwood, NY: St. Vladimir's, 1983).

[3] *Didascalia Apostolorum,* trans. R. Hugh Connoly (Oxford: Clarendon, 1929).

[4] *Ethiopic Didascalia,* trans. J.M. Harden (London: SPCK, 1920).

[5] *Apostolic Constitutions,* ed. James Donaldson (Edinburgh: T&T Clark, 1870).

[6] *Testament of Our Lord Jesus Christ* (Edinburgh: T. Clark, 1902).

[7] Gvosdev, *The Female Diaconate,* 9-19.

[8] See vol. 1 of *The Decrees of the Ecumenical Councils,* ed. Norman P. Tanner (Washington, DC: Georgetown, 1990). See also canon 19 of Nicaea (325).

[9] See *St. Basil: Letters and Selected Works, A Select Library of Nicene and Post-Nicene Fathers of the Christian Church* 8, 2d series (Grand Rapids, MI: Eerdmans, 1974–1983).

[10] *Panaria,* Corpus haereseologici, 2 vols. (1856–61).

[11] Letter 197, in *Cyril of Jerusalem and Gregory of Nazianzen, A Select Library of Nicene and Post-Nicene Fathers of the Christian Church* 7, 2d series (Grand Rapids, MI: Eerdmans, 1974–1983).

[12] See *John Chrysostom, A Select Library of Nicene and Post-Nicene Fathers of the Christian Church* 9, 2d series (Grand Rapids, MI: Eerdmans, 1974–1983).

[13] The primary sources are Sozemon (Sozemnos), *The Ecclesiastical History of Sozemon,* trans. C.D. Hartranft (Grand Rapids, MI: Eerdmans, 1989); and Palladios of Helenopolis, *The Lausiac History,* 2 vols, trans. R.T. Meyer (Westminster: Newman, 1965).

[14] Palladios.

[15] Ibid.

[16] Book 3.10 in *Theodoret, Jerome Gennadius, Rufinus* [etc.], *A Select Library of Nicene and Post-Nicene Fathers of the Christian Church* 3, 2d series (Grand Rapids, MI: Eerdmans, 1974–1983).

[17] Cf. Kyriaki Karidoyanes FitzGerald, "The Characteristics and Nature of the Order of the Deaconess," in *Women and the Priesthood,* ed. Thomas Hopko (Crestwood, NY: St. Vladimir's, 1983), 78–79.

[18] All citations from Jacob of Edessa can be found in *A Letter From Jacob of Edessa to John the Stylite of Litareb Concerning Ecclesiastical Canons,* trans. K.E. Rignell (Lund: CWK Gleerup, 1979).

[19] A standard English reference volume for Orthodox services is *Service Book of the Holy Orthodox-Catholic Apostolic Church,* 6th ed., trans. Isabel Florence Hapgood (Englewood, NJ: Antiochian Orthodox Christian Archdiocese, 1983).

[20] For a discussion of this process in early twentieth century Russia see James W. Cunningham, *A Vanquished Hope: The Movement for Church Renewal in Russia, 1905–1906* (Crestwood, NY: St. Vladimir's, 1981).

[21] See Constance Tarasar and Irina Kirillova, eds., *Orthodox Women: Their Role and Participation in the Orthodox Church* (Geneva: WCC, 1976).

[22] Inter-Orthodox Consultation on "The Place of Women in the Orthodox Church, and the Question of the Ordination of Women," *Orthodox Visions of Ecumenism,* ed. Gennadios Limouris (Geneva: WCC, 1994), 133–140.

[23] The increasing movement in favour of a restored female diaconate is evidenced by recent events. On November 15, 2000, a prominent group of French Orthodox clerics and theologians sent a letter to the primates of all Orthodox Churches appealing for the "creative restoration of a female diaconate." *Service Orthodoxe de Press* #254 (Janvier, 2001): 7–8.

VII. Meeting Christ in the Divine Liturgy (1999)

Chapter 11

Meeting Christ in the Divine Liturgy

LAWRENCE HUCULAK

Bishop Lawrence is the Ukrainian Catholic Bishop of Edmonton. He holds a doctorate in Liturgical Theology from the Pontifical Oriental Institute, Rome. In addition to his pastoral responsibilities, he also is adjunct lecturer at Newman Theological College in Edmonton.

An essential theme for Christians to consider is that of "Meeting Christ" – a personal encounter with Christ. Every individual who claims to be a Christian has to be concerned with meeting and nurturing a personal encounter with Jesus Christ. Nevertheless, we in the Eastern Churches who are much attached to our liturgical life recognize that this encounter is not just about "me and Jesus," but has a communal, liturgical aspect as well. I propose to reflect upon both of these "arms" of the encounter with Christ: both the "me and Jesus" and the "we and Jesus."

The Jesus the Apostles Saw

Let us first review the historical perspective. Imagine living at the time of Jesus Christ. Imagine what his followers, the apostles and disciples, would have gone through. They journeyed with Jesus during those three years of his public life, and their hopes grew that indeed this was the Messiah; this was the one who was going to save Israel and fulfil all of their expectations. Then they go through that great shocking experience of the last days, of the Crucifixion, of seeing him die on the cross, and of seeing him buried. When the stone is rolled in front of the grave it is as if on TV when the film comes to the finale and you see the words, "The End." You can go home now; it is all over. Then, inexplicably, joy comes to them. They are confronted with the idea that this Jesus whom they saw buried had risen. That joy would remain with them and Jesus would be with them, and again they would be encouraged and strengthened in their faith. But then again they would go through another difficult period when Jesus would tell them, "I can no longer stay with you on earth in this same fashion." Jesus returns to his heavenly Father, as we celebrate in the feast of the Ascension; he returns to the Kingdom of God. Once again, the followers feel abandoned. They huddle together full of fear in that upper room until the great event of Pentecost, when the Spirit of God comes down upon them. With that Spirit of God in them, they are able to go out and preach the Good News, to share this Good News with so many others. They believe that in a short time Jesus will come again, as he said, and will take all of humanity to God. The second coming is near!

Yet again they experience a setback: they realize that it is not so near after all. The second coming of the Lord is not going to be immediate. They have to then begin to change some of their outlook and some of their attitudes, because initially, the apostles and disciples are people who know Jesus Christ as a person, as an individual. They had walked with him, listened to him, and touched him. Now they begin to attract other followers who are taken up with this message about Jesus Christ. These new followers have never had that opportunity to meet Jesus in that same personal way. So two things begin to happen for the early Christian community: they recognize the need to write down what Jesus had said, done and taught and they realize the need to pass this message on to new followers of Jesus Christ.

Thus, we have the development of the four gospels: Matthew, Mark, Luke and John. These Gospels were written after the Resurrection as the community's memory of the events surrounding Jesus Christ. They were guided by the Holy Spirit to give us the record that we call the Gospels. With that also came records, written letters, generally called epistles, that offered advice to the communities which followed Christ. This developed into an entire corpus: a collection of works telling the story of Jesus Christ and his meaning for his followers.

The early Christians also had to reflect further on their lives. Initially they knew that Jesus had gone to return to his heavenly Father and they too expected to go immediately. However, they then realized this would not happen. They would have to wait and so what would they do? The early Christians began to reflect more and more upon the event and the person of Jesus and what his mission meant to them. They began to realize the value of being a community. It was not enough just to be alone in their homes and reflect upon Jesus. They needed to come together as a community, to remember, share, think and pray together about what Jesus had done.

The day that they picked for this assembly was a very natural choice; it was Sunday. After all Sunday was the day of the Resurrection. Jesus had risen from the dead on this day. They knew the Jewish Tradition that the Sabbath, the day of rest – the Lord's Day – was the seventh day. Jesus had in fact kept that Sabbath day sacred as well. This was the day Christ rested in the grave; but on the first day of the week, he rose from the dead. For the early Christians, not only was it the first day of a given week, but also it was the first day of a whole new era. That first Resurrection Sunday was the first day of the renewal of all creation. Everything that God had created was now renewed and seen in a very new light through the work of Jesus. Therefore, each Sunday became this most important day, this Lord's Day, this day of gathering when they would celebrate creation as it had been renewed in Jesus Christ. It became a day for them to gather to praise the Lord, to praise God, to give thanks for the specific blessings that they could see in their individual lives. It was also an occasion to remember what Jesus had taught them: to pray for their daily bread, to realize that before God each and every one of them was but a creature of God, a child of God, and that they were dependant on God for absolutely everything. So came about the Christian practice of regular Sunday liturgy.

It is during these regular liturgies that the community came to struggle with how to speak of their Lord Jesus Christ. Just what did it mean when Paul said, "He was like us in everything except sin." They had to work out an understanding of how Jesus on the one hand was divine, was God, and on the other hand, was human. What did it mean to speak during the liturgy of a God-human who suffered and died? They knew that the Old Testament spoke about sacrifice, but how was Jesus' death a sacrifice? The early Church reflected long and hard on just who Jesus was, how he was related to God, and how God worked through him. Many, many new questions were posed and slowly answered.

They soon recognized that although Jesus was not visibly present among them they were not alone. Jesus was with them. The love of God was with them. They found the words to express this: the Holy Spirit dwelt among them! This was the Spirit given to the apostles on that first Pentecost. That same Spirit Jesus promised would be given to all those who followed him, who came together in his name.

The concept of God as Trinity, as three important and powerful beings or persons in one God, developed gradually. It took time for the early Christians to think out, to work out, this new language about God, but they came to it and recognized it as a valid way of speaking. They now assembled to praise the God of Trinity who came and was part of human life, of this created order, so that we all would be restored to the Creator.

Finally, that early Christianity came to realize that although their words were new, their ideas were not. They would take the Old Testament, such works as those of the prophet Isaiah, and say, "Now I understand what Isaiah was talking about. Before it was not clear. But now when I believe in the resurrection of Jesus and understand who Jesus is, now a lot of this in the Old Testament makes sense to me." So, they would include in their prayer-gatherings readings from the Old Testament, whether it was portions of the works of the prophets, or the Psalms. They found that the Old Testament foreshadowed the New. The Trinitarian God was Yahweh!

The Liturgy of the Word

These developments are the basis of the liturgy of the Word. The first part of the eucharistic liturgy is our opportunity to reflect on all that has been done for us. It is the story of salvation!

This part of the liturgy developed not only in relation to the understanding of the Word, but also in relation to local customs and practices. One of the cities with the strongest influence was the capital of the Eastern Roman Empire, Constantinople, today Istanbul. One of the most popular practices in the Roman Empire, and especially in the capital, was processions. In Christian practice, these processions are called stationary liturgies. In Constantinople, or Jerusalem, or Antioch, the Christians would gather to pray at particularly important sites and then move together from site to site. Finally, they would conclude these processions at the most important church of the city: the Holy Sepulchre (Jerusalem) or Hagia Sophia (Constantinople). During the processions the people would sing sections from the Psalms. These refrains formed the first part of the liturgy. They give us many of the antiphonals or responsorials that we have in our liturgies.

When everyone got to the main church, the service continued, but not yet in the sanctuary. Often the patriarch and the whole court would wait in the centre of the church, and from there the readings of Scripture were given, and then the homily. A remnant of this remains in the Byzantine Tradition when the bishop celebrates the first part of the liturgy while remaining outside the sanctuary. He enters the church, but initially he and the clergy sit outside the sanctuary for the climax of the liturgy of the Word – the proclamation of the Gospel.

Therefore, this first part of the eucharistic liturgy gathers the community together, from all corners of the city or region. The community comes to share their experiences of and faith in Jesus Christ. They do this first by proclaiming the Word. Hearing the Word of God in the old and new scriptural texts prepares us for the reflection or homily. The purpose of the homily is for the whole community to reflect together on their common experience of the Living Word. This prepares the assembly to move on to the eucharistic liturgy's second section: the liturgy of the Eucharist itself.

Before the commencement of the second part of the eucharistic liturgy we have an interesting remnant of an ancient Christian practice: the *ektenia* (or litany) of the catechumens. This is a series of short petitions intoned by the deacon with the community. These are prayers for the catechumens, those who were preparing for Baptism. Near the end of that litany, we have that very beautiful and interesting text which would instruct all the catechumens to leave the Church. The deacon would say, "Catechumens, leave; catechumens, depart; let only the faithful remain, all the catechumens leave!" Although at times today the placement of these elements varies, the text remains and it is a very good reminder of this division of the liturgy. Indeed this *ektenia* marks the completion of the liturgy of the Word, which was open to all those who had an initial preparation for faith (were part of the catechumenate) and also to other groups such as certain groups of sinners. It reminds us that the eucharistic liturgy was an inclusive action, but full participation was only for those persons who were in good standing.

The Great Entrance

At this point in the Byzantine liturgy, what we have is the section called the Great Entrance. This is quite a solemn moment: a unique combination of prayer, of action or rubric, of music – a combination of what the celebrant does, what the deacon does, what the people do, and what the choir does. This harmonious great pageantry takes place along with the hymn, "Let us who mystically represent the Cherubim and sing the thrice-holy hymn to the life-creating Trinity, now set aside all earthly cares that we may welcome the King of all, invisibly escorted by angelic hosts. Alleluia." This hymn reminds the faithful of what is going to happen. In a very concrete and immediate way, a simple event becomes a mystical event. The gifts of bread and wine are brought from the side altar, where they have been prepared, to the main altar for the consecration. However, the liturgical tradition of Constantinople has developed a very beautiful procession around this simple act of transference.[1] This solemn but simple action prepares the celebrants and the people for what is about to begin. They are now going to be participants in something very holy, something very awesome, something that unites us with the work of the angels, the cherubim and the seraphim. The assembly is now moving from reflection on the Word to living in union with the Word. The Word, Christ, is in heaven and we are now joining the angels in their unending praise of God in the heavenly kingdom.

Next, we have the presentation of the Nicene Creed. The Creed, which comes from the early Church's Council of Nicaea (325), is very important because it gives us the summary or the synthesis of the main doctrines of our belief as Christians. The Creed was introduced into the Byzantine Divine Liturgy in the year 511. This Creed also became an important part of the rites of initiation. When the candidates, the catechumens, were being prepared for Baptism, they were not "presented" the Creed until near the end when the community was certain of their appropriateness. Thus, it came to be a sign of membership in the eucharistic community (only the baptized could be full participants). The recitation, the execution, the singing of the creed, is a reminder to all, repeatedly, that they are true followers of Jesus Christ – full members of the eucharistic assembly.

The Anaphora

We now move to the core portion of the eucharistic liturgy that we call the *anaphora* or eucharistic prayer. Many people familiar with the terms, as used in the Roman Catholic Church, will understand this as the canon of the mass. In the Roman Catholic rite there are a number of different canons, different central core prayers that they may choose from at a given Eucharist. For the Byzantine rite, we have the two *anaphora*, or the two core central prayers of our Sunday liturgy. The most common one is the one we attribute to John Chrysostom. The other, and the one I will focus on, is that of Basil the Great.[2] It is such a beautiful, rich and exquisite liturgical, theological, spiritual work that sums up for us the importance of Scripture, the importance of knowing what God intended right from the beginning of creation, what was involved with the Jesus event, and where we stand now.

Basil the Great is an excellent example of the degree to which the people of the early Church knew and used both the Old and New Testaments, for many sections of this *anaphora* are paraphrases of Scripture. This *anaphora*, which now is mainly used during Great Lent, is longer than that of Chrysostom, and it begins with a beautiful prayer addressed to God the Father. It speaks of and to God of the Old Testament creation, and it goes through God's whole plan of salvation. It literally recounts everything God has done for us.

The prayer is structured in such a way that the Christian understanding of a trinitarian God is also clearly present. This trinitarian God is active both in history and in our personal lives. This God has not simply set things in motion and retreated; the Holy One of Israel has never departed this world. However, it is not just a story about God and humanity. This epic story involves all creation and all the heavens. All created beings offer adoration, praise and glory to their Creator. So too does humanity:

> With these blessed powers, O Master and Lover of mankind, we sinners also cry out and say, "Holy are you, truly most holy. Immeasurable is the majesty of your holiness. You are revered in all your deeds for with truth and just judgment you have brought all things to pass for us."[3]

The account then turns to Genesis:

> Taking dust from the earth, O God, you formed man and honoured him with your own image. You placed him in a garden of delight and promised him the never-ending enjoyment of blessings and immortality for the observance of your commandments.

Notice what happens here. This is an instruction, a reminder for the faithful:

> But man disobeyed you, the true God, who created him. He was led astray by the cunning of the serpent and by his own transgressions was subjected to death. By your just judgment, O God, you expelled him from paradise into this world and returned him to the earth from which he had been taken.

Is that not an interesting comment? He was made from dust, from dirt, and he was sent back there. "God devised for him the salvation of regeneration which is in your Christ." God so values each and every human being that in spite of all human error, inadequacy and sin, humanity is still worth saving, and is still worth God's sending his only Son, Jesus Christ, to save those who have sinned. "And yet, O gracious Lord, you did not turn away from your creation, nor did you forget the work of your hands. You visited man in various ways because of your merciful loving kindness."

The prayer continues:

You did not give up on us. You sent prophets and wrought mighty works through the saints, who in every generation have been pleasing to you. You spoke to us through your servants, the prophets, who foretold the salvation that was to come. You gave the law as an aid and appointed angels as our guardians. When the fullness of time had come, you spoke to us through your Son himself, through whom you created the temporal world.

This wonderful prayer goes through the entire history of salvation and culminates in the person of Jesus Christ, the Incarnate One. However, Jesus' story climaxes when he is about to go to his voluntary and ever-memorable and life-giving death:

On the night on when he surrendered himself for the life of the world, he took bread into his holy and most-pure hands and having offered it to you, God and Father, he gave thanks, blessed it, sanctified it, and broke it. He gave it to his holy disciples and apostles, saying, "Take, eat, this is my body," [and then it continues,] "drink of this all of you, this is my blood. Do this in remembrance of me. For as often as you eat this bread and drink this chalice, you proclaim my death and profess my resurrection."

This command, or mandate, to the Christians became central for the first followers of Jesus. For those early followers, the Eucharist came to be a way of entering into Jesus' death, burial and resurrection. The Eucharist became a source of comfort for the followers; it was spiritual nourishment, which offered them experience of his own presence. So through two simple elements from their daily lives, bread and wine, Jesus became forever present to his followers. The bread and wine, these very basic forms of nourishment, became through Jesus' divine action his body and blood, his eternal presence to his followers.

Jesus nourishes his followers, gives them life by being present to them and allowing them to "take and eat." Just as babies are nourished, given life by their mother's breast milk, the Christian is brought to life by eating the Body and Blood of Christ. The prayer continues with a call upon the Holy Spirit (*epiclesis*) to descend upon these gifts of bread and wine and make them be the Body and Blood of Jesus Christ. The community calls upon the life of God, the Spirit of God, to come upon these gifts to truly become the Body and Blood of Christ. Thus we in the Christian churches, Eastern Catholic, Orthodox, Roman Catholic, believe so strongly that the bread and wine consecrated at the Divine Liturgy is permanently so. It is not just something we say, "Well, for the time being, let us pretend that this is the body and blood of Jesus. And after the service is over, well, it is back to being bread and wine." This act is very fundamental and intrinsic to the life of the Christian community. It is the lifeblood of the community.

Thus after this prayer to the Holy Spirit (the *epiclesis*), the prayer moves our attention to the entire community. It begins with Mary the Mother of God, the saints, those who have already passed on, and then those who live now. Basil's prayer remembers all the different people:

> Remember, O Lord, those who are in deserts and mountains, and in the dens and caves of the earth. Remember, Lord, those who live in virginity and piety, those who practice asceticism.... And Lord, for those that I cannot even remember, you remember, O Lord.

I call this a cosmic prayer, because it reminds us that the event of Jesus Christ was not only for me personally, but also for everyone (every human being that has ever walked this earth or ever will walk this earth). The event of Jesus Christ is a cosmic one meant for all humanity.

The Lord's Prayer and the Communion Rite

The next section of the liturgy contains the "Our Father" and the communion rite. The rite of sharing the Eucharist concludes with an interesting prayer by the priest:

> The mystery of your plan, O Christ our God, has been completed and perfected as far as it was in our power. We have done what we could do. We have commemorated your death. We have seen the figure of your resurrection.

We have been filled with your unending life. We have enjoyed your inexhaustible delights. Grant that we may be made worthy of all of this in the world to come through the grace of your eternal Father, and of your holy and gracious and life-giving Spirit, now and forever.

Then comes a phrase that I have always liked:

We thank you, O Lord our God, for having partaken of your holy, most-pure, immortal, and heavenly mysteries, which you have given us for the benefit, sanctification, and healing of our souls and bodies. O Master of all, grant that the communion of the holy body and blood of your Christ may be for faith that cannot be confounded ... for love that does not pretend ... for wisdom that is complete, ...and for healing of our souls and bodies.

The reception of the Eucharist is not simply a matter of eating and that is it. Consuming the Eucharist strengthens us physically and spiritually. It is our food for living. Meeting Christ in the Eucharist is thus about participating in, and consuming the Body of Christ. Meeting Christ in the common assembly is about being nourished and strengthened. Thus, the Eucharist truly is life, and life in abundance.

For Further Reading

Cabasilas, Nicholas. *A Commentary on the Divine Liturgy.* Trans. J.M. Hussey and P.A. McNulty. London: SPCK, 1978.

Gogol, Nikolai. *Meditations on the Divine Liturgy.* New York: American Review of Eastern Orthodoxy, 1964.

Huculak, Lawrence. *The Divine Liturgy of St. John Chrysostom in the Kievan Metropolitan Province during the Period of Union with Rome* (1596–1805). Analecta OSBM 47. Rome: P.P. Basiliani, 1990.

Ignatius IV, Patriarch of Antioch. *The Resurrection and Modern Man.* Crestwood, NY: St. Vladmir's, 1985.

Kucharek, Casimir. *The Byzantine-Slav Liturgy of St. John Chrysostom.* Combermere: Alleluia Press, 1971.

Schulz, Hans-Joachim. *The Byzantine Liturgy.* Trans. M. O'Connell. New York: Pueblo, 1986.

Taft, Robert F. *The Byzantine Rite: A Short History.* Collegeville: Liturgical Press, 1992.

Taft, Robert F. *The Great Entrance: A History of the Transfer of Gifts and Other Preanaphoral Rites of the Liturgy of St. John Chrysostom.* Orientalia Christiana Analecta 200. Rome: Pontifical Oriental Institute, 1975.

---

[1] Robert F. Taft, *The Great Entrance: A History of the Transfer of Gifts and Other Preanaphoral Rites of the Liturgy of St. John Chrysostom,* Orientalia Christiana Analecta 200 (Rome: Pontifical Oriental Institute, 1975).

[2] In the Slavic Churches, the Liturgy of St. Basil the Great is used ten times a year: on the five Sundays of Great Lent, the Feast of St. Basil, with Vespers on Holy Thursday and Holy Saturday and on the eves of the Nativity and Theophany.

[3] These excerpts are taken from the Liturgy of St. Basil.

Chapter 12

Seeing Christ

DANIEL GUENTHER

Father Guenther completed his Master's degree at St. Vladimir's Orthodox Theological Seminary. Currently he has pastoral charge of a number of parishes of the Orthodox Church of America in central Saskatchewan.

"Seeing Christ" – The Scriptural Witness

This topic, "seeing Christ," compels us to look beyond the Eastern Christian Churches, to face the "utter East," as C. S. Lewis called it in his timeless classic series, *The Chronicles of Narnia.* In other words, in order to see Christ, we must of necessity look to the source for all Christian Tradition, both East and West, that is to the Scriptures, which by faith we identify and recognize as the Word of God. At the very outset, at the risk of sounding trite, I must make the point that "Christ" is not a surname, as it is often treated, but a title for the ancient Jewish scriptural hope of deliverance by God through an "anointed" deliverer.

Following the Baptism of Jesus by John, in the account given in the Gospel of John, Andrew, after hearing John the Baptist speak, found his brother Simon Peter, and told him, "We have found the Messiah" (John 1:41). The following day, in the same account, Jesus calls Philip to follow him. Whereupon, Philip finds Nathaniel and convinces him to "come and see" with the following telling words, "We have found Him of whom Moses, in

267

the law, and also the prophets wrote – Jesus of Nazareth, the son of Joseph."

Clearly, then, the recognition of the person Jesus, the son of Joseph of the city of Nazareth, as the Messiah required the ability to make the connection between him and the Old Testament writings, here referred to as "Moses and the prophets." In other words, "seeing" involved, even for the ones who interacted with him directly according to the flesh, more than apprehension through the physical sense of sight.

Seeing Christ in the Word

That brings us then to the title, "Seeing Christ." Each word of this two-word phrase needs some detailed attention. Now one might say that indeed in the Orthodox faith it is possible to apprehend something of Christ through the faculty of physical sight, for we confess, according to the Seventh Ecumenical Council, the value of icons, or "windows to heaven," as we call them. However, even here, we find ourselves at the same disadvantage that the original disciples did. That is, we simply cannot do without words. For example, what happens in our home with our children when they ask us to identify the personages on the icons they see? Do we respond, "Why, Jimmy just look and you will see"? No, we take the time with many words to explain who the saint is that is venerated and that we consider them saints because by their lives they communicated the truth about Christ.

Now could that have been communicated without the icon? The answer obviously is yes, it could. This is not to belittle the importance of that which can be communicated through the aid of the physical senses. Rather it serves to underline the fact that all symbols become meaningless without prior elucidation through word.

To put this another way, the sign by which God communicated Himself ultimately and perfectly was the Logos, the very Word of God. Yes, indeed, the Word of God spoke most eloquently when he hung silently upon the cross, yet we use 50 words in our hymn to say just that. To use another example, at every feast of Christ and of Mary, we do not just bring out the icon, rather we sing many hymns explaining the meaning of the feast that we are being encouraged to celebrate. What stands between the liturgy of the Word and the liturgy of the faithful if not the homily, wherein the truth of the Gospel of Christ crucified for us is to be proclaimed? What would the services of the Church be, without the words about Christ the Word, but empty ritual?

Seeing Christ – The Scriptural Vision

Well, by now you are asking, why are you belabouring this matter of seeing as understanding by communication through words? It is just this. I began by saying that the two words "seeing Christ" both need some explanation. We have talked about the former "seeing" as meaning "understanding," to get to the meaning of the second, "Christ." Jesus Christ was known to his disciples by the name Jesus, or Yeshua, which we transliterate from the Hebrew as Joshua, a name that was relatively common in those days, as it is still today. The title Christ means "anointed," arising out of the Old Testament as an appellation of the Messiah, the promised deliverer whom God would send to free his people from their bondage.

In the Gospel of Mark, Jesus is called the "Son of God" three times: the first time by the author in verse one of chapter one where he introduces the book as "the beginning of Jesus Christ the Son of God"; then by the demon whom Jesus drives out of the demoniac; and finally by the centurion who, after witnessing the crucifixion, says, "surely this was the Son of God" (Matt. 27:54). However, never do the disciples of the Lord call him Son of God, not even after the Resurrection. In fact, the only confession of faith by a disciple in Mark is by Peter who confesses that Jesus is "the Christ" (Mark 8:29).

The scales never lift from the eyes of the disciples in Mark, for even after the announcement of the empty tomb to the women by the angels, they depart with fear and trembling. The Gospel concludes with their fearful amazement and the invitation that the disciples are to return to Galilee, the place of the Lord's ministry in Mark, where he will meet them. This is also the invitation of the Gospel's author for us to meet Christ in the

Gospel. The early Church recognized this invitation most clearly. Thus, the earliest sub-apostolic writers, Ignatius, Justin and Irenaeus, refer the recipients of their instruction to the Gospel of our Lord Jesus Christ as containing the whole truth of God for our salvation.

The Scriptures then were the instrument for seeing Christ. For the disciples these Scriptures were exclusively those that we call the Old Testament. It was through the story of Yahweh and his people that they came to see Christ. This is so even for us today. The Scriptures have always been in the faith of the Eastern Tradition, the primary means by which we "see Christ."

Without a knowledge of them, we are subject to seeing Christ according to our own preconceptions, fashioned by images of our own day, images foreign first of all to the disciples, foreign to those who first preached the gospel, foreign to the authors of the New Testament, and foreign to the patristic writers. Without a knowledge of the Scriptures, we may be seeing the wrong Christ, and this was already a problem for many at the time of Paul (1 Cor. 1:12).

In the middle of the Luke/Acts narrative, we see how the first disciples were able finally to see Jesus as the Christ. Following the crucifixion and resurrection of Jesus Christ, Jesus appears to two of the disciples as they walk along the way to Emmaus. After joining them, Jesus asks them, "Why are you so downcast?" They respond by asking him if he is the only one in Jerusalem who is unaware of the death of their master and teacher, and proceed to tell him that they had hoped that he was the one of whom the Scriptures had prophesied, that he should be the redeemer of Israel. To this Jesus responds, "'O foolish and slow of heart to believe in all that the prophets have spoken! Ought not the Christ to have suffered these things and to enter into His glory?' And beginning at Moses and all the prophets, He expounded to them in all the Scriptures the things concerning Himself" (Luke 24:25, 26). As the disciples reach their intended destination, they prevail upon Jesus to join them at table, and as he breaks bread, their eyes are opened, and they recognize him. Whereupon they ask each other, "Did not our hearts burn within us as he talked with us on the way and opened to us the Scriptures?" (Luke 24:32). Scripture and its proper interpretation is central to truly seeing Christ.

The astonishing thing is that in the continuation of the Luke/ Acts narrative in the opening chapter of Acts, as the disciples stand with Jesus on the Mount of Olives just before his Ascent, they ask him, "Lord, will you at this time restore the nation to Israel?" (Acts 1:6). The full import of who Jesus was as the Christ was still not clear to them. Clearly, the Holy Spirit's descent upon the disciples played a role in this account in the disciples' ability to finally see Christ, but a full examination of the role of the Holy Spirit in this account is beyond the scope of this lecture.

It is enough to point out here that seeing Christ is not aided by physical sight. Rather, seeing Jesus in the flesh does not enable the disciples to see Christ. The disciples go to Jerusalem, hiding in the upper room, as uncertain and confused as ever. There they await the fulfilment of Jesus' promise of the Comforter. In Acts, it is this descent of the Holy Spirit that brings to them understanding and insight regarding the meaning of Scripture as it witnesses to Jesus as the Christ.

Now Peter, the one who denied Jesus at his trial, is able to stand before the Jerusalem throng and proclaim Jesus as the fulfilment of the prophetic expectation:

> [David], foreseeing this, spoke concerning the resurrection of the Christ, that His soul was not left in Hades, nor did His flesh see corruption. This Jesus God has raised up, of which we are all witnesses. Therefore being exalted to the right hand of God, and having received from the Father the promise of the Holy Spirit, He poured out this, which you now see and hear.... Therefore, let all the house of Israel know assuredly that God has made this Jesus, whom you crucified, both Lord and Christ. (Acts 2:31-33, 36)

Thus, the disciples were able finally, through a corrected understanding of the passion and resurrection of Jesus Christ according to the Scriptures, to perceive and understand that which they had not been able to perceive with their physical faculty of sight. This means, among other things, that the access to seeing Christ is as open to us who have never seen Jesus in the flesh as it was for the disciples. One might even argue that seeing him in the flesh was a handicap for such seeing. However, most significantly, without the Scriptures, we cannot see Christ.

It is interesting in this connection that after Pentecost, Peter preaches Christ to the Jews as Jesus had, by declaring to them from Moses and the Prophets that this One whom they had crucified was the Christ. In fact, the New Testament is the revelation of Jesus as Christ by the portrayal of him as the fulfilment of the Old Testament messianic expectation, a fulfilment which occurs through the death and resurrection of Christ. In Galatians, for example, the central Pauline epistle, the case is made by Paul for the Gospel of Jesus Christ based entirely on the text of the Old Testament.

If we look for examples in the patristic teaching of the role of the Scripture in the revealing of Christ to its hearers, we notice that they too focused on the Old Testament. Without going into detail at this point, we may conclude those who have read the Fathers, in particular those of the first five or six centuries, will easily affirm this. For our purposes here it will be enough to point to the practice of John Chrysostom, the fifth century patriarch of Constantinople. Chrysostom continually reminds his hearers that in order to understand anything in church, they must read the Scriptures in advance of coming to the Liturgy, else they will not know the questions and will therefore not understand the answers he will give them in the homily. In fact, the writings of Chrysostom make up the largest single portion of the patristic writings, and they are almost entirely a verse by verse exegesis of the Scriptures – this in a time when the ability to read and write was in no way as common as it is today.

Seeing the Christ: The Liturgical Dimension

One of the first obvious features of the Gospel accounts that stands out for the student of the New Testament is that the passion narratives form the bulk of each Gospel. It is commonplace to say that these passion narratives are understood in New Testament scholarship to be the original narratives about Christ, which were expanded to include some of the details of his life and ministry before his passion.

With this in mind, it is interesting to note just how the passion narratives are developed. Each of the four Gospels is an intricate interweaving of Old Testament messianic prophecies and their fulfilment in the details of the passion as narrated by the authors. These details are not always the same, but each author uses some differing detail to narrate Jesus' passion as a fulfilment of the messianic role. However, as we noted above, it was a particular vision or "reading" of the Old Testament that enabled this particular "seeing" of Christ. In the Lukan account, even at the account of the Ascension of Christ, the disciples are still looking for a messianic fulfilment that included a restoration of the nationhood of Israel in a temporal sense. (This is a particular vision or reading that still prevails to this day, not only in Jewish cultic and nationalistic circles, but also, surprisingly, in some Christian theologies.) I point it out here because it highlights the problem surrounding this matter of "seeing Christ." If it was difficult for the disciples to focus correctly on Christ as Saviour and Lamb of God, it is no wonder that it is difficult also for us.

Here the Eastern Christian liturgical expression of the Gospel of Jesus Christ can be particularly helpful in correctly "seeing Christ." I say this primarily because the eucharistic liturgy in particular is focused on the Scripture, focused according to the Gospel of Jesus Christ on the Saviour and "Lamb of God who takes away the sins of the world" (John 1:9).

Before making a few specific points to demonstrate what I mean, I would like to make a few general observations about the eucharistic liturgy in the Eastern Christian Tradition. The first is that the eucharistic liturgy proper, or the "liturgy of the faithful," is preceded by what is called the "liturgy of the Word." In Justin Martyr's description of the liturgy, the earliest systematic account of the Christian eucharistic practice (outside of possibly the *Didache* account), we are told that when the Christians gathered on Sunday before dawn, they first sang hymns to Christ as God. Then they read the Scriptures for as long as time permitted. Subsequently, one who was capable expounded on the Scriptures for the edification of the assembled, before the eucharistic meal itself. This basic structure remains the same today.

This preparation for the eucharistic meal by the liturgy of the Word defines the meaning of the meal itself, and without it, the meal could not take place, for it would have no meaning in and of itself, at least not a meaning that would enable seeing and communing with Christ. This follows the pattern that we have already seen in the Lukan account of the two disciples on the way to Emmaus. That is, before recognizing him in the breaking of the bread, they had to have the Scriptures expounded for them by the Lord, i.e., by the Gospel of the Lord.

The second general observation is a comment on the hierarchical eucharistic liturgy. After the singing of the antiphons, the entrance is made with the Gospel. In the Eastern rite, this is a pronounced affair, with the Gospel book being carried around the nave from the altar to the ambo. As the Gospel is carried into the altar, all are led by the bishop and clergy in the singing of the hymn "O come, let us worship and fall down before Christ, save us O Son of God who sing to Thee, Alleluia!" Then following the *tropar* and *kondak* (hymns of the day), the deacon censes the altar. In fact, it is not the altar that he is censing, but the Gospel, representative of the Lord. Then follows a very important rubric. The deacon carries the Gospel from the altar out the royal doors to the centre of the nave, and turns to face the bishop who stands on the ambo facing the deacon. The deacon then reads the Gospel to the bishop, with the bishop giving full attention.

In other words, in the homily to follow, the presider, in this case the bishop, is told what he must proclaim: the Gospel. The homily is as much a liturgical act as all the other rubrics and texts of the liturgy. The bishop at the liturgy does not have licence to say whatever he wishes. He is bound, if he wishes to be faithful to the text and the rite, as we have received it down to our own day, to proclaim the Good News, the *evangelion* of Jesus as the Christ, in order that the hearers will also be enabled to "see Christ." This cannot happen without a vision that arises out of the Old Testament messianic hope, as seen through the lens of the passion of Jesus Christ.

With the above general observations in mind I would like to make a few brief points concerning the centrality of the passion of Jesus Christ in our being able to "see Christ." As a general note, I would recommend a careful reading of the services for Holy Week and Pascha in the texts of the Eastern Christian Church. These services are compiled in their entirety in one volume, and are an excellent source for an understanding of the eucharistic liturgy celebrated every Sunday, for each eucharistic liturgy is in microcosm a celebration of Pascha, the passion of the Lord Jesus Christ.

This vision of the central importance of the passion, and especially the eucharistic liturgy, is profoundly scriptural. In the Emmaus story, the disciples finally recognize Christ "in the breaking of the bread" (Luke 24:35). Even more powerfully, the elaborately constructed Gospel of John is built around the importance of the eucharistic banquet. The eucharistic vision lies at the chiastic centre of the book. The Gospel's centre, found at 6:16-21, follows the multiplication of loaves story and leads into the Bread of Life discourse. The centre is the miraculous walking on water story. It parallels the Red Sea episode in the Exodus, and it is John's way of demonstrating that eating a meal with Jesus (6:1-5) and consuming, or uniting with Christ (6:26-40), is the continuation and fulfilment of the salvation wrought in the Exodus. Just as Yahweh delivered the Hebrews from the bondage of Egypt, so now Jesus Christ delivers the baptized from the enemy. This deliverance is predicated on recognizing that He is the "bread of life" (6:35).

Christ in Holy Week

The importance of repentance as preparation for meeting and seeing Christ is also emphasized in the services of Holy Week. Vespers from Holy Thursday morning challenge us to be adequately prepared for this liturgical meeting. They challenge us by placing before us the example of Judas:

> The transgressor, Judas, O lord, who at supper dipped his hand into the dish with you, unlawfully stretched out his hand to receive silver. And he who calculated the price of the myrrh did not shudder to sell you who are beyond all price. He who submitted his feet to your washing treacherously kissed you, the Master, in order to deliver you to the enemy. When he left the apostles and cast down the thirty pieces of silver, he saw not your resurrection on the third day. By this, have mercy on us.

I emphasize the role of repentance in these services because of the necessity of repentance as a prerequisite for our own participation in Christ's death through our Baptism. In Romans

6, the Apostle Paul spends a great deal of time reorienting the minds of his readers, asking them if they do not "know," orienting their perspectives to the death and resurrection of Christ. In other words, as we seek to see Christ, we are called to see ourselves as being identified with him in his passion. According to Paul, Baptism means nothing if it does not involve an active, ongoing orientation of our perspective to a new identity, an identity shaped by Christ's passion and resurrection.

This dimension of repentance and preparation flows out of the Old Testament Scriptures. In a reading on Holy Thursday from Exodus 19:10f. God instructs Moses to tell his people to prepare themselves: "Go to the people and have them sanctify themselves today and tomorrow. Make them wash their garments and be ready for the third day; for on the third day the Lord will come down on Mount Sinai before the eyes of all the people." Holy Thursday, as preparation for the events of the Passion and so too the liturgy of Pascha, prepares us for the profound events that have taken place on our behalf, and also reminds us that each of us needs to prepare to meet the Lord.

The Matins service of the Twelve Gospels also directs our attention to our preparation for hearing the final teaching of Christ (i.e. "seeing" Christ). During the readings, we hear the account of the washing of the disciples' feet by Jesus, and then the mention of the betrayal by Judas. Again the message of the texts of the service calls us to prepare by choosing – choosing to obey the command of Christ to love one another, or to betray him. This passage leads then to the central promise of Jesus that "He who has my commandments [love one another as I have loved you] and keeps them, it is he who loves Me. And he who loves Me will be loved by My Father, and I will love him and manifest Myself to him" (John 14:21). Seeing Christ then requires that as our eyes are opened by the Scriptures to hear his voice and truly "see" him, we must then choose to obey him as he reveals himself, or to deny him. To see him is not enough. Rather, to see him is to truly follow him by obeying his commandments.

These services of Holy Week lead us forward to the ultimate event of Pascha, the death and resurrection of Jesus Christ, which is the perfect expression of divine and human love. As Paul says in Galatians 2:20, "I am crucified with Christ, and it is no longer I who live, but Christ who lives in me. And the life which I now live in the flesh, I live by faith in the Son of God who loved me and gave himself for me." This sums up succinctly the whole matter of the baptized community, who in seeing Christ, choose to follow him as Lord and master, as the one who "loved them and gave himself for them." They are willing bond servants, or servants who have chosen of their own will be slaves to Christ as chosen Lord.

The services of Holy Week and Pascha, the Johannine focus on the eucharistic banquet, the Lukan Emmaus story, all lead us to the cross and the empty tomb. As Paul sums it up,

> I handed on to you first of all what I myself received, that Christ died for our sins in accordance with Scriptures; that he was buried and, in accordance with the Scriptures, rose on the third day. (1 Cor. 15:3-4)

What stands then at the centre of all Christian life if not the death and resurrection of Jesus Christ? Is not all liturgy, after Baptism, an invitation to make the reality of his death and resurrection a living reality for our life? We see Christ and meet Christ through participation in his life, as he is revealed to us through the Scriptures. Inasmuch as the Liturgy of Baptism, Eucharist and Pascha direct our attention to the revelation of Christ that proceeds from the Scriptural witness, they serve to illumine our understanding and knowledge by faith that Jesus is indeed the Christ, "the Lamb of God who takes away the sins of the world" (John 1:9). In this way liturgical seeing focuses our reading of Scripture so that we can see, understand and follow Jesus the Christ.

For Further Reading

Barrois, Georges Augustin. *The Face of Christ in the Old Testament.* Crestwood, NY: St. Vladimir's, 1974.

Barrois, Georges Augustin. *Scripture Readings in Orthodox Worship.* Crestwood, NY: St. Vladimir's, 1977.

Breck, J. *The Power of the Word: In the Worshiping Church.* Crestwood, NY: St. Vladimir's, 1986.

Doherty, Catherine de Hueck. *The People of the Towel and the Water.* Denville, NJ: Dimension Books, 1978.

Matthew the Poor. *The Communion of Love.* Crestwood, NY: St. Vladimir's, 1984.

VIII. Eastern Christianity in a Post-Modern World (2000)

Chapter 13

Iconography

MARIANNA SAVARYN

Ms. Savaryn is an iconographer living in Edmonton, Alberta. Her presentations were entitled "Becoming an Iconographer: The Transition from Artist to Iconographer" and "Being an Iconographer: Faith, Art, Theology." Rather than including an article, we feature her icons in the centre of this volume.

Chapter 14

Living in Skin:
Sex, Spirituality and the Christian Male

ANTHONY UGOLNIK

Father Ugolnik is Professor of English, Elijah Kresge Chair at Franklin and Marshall College. Among his many professional honours are a Woodrow Wilson Fellowship and a Fellowship at the Institute for Ecumenical Research.

Whose Temple?

"The body is the Temple of the Holy Spirit" (1 Cor. 6:19). However abstractly modern believers may tend to conceive of the term "body," our bodies remind us of their resistance to abstraction. At puberty, each body embraces even more insistently the stuff of which gender is made. The Holy Spirit, Christians maintain, is fully accessible to both women and men. The body, however, is clearly the least androgynous of our attributes. Thus men and women dwell within "temples" of a distinctly different architecture. The male body, with its own peculiar configuration of muscle, gristle, flesh and bone (and endowed with a phallus invisible in most religious discourse) is the specific temple that we men indeed inhabit.

The male mind, it is said, has dominated the organizational Church. Nonetheless, the male body has been exiled from the temple. In the rich "temple" imagery of the Christian canon, the Christian mind turns for its prime frame of reference to the female body.[1] In the iconographic imagery of the Christian East, the Theotokos or "God-bearing" Mother of God encircles or encloses the child-Christ. In both secular and Orthodox Christian discourse, women identify this "God bearing" image with her "earth goddess" prototype.[2] Her body is the frame, the context, within which we receive the Incarnate Word; and from childhood Eastern Orthodox Christians connect the manifestation of God among us with the enclosing, nurturing "enwombment" of the female body.

Some feminist scholars concentrate on Western images of the "Virgin Mary" popularized by celibate men. They have been critical, even bitter, over the role of Mary in Christian lore. Mary Daly, at the beginning of her estrangement from Christianity, notes,

> Is it mere coincidence that the countries most noted for their "devotion to Mary" are those in which the clergy have the greatest power and in which the legal and social situation of women is demonstrably the most retarded?[3]

In her later work, she recreates in inverse form the very metaphysics of gender she had early critiqued. She cites patristic sources, which identify Eve and woman as the source of evil and discord in the universe. Later, she herself identifies males as by their nature the agents of evil and sowers of disharmony. She indicts by definition, then, any male portrayal of the female body, whether it be sexual or maternal or virginal. As "symbol," argues Daly and her school, woman is by nature "object," and Mary is the prime woman-symbol. Rosemary Reuther is particularly critical of what she sees as a cultic male focus upon Mary's virginity.[4]

However problematic the theological envisioning of the female incarnation, we men have no such frame of reference available to us in our own bodies. We may turn, with an idealizing enthusiasm, to imagery of motherhood and the nurturing female body for our models of virtue. We have even, in our ancient Syriac Tradition, relied quite regularly upon female references to describe the action of the Spirit.[5] On the other hand, we may also turn to the imagery of the sexually inviting female body for our models of delight, contempt and sin. Indeed, the positive and negative attributes may be intimately connected. Through a kind of "linguistic blackmail," we men tend to undo in our profanity the very dignity we provide in other conventions. (Terms so sexually connotative as "harlot," "tart" and "mistress" were once, for example, terms either neutral or complimentary in meaning.)[6]

Currently, men face difficulties whenever they express their religious attitudes toward women, for feminists have critiqued us for both exercises: we are damned for exalting women's bodies as the purest form of the "temple of the Spirit," and we are likewise damned for denigrating women's bodies as the occasions of sin. However, the real revelation in these studies is our studied neglect of our own bodies. Possibilities for our own male bodies as "temples," as dwelling places for the Spirit, have by and large escaped us. This is not for any lack of incarnate imagery, of course. Males "engender." Males "seminate." Males "penetrate," "fertilize" and "enact" in all those verbal permutations which radical feminists see as a burden upon the language. All of these acts, and much of the male organism which makes them possible, is purged from our imagery which builds up the Temple of God. In religious terms, we men have lost the connection between our bodies and religious meaning. This is a primary reason why lay Christian men have exiled so much of their language from their piety.

Language has a distinct relationship to the body: the "temple" within which we men dwell relates directly to the articulated worship we offer the God in whom we believe. There is an abundance of modern research which documents the ways in which men speak and articulate that are distinct from those of women.[7] It is often clear to us as men, in fact, when we do speak from within our gender among ourselves, "with the guys," we unconsciously and deliberately engage in certain habits of discourse that can be clearly marked. In brief, we tend to pitch our dialect "down-wards," into the realm of a working class speech we ourselves perceive as conveying a greater physical power, and we also assign to those speech patterns a "covert prestige" which we award among ourselves, even as it is discouraged among us by others (often mothers and female teachers) who reinforce linguistic norms. Thus what men recognize as "proper" is, in the codes we employ, often also perceived as less than masculine. This has, as we shall see, analogues in the realm of piety and faith.

Spiritual Cross-Dressing

Despite the profound attention in recent days to gender and Christology, as a man, Christ has now become almost invisible to men. Men, it is true, in effect preside over the traditional churches. They have taken up a sacerdotal and sacramental role. Until recently, they even controlled discourse in the Church. Nevertheless, despite this – if not because of it – males have at the same time become radically estranged from their own voice in Christian piety.

For well over twenty years, women have pointed out an estrangement of women from the "sociolinguistics" of theological discourse. Mary Daly has consistently seen a parallel between male power and the male body. As early as her still-Christian work in 1968, she identified a "phallocentric" dimension to male theological discourse essentially in the language of metaphor.[8] In her later work, she herself mythologizes the penis into the emblem of a male "phallocracy," and "phallocratic technology." Daly sees patriarchy as a "Religion of Rapism," and the technology of modern war as a paradigm of rape. Male language in her system begets male myth, and that myth suffuses the world with death and despoliation. In *Gyn/Ecology,* Daly interprets Dr. Frankenstein, the character in Mary Shelley's novel, as an emblem of the hysteric man-technocrat enraged by his "inherent male sterility":

> Today the Frankenstein phenomenon is omnipresent not only in religious myth, but in its offspring, phallocratic technology. The insane desire for power, the madness of boundary violation, is the mark of necrophiliacs who sense the lack of soul/spirit/life-loving principle with themselves and therefore try to invade and kill off all spirit, substituting conglomerates of corpses.[9]

Male language, in the mythos of much feminist literature, begets male violence. The extent of its condemnation also begets a postmodern heresy, a kind of "gender Donatism" whereby any concept issuing from a male source bears a taint. The category of "sin" becomes a function of gender rather than the human condition. The genesis of the "sin of maleness" is inherent, begotten in men by the nature of the male body. Males are "enphallicized," endowed with a penis, and hence in their very incarnation males are "those who violate boundaries" in body, word and act. A bitter irony becomes apparent in this demonization of the penis. The penis emerges with such symbolic insistence, after all, in the concealed, only implicit metaphor of descriptive language. In religious portrayals of the male body, however, energies are focused upon suppressing rather than enhancing the penis. As we shall soon observe, much of the energy of spirituality has been spent in casting the souls of men as women. Thus, "phallocentrism" is more a problem in radical feminist myth than in male Christian spirituality, where an effort is needed to restore and redeem male sexual discourse rather than condemn or suppress it.

Daly and Origen, the self-castrating Christian Father, share a common obsession. The penis, in itself, is no more wicked than the womb. If the male imagination has made it into a weapon, so also has the male imagination (long before Mary Daly) made it into an emblem of evil. That "phallic resonances" can be discerned in the subliminal symbol and metaphor of male discourse is no more to be condemned than the presence of the "vaginal dimension" in female discourse, which feminists foster and encourage.[10]

The legitimate complaint consists in the fact that male theologians have imposed male language upon females who wish to engage in theological discourse of their own. Theology is, in effect, an exercise which males have dominated. Women should engage it in their own terms. However, many students of gender have utterly missed a no less startling point. While male *language* dominates theology, the male *voice* has been suppressed in Christian piety. When we discuss *language*, we consider words objectively; when we discuss *voice*, we consider the personality or "persona" those words convey. (In the "epic voice" of the ancient songs, men sought *lof*, the Anglo-Saxon ancestor of our modern word "love." *Lof*, however, meant the praise and honour men earned from their deeds: it is devoid of the dialogic mutuality implicit in the word "love".) As men, theologians may dogmatize "logocentrally." However, as men, they find it difficult to communicate with their Lord. As the Psalms make so clear, the voice of our prayer is the vital link to our God. Our male "voice" is caught in our throats before the throne of God. As men, deep within the private chambers of our own bodies, we find it hard to pray.

We can look first to the image as an index of the word. The bodies of women, as has often been pointed out, have been exploited in art and metaphor.[11] Yet, the bodies of men have been distorted as well. The images of Jesus Christ evident in a Western context have shown, in past centuries, an ever more insistent trend not toward maleness, but rather toward feminization. Saintly figures in this tradition of "Christian kitsch" display an exaggeration of romantic detail: faces are placid and rouged; hair is curled; lips are a brilliant red. In a culture which values vigour and health in the human form, the skin of the saints is white and anaemic, their limbs painfully thin. Mary as womb-encompassing Mother has given way to Mary as child-virgin, ethereal and insubstantial as moonlight. The bodies of the female saints, robed as they are in folds of cool and placid colours, are the inverse mirrors of male eroticism. They are relatively fleshless, without substance beneath their robes. Jesus Christ and the male saints, not saved from this fate by their combed and silky beards, take on the forms and shapes of this "erotically cleansed" female paradigm. Pious men whose imaginations are shaped by this art must, in effect, undertake a spiritual "cross-dressing," passing into the realm of the holy by virtue of a shape and demeanour which they themselves have usually assigned to pious women.

Satiric films, like Monty Python's *Life of Brian* (1979), lampoon not only a treacly pietism, they also presume a subtext which has become a convention among us: "piety" presumes a kind of image and behaviour which men find laughable in men. This vision of piety is, of course, a distorted one; yet, in large measure, the "bearded lady" image of Jesus Christ is responsible for the distortion. Men who struggle to express their piety, their love of God, do so burdened by conventions that violate their masculinity. This image has applied "covert prestige," that same dynamic evident in male language, to the realm of religious burlesque. Piety, clothed in feminine dress, was urged upon young men who were expected to reject it. Thus, piety itself became remote from many men who sought, as men, to pray. Catholics and Orthodox in America still often see in our houses of worship a remote, uninvolved male liturgics, as the men folk "hover" at the back of the Church in a curious counterpoint to the robed, presiding clergymen at the altar. In the midst churns a sea of women, often aching for greater empowerment in the ministry of the Church.

The tension between piety and gender has led to some overwhelming ambiguities and mixed signals about sex. Piety's greatest enemy is still puberty, not only because of a bad theology of sin, but also because sexuality distances the Christian male and female from the "hyper-feminine" asexuality implicit in Christian imagery. The proof of the connection, and of the challenges in sexuality which it implies, now lies in the visual imagery surrounding explicit sexuality, both heterosexual and homosexual.

A high camp tradition in gay San Francisco marches men in drag, dressed as nuns, in a yearly Gay Pride parade. The pop icon Madonna (presumably only before she became an icon of motherhood) highlights her cleavage with a cascade of rosaries. As a feature of his early work, the homoerotic photographer Mapplethorpe creates shadow boxes out of traditional Catholic, popular sacred art. In pornographic imagery, religious articles are draped over and around male and female genitalia. The artist Andres Serrano, in a work which estranged artist from patron, immerses a crucifix in a jar of urine and calls it "Piss Christ." Images of a charged, aggressive sexuality, implied and explicit, bounce crazily off the symbols of a passive, asexual piety. The most liberal of Christians can balk in this maze of distorted images.

We have, I believe, asked the wrong questions in the aftermath of our outrage. We may ask why the artist or performer would deliberately violate our sensibilities in the way he or she has. However, the deeper question is, what satisfaction does the artist or performer meet in doing so? What new *convention* has our culture spawned? Women have themselves spoken of the way in which they have been symbolically stripped, used by men who exploited them: feminist piety in many ways now seeks to "reclaim" the female body in order to return it to its custodian. Men, however, undergo a reverse process. Their own bodies have, in religious imagery, been swathed and muffled in robes of silk; their faces have been hidden behind a cosmetic mask. They are deprived in their piety of those sexual attributes, which they bear in their own flesh, and in their eroticism men struggle to break free of that which has bound them. Male misogyny is aggravated by the act of "spiritual cross-dressing," by a piety redolent of a sweet, hyper-feminine romanticism.

To reclaim our piety, then, men must reclaim their sexuality. In our male "genderlect" or use of language, there is much to repent. Women have shown us the way in which we have objectified them, parcelled their bodies, and rendered their anatomy as "obscene." Our competitiveness can degenerate into a worship of power. Yet, there is also within us a desire for integration, a willingness to persevere and respond to challenge. Our spirituality has not helped us to realize our own dignity and self-worth as males.

Prayer as Impersonation

As a result of the problems with gender afflicting his "speaking voice," the male lover of God undergoes an experience just as estranging as that of a woman who endures a "phallocentric" theology. Looking in the mirror of piety offered by the art and diction of his Church, he sees a face which he himself has in large part created: it is a "womanly" countenance, a face to which he does not aspire in public. If, in his private moments of loving longing, a male Christian takes up the prayers to his God offered him by the devotional genre in his Christian literature and tradition, he raises a voice he may barely recognize. In effect, he prays in a falsetto. The tradition of his piety asks him, in sociolinguistic terms, to pray in a female voice, which, according to all the data, he would strive to avoid in all his public discourse. There is, then, a schizophrenia in male Christian piety; the Church has estranged males from their own voice in prayer.

Daly once complained, with oft-echoed irony, "Whereas the idea of a 'theology of woman' is frequently proposed, few would seriously suggest that there should be a 'theology of man.'"[12] Spiritual and ascetic writers, however, have in fact given men specific criteria for sanctity, which estrange them from their own paradigms of maleness, their sexuality, and their own habits of language. Men have done themselves violence in depriving their own bodies of a sacral dimension.

In the phenomenon of "sacrament," symbol weds reality. The Christian East has long observed a disjunction in language and understanding between itself and the West (like that between men and women).[13] Alexander Schmemann but articulated an old Orthodox critique when he noted, "It is indeed one of the defects of sacramental theology that instead of following the eucharistic journey with its progressive revelation of meaning, theologians applied to the Eucharist a set of abstract questions in order to squeeze it into their own intellectual framework."[14] Representation here implodes: bread *means* body so intensely, and wine means blood with such power, that body and blood come to be among us. Women in the particular reality of their gender have been made to "mean" both sin and virtue. Male patristic writers and theologians have, in now frequently quoted interludes, invested the bodies of women with a particular, peculiar sinfulness. Yet the Church has also given the bodies of women a rich sacramental dimension, a dimension denied to men. The male anatomy in fact has experienced a progressive estrangement from the idea of sacrament.

Married, sexually active males fuse sex and sacrament with the women to whom they are "crowned" in marriage – they make of sex itself a sacramental act. *Sacramentality demands "embodiment."* Instead, the language of our piety and devotion "disembodies" us or estranges us from our male bodies and male sexuality in an attempt to render us more holy. The result is the radical estrangement many men feel from the piety which the Church seems to offer us.

Feminist literature has done us all a service in calling attention to gender as a dimension of theology. That literature tends, however, to interpret this projected male voice from the perspective of middle-class women. Power is the focus of this middle-class feminist critique. Thus, the elements of power, threat and intimidation in the complex dance of male discourse and interaction are in themselves an indictment of the gender as a whole.

Yet some feminists have observed that women of the working class perceive this power-dynamic quite differently.[15] In the eyes of these women, power is relative to those who wield it. Since working-class men exercise little public authority, the home is the place where that authority is most consistently reinforced, by women as well as men.[16] Working-class women, in fact, have more negotiated power relative to men than middle-class women do, since their work and earning power are more needed within the home.[17] Thus, this assertive male voice has, in some class contexts, a meaning different from that which many critics assign it.

Social class plays an important role in the critique of male identity. The male gender projects a voice, that of the strong, embodied male. Feminists of the middle class, who have identified the many injustices wrought upon women by men, may perceive this voice as the source of oppression and abuse. However, men employ this voice itself, we have seen, most consistently among other men. We men, like working-class women, can look for the positive attributes within this voice, which we project. If men test themselves against each other, they also defend principles, protect the weak, bond with other men, and pledge themselves to commitments. The authority of the traditional, ethically bound, working-class male is, after all, negotiated: the father who projects an authoritative voice is present to his family, supportive of his means, and (in working-class environments, at least) given a sphere to his authority which need not violate the integrity of the female in the household. Social class also plays an important role in the language of devotion. When we speak of prayer, we speak of a voice stripped insomuch as possible of its social dimensions; yet insofar as God has commerce with us, prayer is also a "social" act. The speaker who encounters God in prayer will wish to use the most "authentic" voice, that voice closest to its centre of his being. Gender is a vital part of the human psychology, and it is a factor in our communication as well as a constituent in our being.

When we look to the literature of private prayer, the genre of devotion, we discover that the voice of prayer is expressed in a manner and tone alien from that which we use with women or each other. We men often pray, in fact, in a way in which we never speak. The spiritual psyche of the Christian male has been torn asunder.

"The Thews and Sinews of the Brain"

The process has been a long and gradual one. In art, we can see its progression from the Jesus resplendent in the majestic, awe-evoking Byzantine iconography to the pale and treacly Jesus of the "holy card." Christian imagery then could treat the naked Jesus as subject. After a naked Jesus emerged briefly once more in the Renaissance, he was decisively reclothed and then progressively feminized. Men subsequently, however, made efforts to rescue his maleness. Victorian males in art and devotional literature attempted to convey Christian thought in an idiom comprehensible to common working people.[18] *Christian Manliness,* published by the Christian Tract Society in 1867, served as a catalyst for the trend. The movement was parodied by its successors, as it often is today, under the description "Muscular Christianity." Significantly, in Charles Kingsley and others of its practitioners, it became a staple element in the anti-Catholicism of the day. Catholic piety, in fact, became in Kingsley's eyes the essence of "unmanliness." As one of the characters in his fiction remarked, upon meeting a frail and flesh-denying Catholic priest, "O, for the thews and sinews of an English brain!"

Though strains of Christian manliness survive in conservative American Protestantism and the shape, at least, of the English public school system, it was a reactive movement, which expired by the beginning of this century. "Christian Manliness," long before the era of feminism, became a thing redolent of irony. The Victorian poet Algernon Charles Swinburne viewed both Christianity and athletic activity with condescension at best. In a letter to his fellow aesthete, Dante Gabriel Rossetti, he described himself after a morning of vigorous riding and swimming as "in a rampant state of muscular Christianity." The movement expired in a ridicule born largely of later Victorian aesthetes who, ironically, lampooned the movement with a homoeroticism which proved its undoing.[19] The voice of male piety, like its portrait in religious art, resumed its estrangement from its own maleness.

The Transsexual Soul

Piety, the process of expressing love and devotion to God, is informed by its own literary genre. Whereas liturgical texts largely follow the biblical precedent of focusing primarily upon the male gender in alluding to God, liturgy rarely assigns a gender to the soul. Liturgy, however, is public prayer in which the individual believer participates with the group. The persona of liturgical prayer is plural; in liturgy, the Christian male is a part of a communal "we." The literature of devotion, however, expresses the voice of a single believer. In addition, the history of devotional texts shows a progressive expunging of the male gender in the voice of Christian prayer.

The Christian East, in its earliest texts on prayer, reflected the Neoplatonic convention of portraying the soul as female. Earlier Eastern devotional texts, such as the "Songs of Love" composed by Symeon the New Theologian (c.949–1022),were rapt in their focus upon the Godhead.[20] Yet, in the subjective language of love, these earlier texts distanced themselves from an imagery which implied gender. In speaking of the soul's attraction to God, Symeon is careful to distinguish between human and divine love, sexuality and love of God, which "turns from the erotic passions of carnal pleasure." Indeed, when figuratively describing the love between human and divine, Symeon most often relies upon inanimate objects like stone and flint, iron and fire, pearl and sand to illustrate his meaning. Thus the language of Symeon the New Theologian differs markedly from the transfigured eroticism of the Spanish Carmelite John of the Cross (1542–91). John in his poetic voice embraces the sexually charged language of human love to express the soul's relationship with God: "How gently and how lovingly Thou awakenest in my bosom, / Where Thou dwellest secretly and alone."[21] This verse alternates with a more distant and dispassionate prose commentary. Yet the prose but explicates the verse. Sexually, the persona of the mystic poem "encloses" and never "projects"; symbolically, the soul of the male lover of God has become transsexual. The soul has become, in effect, a woman.

A Boisterousness of Body

We live out our masculinity through a process of integration through assertion. In our interrelationships with other men, in particular, there is a level of competitiveness that is a prelude to our finding a place relative to each other. Language addressed to God, however, is not the same as speaking among ourselves. In interrelationship with women, we men of the ancient Christian traditions sometimes engage in a curious twist of logic. On the one hand, we recognize that we cannot relate to God as we would to another male because, as men, we struggle against each other for precedence. On the other hand, we cling to the traditional gender language as applied to God in order to justify a precedence in some form over women. In dealing with language and male identity, we can immediately recognize how our spirituality has suffered a disjunction from our gender.

Some scholars have drawn attention to the way in which women in particular escaped the strictures of their gender by embracing celibacy in the religious life. It is clear from spiritual narratives by males that men, too, found themselves freed of a kind of tyranny of gender through their separation from "the world," that is, the political and social dominance which they would otherwise be called upon to assume. Caroline Bynum points out that men, more often than women, developed the theme of "Jesus as Mother" in the Middle Ages.[22] Quite contrary to the primacy and honour that men consciously sought, and which the canons of the medieval Church assured them, those men dedicated to a spiritual life were to regard themselves as inferior, even vile, in comparison to women.

Walter Hilton, in his *Ladder of Perfection*, undoes the male quest for dominance and self-esteem. Men who lead the active life, he says, seek authority and power over others. Men who lead the contemplative life lie, like John the Evangelist at the Last Supper, recumbent on the breast of God.[23] The "anchorite literature" of the medieval period, in fact, intensified the abandonment of sexuality for those who sought to love God in solitary life and more deeply. *The Cloud of Unknowing* argues that a "boisterousness of body" may lead young men and young women to interpret spiritual yearnings in a bodily way. "Their physical hearts are then greatly excited in their breasts."[24] Men in active monastic or lay communities, in the genre of anti-feminist literature now so frequently cited, identified women as the source of enslavement to the body and the source of sexual temptation. The mystic writers, on the other hand, distanced men from the hierarchies, which their anti-feminist cohorts supported. Anchorites were more than celibate, for a celibate male is "male" nonetheless. They sought a divorce from sexuality and gender itself.

Richard Rolle (c.1300–49) in his *Fire of Love,* for example, does assert that women who love men "go mad because they do not know how to keep measure in their loving."[25] Yet women's excesses are those of reason and the affections. Male temptations in his view are clearly centred on the body: "temptations of the flesh" and an inflammation of "depraved delights" (29.200). Men must always beware, lest "evil motions should surge up" (39.246). Thus, sexuality in his work suffers an intrinsic vileness, expressed in thinly veiled phallic metaphors. The male erection drives away the presence of the Spirit; tumescence is a symbol of depravity.

Philothea and the Elephant

Popular spiritual works of the Renaissance and early modern era addressed an audience living "in the world," not apart from it. Having made the male body a desert of mortification, the soul continues its shift in gender. Females of the aristocracy or upper middle class, free of at least part of domestic labour and now able to read books of prayer in the vernacular, were the overt audience whom devotional authors addressed. In both English and continental editions, books of private prayer and devotion appeared primarily for female readers.

Like the earlier Walter Hilton, Francis de Sales (1567–1622) addresses his *Introduction to a Devout Life* to a female.[26] Unlike Walter Hilton's in-the-flesh "ghostly sister," however, the woman whom Francis addresses is a laywoman, emblematic of the soul. She stands for us all: she is "the soul from her first desire till she be brought to a full resolution to embrace a devout life." In the symbolic significance of her name ("lover of God"), and in the breadth of his advice, the work is clearly intended to apply to souls of both genders. For a male to become "Philothea," however, he must go beyond even the "Origen complex." He must become female "in imagination."

This work, unlike the previous examples in the genre, allows for a sex life in marriage. In fact, de Sales freely encourages affection and bodily embrace between lovers. Yet he compares men to bitter fruits like the quince, which need sweetness to make them palatable: "Thus wives ought to wish that their husbands should be preserved with the sugar of devotion. A man without devotion is a creature severe, harsh, and rough" (38.219). Sexual pleasures even in marriage, "by reason of their brutal vehemence," bring danger to the soul.

When his reader is clothed in female gender, de Sales can speak with some mild indulgence of sexual activity. When he speaks of males, however, sex becomes a kind of pollution. Men are counselled to occupy the mind with sex only when they actually have intercourse. Further, intercourse, it is to be hoped, will occur relatively infrequently. As a model for sexually active males, de Sales relies upon the elephant (at least as his era's bestiaries understood the creature):

> Although a huge beast, the elephant is yet the most decent and sensible of all who live upon the earth. I will give you an instance of his chastity. Although he never changes his mate and has a tender love for her whom he has chosen, he couples with her only at the end of every three years, and then only for the space of five days and so privately that he is never seen in the act. When he makes his appearance again on the sixth day, the first thing he does is to go directly to a river. There he washes his body entirely, for he is unwilling to return to the herd until quite purified. (39.222–23)

It is no coincidence that the poor elephant, who cannot hide his phallic character even in a book of devotion, is the creature who represents sexually (in)active men. Philothea, in her loving and modest female body, is the emblem of the soul. The elephant in his size and strength and yes, in his "trunk," is the emblem of the male body. In that common pattern of body-soul dualism which marks both Christian piety and radical feminism, men must do penance for their physiology. Hermeneutically there is a "phallic problem," and every man bears it between his legs. The story of Philothea and the elephant is the tale of Beauty and the Beast.

The soul's language itself conveys a sense of its gender; mystic poetry in English assists the transmutation. John Donne (1572–1631) writes lyrics dealing with both human and divine love. Lyrics of each kind employ a vivid, even discomfiting sexual imagery. Yet, there is a radical difference between Donne's "voices" in each kind of poem. In the poems in which he expresses his love for a woman, Donne confidently assumes the voice of a male lover. He spins out his eroticism through a persona who possesses a power, a mastery, even a *dominion* in his possession of the beloved. In the famous "Sun Rising," the morning sun has shone in the bedroom window and awakened a couple in bed. The male lover mocks the sun's mastery in his circuit of the globe, and he challenges the sun like a rival to survey his world and compare it to the lover's own "domain":

> She's all states, and all princes I,
> Nothing else is.
> Princes do but play us; compared to this,
> All honor's mimic, all wealth alchemy. (21-24)[27]

The metaphorical conceit depends upon the confident male sense of regency and possession. The "eroticism of power" which underlies the male sexual imagination extends itself through Donne's poetry. His love for women, then, and the sexuality which energizes that love emerge in a voice which assumes his power.

That very assumption, however, is undone in Donne's religious poetry. His "Holy Sonnets" express his love of God. If as a male his sense of his own power becomes a function of his sexuality and his love, then before God he abandons his maleness. In "Batter my heart," Holy Sonnet 14, Donne speaks as one who dwells in a town under siege. The "three-personed" God is the assailant, and the persona pleads with the champion warrior to "batter my heart," "o'erthrow me," "bend your force to break, blow, burn and make me new." The last six lines of the sonnet show Donne's complete transformation as a lover:

> Yet dearly I love You, and would be loved fain,
> But am betrothed unto Your enemy:
> Divorce me, untie or break that knot again,
> Take me to you, imprison me, for I
> Except you enthrall me, never shall be free,
> Nor ever chaste, except you ravish me.

Thus the poem conveys a dark paradox. The words "enthrall" and "ravish" have borrowed their power from our male eroticism; they have now come to surrender their deepest meanings of enslavement and rape because we imagine both, at some deep level, to be somehow desirable. The voice of the poem, as a betrothed female lover, begs the Lord for whom she longs to "enslave" her in order to "free" her, to "rape" her in order to render her "pure." Though critics in our day too have recoiled from the metaphor in the poem, its power rests in the dark contradictions of our male eroticism. Donne takes that very quality Francis de Sales feared in sexuality, its "brutal vehemence," and injects it into the voice of his love for God. The soul becomes female because the voice of the soul longs to be possessed.

The Soul as Woman of Leisure

William Law (1686–1781), especially in his classic work *A Serious Call to a Devout and Holy Life* (1728), has a clear, stated preference for women as the gender most susceptible to piety.[28] Like proto-feminists of his own age and shortly thereafter, Law condemns the kind of frivolous education given to women of leisure in his day:

> They are not suffered to compete with us in the arts and sciences of learning and eloquence, in which I have much suspicion they would often prove our superiors. But we turn them over to the study of beauty and dress, and the whole world conspires to make them think of nothing else. (19.120-121)

Law's examples and counsels for a devout life, in fact, depend heavily upon women, whom he deems to possess "a finer sense, a clearer mind, a readier apprehension, and gentler dispositions" than the generality of men (19.121). The "pious woman," married or single, is distant from her sexuality and imagined to be totally fulfilled in her charitable labours. The male, however, is afflicted with his sexuality and immersed in the business of a mercantile world. Significantly, the male's labour for profit estranges him from God. The "clearer sense" and greater virtue of the female is, in this emerging literature of "devotional leisure," the product of her gender. Her virtue subsists in her commerce-free subjection.

A generation after William Law, the Catholic St. Alphonsus Liguori in Naples published a seminal devotional work, *The Glories of Mary* (1750). Though the imagery of the Marian cult emphasizes her virginity, the voices of the devotees exalt her motherhood. Male devotees deal with their own problematic sexuality by sublimating its urges in a "pure" object, at once beautiful in youth and mature in maternity. "Mary is our Mother," says Liguori, "not according to the flesh, but through love: 'I am the mother of fair love' (Prov. 24:24)."[29] Her love is "fair" by virtue of its being not "of the flesh."

The closer we approach our own era, the more "gender-bending" becomes the voice of Catholic male devotion. When the voice of prayer habitually or exclusively addresses a virginal mother of sublime perfection, men grow even more distant from their own sexuality. The male, of course, has an eventual need to define himself against his mother, to identify with the father who is a precursor of himself. Thus, the "bourgeois niceties" of an increasingly romanticized Catholic devotion grew to conflict more and more with the expectations of mature male behaviour.

Generations of Catholic men have absorbed signals at conflict with their own gender identification. They have been raised in a "dialect of piety" at odds with a "genderlect" powerful in their own male socialization. At times it is a factor in their failure to develop a deeper prayer life: many young men, associating a preciousness or extravagance of devotional imagery with the nuns who were its first vehicles, reject piety as itself "unmanly." Nun-baiting, like mother-rejection, is a stage in "spiritual puberty" for men. Yet the values which underlie the piety, however saccharine it might be, escape men because they are lost in a blizzard of flowers, a fog of perfumed essences, an avalanche of honeyed images which now elude both genders, but which once were the hallmark of feminine sensibilities.[30]

Thus into the present era, with its return to the celibate monastic models made known anew by Thomas Merton, the voice of the sexually active male has been virtually absent in Catholic piety. Their canonical tradition gives men a sanctioned "headship" over females, which their spirituality urges them to renounce. They cannot do so without assuming, themselves, a female voice. Their male bodies are endowed with a strength which they are driven to exercise competitively, and their eroticism gives them an urge to mastery. They cannot present this gift of Self to God without stripping the soul of the rags of its maleness. Sexually experienced men, without their own male ethos, are mute before the Spirit. Embodied, they conceive of their bodies as an affront to God. Bodiless, they have no voice.

"Trusty" Jesus

Protestant spirituality, like the commentaries of John of the Cross, has a voice of prose and a voice of poetry. Relentlessly drawn to exposition, even the spiritual narratives of the Reformation mind tend toward explanation rather than devotion. *Pilgrim's Progress* (1678), for example, is a classic of Reformation piety. In a dream vision reminiscent of the medieval convention, its author John Bunyan (1628–88) describes in Part I the journey of Christian "from this world to that which is to come." Christian is a married man, with children, and his relationship to his family shows a deep affection.

Yet, Christian leaves his wife and family in order to wander through his allegory and forestall the great disaster that he fears is to come. We gain deep insight into his experience, but not into his affections, and least of all into his sexuality. Indeed, his leaving his wife was a kind of precondition for his spiritual apprehension. (She too, in Part II of the same work, comes after him on her own spiritual journey.) His distance from her allows him to perceive truth the more directly. His wife lies at one pole of the narrative, and God at the other. Indeed, when she meditates upon his departure she admits to her children, "I have sinned away your Father, and he is gone...."[31] As a married man, then, Christian is no less estranged from the object of his sexual desire than a monk. When his head is turned toward the Heavenly City, it is turned away from the woman to whom he is joined in body.

Bunyan finds it difficult in his work to express an affective relationship with God. The allegory is cast in terms of a pilgrimage to a *place* rather than a quest for a *person*. Eastern Orthodox spirituality, in its trinitarian emphasis, focuses upon God as a loving intercommunion among consubstantial Persons. In that sense the souls of males, then, participate in an interrelationship with God; they become drawn into that love which is "God-life." Western spirituality, as we have seen, comes to conceive of the spiritual life as a relationship with Christ, specifically. Gender, then, becomes a factor in approaching a human God incarnate in a male body. In Reformation spirituality as well, this love encounters the problem of gender; Bunyan, for example, compares love for Christ with a male's love for a young girl in *Come and Welcome Lord Jesus Christ* (1678). Yet, his "voice" cannot match the analogy.

Bunyan's problem was the male eroticism of power, which could not coexist with a state of grace. In one of his posthumous works he reveals his belief that men could not escape that eroticism: "Who that shall meet ... a comely and delicate woman ... in a wood, unless he feared God, but would seek to ravish and defile her."[32] Any man, given a chance and the knowledge that he would escape God's punishment, would rape a strange girl in the woods. The fear of God thus constrains a universal male desire to "ravish" and "defile," but it does not eliminate it. The potential for sin is no further away from a man than his next erection.

With the rise of the middle class, which accompanied the Reformation, male writers like Bunyan emphasized a new kind of relationship with God. Distant from sexual implication, it was based on a capito-covenant theology, a moral order that was a reflection of the new commercial one. A liberal use of commercial metaphor cast the relationship of the soul to God in everyday mercantile terms. Scholars in the modern era emphasize the social and economic implications of religion's hospitality to capitalism. For Bunyan and other male devotional authors, however, the debit-credit relationship of the soul to God raised new possibilities for relationship between men and their Lord. If male sexuality was problematic in conceiving of love for a God understood in male terms, then indebtedness, or gratitude, or even collaboration could offer men an alternate sense of kinship to the Divine.

The character Hopeful in *Pilgrim's Progress* tells us that we cannot, by our own efforts in keeping the Law, expect to reach God's Kingdom: "If a man runs £100 into the shopkeeper's debt, and after that shall pay for all that he shall fetch, yet his old debt stands still in the book uncrossed" (181). The "trusty Jesus" becomes in effect the friendly trustee of our salvation. The sacraments, in Bunyan's theology, are the marketplace within which we trade for grace. In *The Advocateship of Jesus Christ* (1688), Bunyan prefigures an affective relationship with God we find in many a pious male Protestant thereafter. Bunyan's Jesus is a friend a man can do business with, a beloved partner who offers unlimited credit on our behalf. He shares with us men the terms of our own economic competitiveness, and with him we can never go into that "bankrupt" state which is Bunyan's contemptuous figure for damnation.

A Curious Knot

Interspersed with the long prose treatises of Reform is a poetic Protestant male voice, continually raising the voice of affections in poems and hymns amidst the prose. Bunyan loved music, and defended it against Puritan condemnation; he himself used, with mixed results, a poetic voice in tandem with his prose. Edward Taylor (d.1725), a Puritan minister of the New World, draws upon the female body and his idealization of female experience ("holy Huswifery" in Meditation 42) for a host of positive metaphors in his private devotional poems. As a male, he is but a "flesh and blood bag" privileged to host the Divine Presence cast in female form (Meditation 30). His own male body, in fact, is consistently a polluted host for his soul:

> Alas! my Soule, product of Breath Divine,
> For to illuminate a Lump of Slime. . . .
> My nobler part, why dost thou laquy to
> The Carnall Whynings of my senses so?
> What? Thou become a Page, a Peasant! nay,
> A Slave unto a Durty Clod of Clay! (1-2; 5-8)[33]

The soul is defiled in the poem by the "nasty wet," "filthy Puddles," "stains" born of the body. If the hints at seminal emission suggest masturbation, then masturbation is but the emblem of a sterile mortality. While the female body in his work is often spiritualized, his own male body but poises his "moldering Heart" between hell and an angry God.

The love, which his meditations so effectively evoke, is expressed in terms of a paradox born of the lowliness of this body and the greatness of God; "should gold wed dung," he says (Meditation 33), God's love for us would be a greater wonder. Yet beneath this negation of the male body, Taylor yet manages to redeem male sexuality. In his poem "Upon Wedlock and the Death of Children," he offers a sensual, botanical metaphor upon conjugal sex:

> A Curious Knot God made in Paradise,
> And drew it out inamled neatly Fresh.
> It was the true-Love knot, more sweet than spice,
> And set with all the flowres of Graces dress.

Taylor describes the birth of children through the "love-knot" metaphor and thus conveys a male dimension of care and nurture.

Christ the Athlete

The growth of female power in the Church through the eighteenth and nineteenth centuries outpaced the power of women in secular society. The Church, in effect, became a place from which women could work to change the social order. Men could tolerate the implicit critique of their gender, which their piety provided, but when women began to control those very structures by which men were socialized into the Church, then piety itself increasingly became a woman's concern. Modernity reveals a series of male attempts to "rescue" piety from the realm of the female. Like the linguistic patterns of imitation revealed in male-to-male speech, the source of this "new male" piety was often the man of the working class.

There are two motifs in this strain of male piety, both of them with antecedents discussed above. The one focuses upon the moral and physical energy of Christ, "Christ as Athlete." Growing out of the "muscular Christian tradition" of the nineteenth century, Thomas Hughes produced one of the first texts in this genre. Hughes sought to harness and mediate both the strength of the male body and the aggressive impulse of the male soul. *The Manliness of Christ* (1896) grew out of Hughes' experience with a Bible study class in the Working Men's College, where he attempted to offer education to labourers.

The other motif focuses upon the more mercantile models we observed in Bunyan. Bruce Barton's *The Man Nobody Knows* (1924) was a work of devotion which permeated Protestant Christian culture in America for some decades and which still leaves a legacy in evangelical and fundamentalist piety. Barton is explicit in his intention to introduce his reader to a Christ who is a "man's man." He took note of the fact that Jesus had attracted to himself many women who were his disciples, but his conclusion offers a lesson to men:

> The important, and too often forgotten, fact in these relationships is this – that women are not drawn by weakness. The sallow-faced, thin-lipped, so-called spiritual type of man may awaken maternal instinct, stirring an emotion which is half regard, half pity. But since the world began no power has more fastened the affection of a woman upon a man than manliness. The men who have been women's men in the finest sense, have been the vital, conquering figures of history.[34]

Barton is no critic of the social order: he is satisfied that through the Gospel, "the world is becoming a fairer, juster and happier living place for the great majority of its inhabitants" (157). In this day of sensitivity to social action, the problematic nature of Jesus as "The Founder of Modern Business" is obvious. Jesus here works as a servant to the "system." He does not operate in tension against it. Jesus in fact can join a man even in the struggle to compete, to find a place in the world. This Jesus avoids the elaborated diction and precious metaphors, which find scant space in the society of men. The "common sense" of Jesus can trivialize that very theology and spirituality which seeks to actualize and reify his personality within us. The inadequacy of this piety is the tragedy of the male dilemma.

Skin and Sacrament

My own Orthodox Tradition fully accepts a "sacramentality" which the Church confers upon human existence. The number of those sacraments, under heavy Western influence, is usually fixed at seven. There is a strong impulse among Orthodox, however, to suspect so numerical a limitation. The number was not fixed, even in the West, until quite late; there remains the sense among us that sacramentality is more a process than a fixed number of "acts."

A blessed existence within the material world constantly engages us with "external signs" like the water of Baptism or the bread and wine of Eucharist. There is a tendency in the rudiments of sacramental theology to regard those material "signs" as phenomena existing outside the body, but having an effect upon it. We wash and lave ourselves with water; we consume bread and wine. Sacraments, we think, act *upon* rather than *within* us. Sex, however, is a phenomenon which allows the body in itself to become "sacramentally engaged." When sex is sacramentalized, there is a wondrous way in which the mutual pleasure of our touching bodies participates in God's process of rendering us holy.[35]

E. Schillebeeckx regards the "flesh/spirit" union as a happy development in New Testament thought:

> This idea is a very rewarding one from the dogmatic point of view; and, from the anthropological point of view...the sex act is not a superficial one, in which the person remains outside – on the contrary, the person is deeply involved. That is why intercourse with a prostitute is not – as the Corinthians, with their false conception of freedom, thought it to be – a "liberation" (1 Cor. 6.12-16), but rather an enslavement of the person.[36]

Schillebeeckx emphasizes that sex is more than an action. It enacts a dynamic state of being, a *synousia* or "consubstantiality" wherein two people participate in each other's very being. Sex with a prostitute, in its virtual anonymity, does not acknowledge the innate power of communion within the act (nor does having sex with a woman whom one regards as "subordinate"). Our spirituality reflects the failure of our theology to embrace the communion implicit in the act. In truth, our male spirituality, in its disembodiment, is not erotic *enough*. Western Christian men live in a cerebral, word-based culture. The concept of "one spirit" may be better understood among us, in fact, than the concept of "one flesh."

The words we men use to describe sex, from the crudest to the most polite, miss the mark. The oft-used New Testament word for sin, *amartia*, means precisely that: "to miss the mark" of our God-given possibility. Christians avoid sexual crudities because words can, in themselves, "sin" in their failure to render an act according to its true nature. Crudely and often, men use the taboo word "f___ [expletive deleted]." Often the verb has an object, as in "Did X f___ [expletive deleted] Y?" The old word itself is derived from Anglo-Saxon roots; it is an act which one inflicts upon another, like striking or beating. The variations in crude slang carry the same weight of infliction: "plank," "bang," "nail," "screw." On one level, the crude, carpenter-like connotations of these words are violent; on the other, they are more appropriate to inanimate objects than to enfleshed persons.

Even the more polite terms carry the weight of a peculiar syntax: "to *make* love," as if love could be "made"; "to *have* sex," "to *have* intercourse," as if sex could be "had," as if an intersection of two beings could be "possessed." (Sex, indeed, "possesses" *us* rather than the other way around.) Our language struggles to be lord over that surging, insistent power of desire for sexual release in us. It too "sins" in resigning all power to us men, and granting none of the agency to our partner. Our language gives our woman-lover no active role. Look at the objects of the verbs. In the crudest language with its violent subtext, the object is the woman: "*he screwed her.*" When the language is polite, the object is sex itself: "*he made love to her.*" The verb's real object in the politest discourse is the pleasure itself. A woman-lover is grammatically but the means to an end.

Sex, however, continually confirms the mutuality of our being. Whenever a human has sex with any other human, an intense, momentous conjoining occurs. Even though we may not desire so profound a link, one occurs by the very nature of our union. When the community of the Church blesses a marriage between a woman and a man, the lifelong process of their coupling participates in a sacramental communion between them. Here the "materiality" embedded within the sacrament does not subsist in any object outside the two people, like bread or wine or oil. Within the blessing, approving community signified in the blessing of the priest or bishop, the couple themselves *in their very bodies* enact that grace and love between God and God's people, Christ and his Church.

When the Church blesses the union of two people, they in their own bodies mutually enact the sacrament. They do so continually, just as the cohesive reality of "Eucharist" subsists in our many consumptions of bread and wine. Sex is itself a type of

Eucharist in that it is a mutual and continual giving. This is not to take away from it its fleshly, embodied nature. The communion of beings, the "consubstantiality" among lovers of God and each other, is enacted at the electric juncture of skin with skin.

If the process is blessed, we must not hesitate to characterize sex theologically. Giving and receiving are mutual in implication. To "touch" too insistently, to "awaken" too abruptly, are initiatives in loving of which women complain. These are spiritual as well as physical problems. In sacramental sex, we love the other *as* ourselves: therein is the completion of the union. For a male to be too focused on his own most sexually sentient organ, to the neglect or obliteration of his partner's bodily sensitivities, is of course a failure in loving. It expresses a selfishness in our being, an appropriation of that pleasure which is to be shared if it is to be savoured. It too is *amartia*, short of the mark: "good" sex can help us understand virtue and sin.

During sex between a male and female, the skin subsists at the border between two sets of sensations. Sex is a communication akin to language, for in dialogic discourse two beings share meaning with each other. The Russian literary philosopher Mikhail Bakhtin (1896–1975), with the sources of his thought embedded deeply in Orthodox Christian theology, developed a dialogic theory, far more satisfying in a Christian context than the isolationism of Freud. Language exists in Bakhtin's system at that space where the consciousness of two speakers meet. The "word," then, is not the "property" of the speaker, for the listener appropriates the word into a new consciousness. Words come into full being at the borders between consciousnesses.

Skin is our incarnate "border." The body in sacramental sex no longer "belongs" to either party, male or female. At that silent border of the embodied consciousness which is our skin, we embrace. In the ensuing exploration of our bodies is a communion of being. It is good that this exploration be prolonged and joyful; it is good that it open the realm of each body to the other. There is thus a physics and a theology to the act of intercourse. The male enters; the female encloses. Whereas a linguist like Bakhtin can concern himself with the *mezhdumir*, "the world between consciousnesses" as expressed in speech, sex defies articulation. Its communion is mute. The act of sex is *not* deployed, like discourse, in the "space between." Rather, the act

308

of loving, mutual intercourse annihilates that space. The skin in sexual embrace and ultimately in that most explosive of orgasmic "touchings" dissipates the *mezhdumir*. Two bodies engage in an act of "oneness"; individuality gives way to mutual personhood.

Sex in its sacramental sense defies a prime tenet of our secular world. Our bodies are not our own. "Or do you not know that your body is the temple of the Holy Spirit who is in you, whom you have from God, and you are not your own?" (1 Cor. 6:19). Whether our laws or our theories of consciousness assume that each person has ownership or proprietorship of his or her body is not the issue. Christianity, in fact, subsisted within legal systems which declared that a master had proprietorship over the life of a slave (as we now subsist in a legal framework which grants a woman effective title to the life in her womb); yet our theology will not capitulate to that assumption. Nor can our theology capitulate here. The act of sex between male and female is "iconic," the sexual paradigm for the whole community. Moreover, in its very essence it surrenders proprietorship of the body to our partner, and through our partner to the Triune God.

To recognize sex as a mutual appropriation of pleasure, rather than as a seizure of sensation for the self, can be difficult for men in our culture. We men have been too well served by the autoerotic industry. It has shaped our attitudes. We have to fight its effects as we open our own bodies to exploration and allow the entire surface of us to become engaged. There must be a patience, a searching, in our seeking the separate points of awakening and engagement in our lover. Promiscuity creates a frantic immediacy in sex. The fidelity to one lover gives us the gift of time: the zealous joy of one communion can succeed the long, slow leisure of another. There is a lifetime together, in the best of cases, to learn the secrets of this body. Like consciousness itself, but much more intimately, it is an entity built on sharing.

In sacramental, erotic love, each orgasmic act is "itself" and "more than itself" at the same time. It takes us out of ourselves in pleasure, and gives of ourselves to another. The entry of male into female creates what some would call an "inevitable sexism of biology." Radical feminists in fact often see marriage itself as a kind of rape.[37] Yet, for us Christian men, the two concepts are antithetical. "Entry" can be seen as concomitant with "rape" only when it is unsought. The greatest joy of this entry, in the process of awakening, which occurs at the skin-contained borders of the Self, is the invitation of the Other.

The male "entry," then, is concomitant with the female "enclosure." The mutual eroticism of sacramental sex opens dimensions of sexuality, which the Church too often fails to discuss, and which the autoeroticism of contemporary culture obscures. The man who explores and comes to know the body of his lover will find a dialogue written in the map of her skin. In this "braille of the body," the male will come to know a different physiological and genital order of being. If he has been attendant to his spouse's own embodiment, he will know not only his own pleasure, but also hers. The mutuality of marriage in fact occurs by the very nature of "good" sex.

Flesh of my Flesh

In Christian marriage, there is a reference not only to union of flesh with flesh, but also to the very identity of flesh with flesh. Adam, when he first encounters Eve, cries out in poetic strophes:

> This is now bone of my bones
> And flesh of my flesh;
> She shall be called Woman,
> Because she was taken out of Man. (Gen. 2:23)

Adam embraces Eve's flesh as his very own. Adam speaks, as did the human author, with a male voice: there is no record of what Eve said or felt. However, in this precursor to what the Orthodox marriage service calls "mystical and undefiled marriage," there is no conquest but a mutual habitation of the same realm. There is a sense in which heterosexual sex, with the two sentient organs of contact in the embrace of enclosure, transcends its own physiology. No part of the body is any longer an "it," but rather subsists in the mutually inhabited realm of the "we."

Genesis is a text often rejected in the radical feminist mythos. The connection between the "garden" motif and marriage helps to explain the tension between marriage and hierarchy. Eden is a state which marriage in the Orthodox Tradition seeks to restore and recapture. The married man and married woman seek in their mutual embodiment, in their "reconstitution" as one flesh in Christ, to veritably "undo the Fall" through their mutual life in Christ's redeeming grace. My own Orthodox Tradition does not identify the Fall in any way with human sexuality. The Eastern reading of the Creation account, however, emphasizes the mutual completion of each gender in the other. That mutuality is itself a sign of its likeness to God: "God created man in his image; in the divine image he created him; male and female he created them" (Gen. 1:27). Though the English pronouns here absorb "male" more definitively into the masculine God, the pure sense of the text is plain. In humanity's "male-and-femaleness" subsists the imaging forth of God.

If males try to take up this burden of "imaging" alone, we cannot sustain it. We thereby distort our male identity and our sexuality. That the word "man" is in English synonymous with maleness is to our own spiritual detriment, for it can deform our theology. As God's communality in love subsists within the consubstantial Trinity, so also our human consubstantiality is most fully reflected in our genderhood. Pavel Evdokimov works from the collectivity embedded in the Hebrew word "Adam-man" to clarify our male and female complementarity:

> The Book of Genesis says literally: "Let us make man [*ha adam*, in the singular] and let them [in the plural] have dominion. And God created man [in the singular] and he created them man-male and man-female [the plural refers to the singular, man]." "Man" transcends the male-female distinction, because the latter is initially not the separation of two individuals that are henceforth isolated from one another.[38]

Neither gender, then, of itself images forth God. In the denial of that reciprocity lies the crux of the Genderist heresy afflicting us in our time. The secular "self-sufficiency" of the individual intellect has begotten a "self-sufficiency" of gender as well. Rather, each human in reciprocity with others reflects that God who has made them all. Every day, in the process of Creation, surveying what God has wrought, "God saw that it was good." The first critique God provides of his own creation occurs when he looks upon the male in isolation. "And the Lord God said, 'It is not good that man should be alone'" (Gen. 2:18). Woman in the Genesis text is hardly a "derivative" being, created as the complement to the male's sense of his own being. Rather, she is "a helper comparable to him," one who does not help him in his own sense of self-completion, but rather one who will work with him in tending the garden which God has entrusted to them both.

The sanctified sex of marriage is hardly, then, a figure for dissolution, but for re-creation and restoration. Intercourse "knits up" the wholeness of Creation; yet it must not be seen as a fusion of two identities. It contains within it a divinely sanctioned sense of "play" which must never be lost: each partner, then, may engage in "roles" at the invitation and for the pleasure of the other. For there to be mutuality, there must also be integral personhood. Male and female must ever "tend," in an engaging variation, toward unity. But that tendency must always preserve the integral personhood of both male and female, so that there indeed can be loving "mutuality" in the encounter. The portrait of the male as "master," a lord of relationship who in effect rules a female partner, is in truth reflected in much of the literature and canons regarding marriage, East and West. Yet, the image of male as "master," sexually or anthropologically, is utterly inconsistent with the concept of *synousia*, consubstantiality. That tension is witnessed, as we have seen, in the male's attitude toward his own body. To demand the prerogatives of the master sunders us from Christ the Servant.

Marriage, in our Tradition at least, is not a fulfilment of the Fall, a harbinger of pain and sorrow. Rather, the liturgy of marriage consistently means to convey joy and fulfilment to the married couple.[39] In its Edenic theology, marriage is "ameliorative"; in co-operation with the saving grace of Christ, marriage is intended to "knit up" creation, and through repentance and mutual love, to put to death that enmity which destroys our links to each other. As married couples often hear from the echoes of their Tradition, marriage provides us with the opportunity to live out in Christ a new stewardship of Eden.

The Orthodox Tradition celebrates the union of the lover and beloved with a ritual "dance," done three times around the marriage table. It is a harbinger of the wedding dance to come, in which the entire community participates. All of us Christian men embrace our sexuality, not only for our own sake but also for the sake of a woman whom we love or may come to love, and for the sake of our most deeply expressed relationship with God. We are all guests at the wedding. We have all drunk the good wine, and we are flush with the joy of our own being. We dance first of all to celebrate that young man and woman whom we have lifted up among us and who are now seated together, at the centre where we have placed them. There they now preside, at the stillness which is the centre of the dance.

Each male then expresses not simply the joy and confidence of his own being. Rather, that truly sexual joy in itself expresses what it is he can become: no longer a male dancer alone, but rather a male-and-female dancing together this union in their being. In that "union of being," we enter into the deepest dialogue with the trinitarian God who draws us unto him. We are male, in all the joy and affirmation of our maleness, not that we may glory in that alone, but that we may be the more joyful in our metamorphosis. For we seek always the Other with whom we will join in the dance. Then the dance, in all its variation and ferocity, will take us up too in its embrace. Then we too will inhabit with our beloved the stillness at the centre, which is *synousia*, consubstantiality, *lof* and love together. Only there in sacred marriage does sex take on the fullness of its paradox. There sex is at once the most private and cosmic of acts.

For Further Reading

Evdokimov, Paul. *Sacrament of Love: The Nuptial Mystery in the Light of the Orthodox Tradition.* Crestwood, NY: St. Vladimir's, 1985.

Meyendorff, John. *Marriage: An Orthodox Perspective.* Crestwood, NY: St. Vladimir's, 1970.

Spidlík, Tomás. *The Spirituality of the Christian East.* Kalamazoo, MI: Cistercian, 1986.

Yannaras, Christos. *The Freedom of Morality.* Crestwood, NY: St. Vladimir's, 1996.

[1] An excellent discussion and bibliography regarding women and Christian imagery is contained in Margaret R. Miles, *Image as Insight: Visual Understanding in Western Christianity and Secular Culture* (Boston: Beacon, 1985).

[2] For a survey of pre-Christian antecedents of the Theotokos and Byzantino-Slavic "earth goddess" mythos, see Joanna Hubbs, *Mother Russia: The Feminine Myth in Russian Culture* (Bloomington, IN: Indiana, 1988).

[3] Mary Daly, *The Church and the Second Sex* (New York: Harper and Row, 1968), 161.

[4] The first sally in Reuther's estrangement from the cult is documented in *Mary: The Feminine Face of the Church* (Philadelphia: Westminster, 1977).

[5] See for example Sebastian Brock and Susan Ashbrook Harvey, ed. and trans., *Holy Women of the Syrian Orient,* The Transformation of Classical Heritage 13 (Berkeley: California, 1987). Some treatment of this theme is in Gabriele Winkler, *Das armenische Initiationsrituale,* Orientalia Christiana Analecta 217 (Rome: Pontifical Oriental Institute, 1982).

[6] Muriel Schultz, "Semantic Derogation of Women," in *Feminism and Linguistic Theory* (London: MacMillan Press, 1985).

[7] In recent years there have been a number of popular texts discussing differences in male and female linguistic patterns. For a clearly written but scientific treatment of the "hard" data, see Peter Trudgill, *Sociolinguistics: An Introduction to Language and Society,* rev. ed. (Harmondsworth: Penguin, 1983); data relevant to this discussion is in Chapter 2, "Language and Social Class," and Chapter 4, "Language and Sex."

[8] Daly, *The Church and the Second Sex,* 74–118.

[9] Mary Daly, *Gyn/Ecology* (Boston: Beacon, 1978), 70-71. The feminist critique of "Phallocentrism" in male language led to a critique of "Phallologocentrism" in male discourse: linear, rational, sequential thought "pointed" toward a goal (ironically, the very kind of discourse which, the data indicate, men shun in their own company and which breaks the code of "covert prestige"). For a discussion of phallologocentrism, see Julia Kristeva, *Desire in Language: A Semiotic Approach to Literature and Art,* trans. T. Gora et al. (NY: Columbia, 1980), and Luce Irigaray, *This Sex Which Is Not One,* trans. Catherine Porter (Ithaca, NY: Cornell, 1985).

[10] Luce Irigaray, however, professes in an interview that there is nothing *other* than masculine discourse, which is why its dominance is so difficult to discern in *The Sex Which Is Not One,* 140.

[11] Men who wish a male's perspective, in images, of the "exploitation" of the female form in Western art can see John Berger [et al.], *Ways of Seeing* (New York: Penguin, 1972), 34–64.

[12] Daly, *The Church and the Second Sex,* 189.

[13] It is interesting to note, in fact, how long Western men have characterized Orthodox Eastern piety and religious forms as in some way "feminine" and less than manly. As early as the Libri Carolini in the eighth century, the Carolingian authors boast that in their armies, "it is the cross, and no effeminate compagination of colours [i.e., the icons of the Greeks], which our soldiers follow into battle."

[14] Alexander Schmemann, *For the Life of the World,* 2d ed. (Crestwood, NY: St. Vladimir's, 1975), 34. The same critique of systematic limitation of the sacramental process, a characteristic of the Orthodox émigré theology of the St. Sergius school, is contained in S.L. Frank, *God With Us: Three Meditations,* trans. Natalie Duddington (London: J. Cape, 1946). The late Prof. John Meyendorff was fond of maintaining in his lectures that the Orthodox adopted the number "seven" in designating sacraments only in response to Western insistence that they choose between the "Reformed" number "two," and the "Catholic" number "seven." When thus pressed, he joked, "what were we to do but choose the higher number?"

[15] See Cheris Kramarae, *Women and Men Speaking: Framework for Analysis* (Rowley: Newbury House, 1981), 135ff.

[16] Kramarae, *Women and Men Speaking,* 135.

[17] Kramarae, *Women and Men Speaking,* 138. (Matters involving class, "negotiated power" and masculinity are also issues of some debate among white and African American feminists).

[18] For literary allusions, see Norman Vance, *Sinews of the Spirit: The Ideal of Christian Manliness in Victorian Literature and Religious Thought* (Cambridge: Cambridge, 1985). In the realm of painting Ford Madox Ford, Holman Hunt and William Morris all faced negative reviews for their portrayals of a muscular, "working class" Jesus figure.

[19] For the gradual sexualization of male nudity and its incorporation into homoerotic convention, see Peter Weirmaier, *The Hidden Image: Photography of the Male Nude in the Nineteenth and Early Twentieth Century,* trans. Charles Nielander (Cambridge, MA: MIT, 1988).

[20] For Greek text of the hymns, see *Hymnen,* ed. Athanoasios Kambilis (Berlin, New York: de Gruyter, 1976).

[21] *Living Flame of Love,* trans. John Venard (New York: E.G. Doyer, 1990), 60.

[22] Caroline Walker Bynum, *Jesus as Mother: Studies in the Spirituality of the High Middle Ages* (Berkeley: California, 1982).

[23] *Ladder of Perfection* (New York, NY: Penguin, 1994), 19. Hilton uses a long textual and artistic tradition of portraying John as a soft, womanly presence among the disciples in contrast to the assertive, impetuous and "manly" Peter.

[24] (Author unknown), *The Cloud of Unknowing,* trans. Ira Progoff (New York: Julian, 1957), 164.

[25] Richard Rolle, *The Fire of Love and the Mending of Life,* trans. and intro. M.L. del Mastro (Garden City: Image, 1981), Ch. 29–30.

[26] Trans. Jeff Lelen (Garden City, NY: Image, 1962). Page and chapter citations are from this edition.

[27] Helen Gardner, ed., *John Donne: The Elegies and the Songs and Sonnets,* and intro. Helen Gardner (Oxford: Clarendon, 1965).

[28] John N. Meister, ed. (Philadelphia, PA: Westminster, 1955). Citations are from this edition.

[29] *The Glories of Mary* (Baltimore: Helicon, 1962), 28.

[30] As illustrations of this genre and to explore its conventions, the larger work explores the texts of Frederick William Faber (1814–1863) and St. Therese of Lisieux (1873–97).

[31] John Bunyan, *Pilgrim's Progress* (Oxford: Clarendon, 1960), 2d ed., 2.189. All citations are from this edition.

[32] *Solomon's Temple Spiritualized; The House of the Forest of Lebanon; The Water of Life,* Miscellaneous Works of John Bunyan 7, ed. Graham Midgley (Oxford: Clarendon, 1989), 302–303.

[33] Edward Taylor, *Poems* (Boston: Twayne, 1988), 78. All citations are from this edition.

[34] *The Man Nobody Knows: A Discovery of the Real Jesus* (Indianapolis: Bobbs Merrill, 1925), 48–49.

[35] The idea that the physicality of sex partakes in the sacramental order occurs in popular Orthodox piety as well as Russian and Ukrainian religious philosophy: see, for example, *The Diary of a Russian Priest,* trans. Helen Iswolsky (Crestwood, NY: St. Vladimir's, 1982), 94ff. The author (Aleksandr Elchaninov, d. 1934) speaks of the physicality as well as the spirituality of marriage as a part of its sacramental character; and he also explicates the tradition that marriage (like monasticism) supersedes the "natural" order of human

relationship and raises it into the realm of the "miraculous" (the Russian carries here the sense of the Edenic, the "God-restored" order). Vigen Guroian in *Incarnate Love: Essays in Orthodox Ethics* (Notre Dame, IN: Notre Dame, 1987), carries the theme into contemporary Orthodox "liturgical piety." Guroian calls the couple united in marriage an "ecclesial entity, one flesh, one body, incorporate of two persons who in freedom and sexual love... image the triune Godhead" through and in Christ (87–88). John Meyendorff in *Marriage: An Orthodox Perspective,* 2d ed. (Crestwood, NY: St. Vladimir's, 1975) explains the text of the marriage rite and discusses the sacramentality of the relationship it initiates.

[36] Edward Schillebeeckx, *Marriage: Human Reality and Saving Mystery* (New York: Sheed & Ward, 1965), 89.

[37] Andrea Dworkin, in *Intercourse* (New York: Free, 1987), 63, expresses this theme (not uncommon in radical feminism) in her analysis of how the act of sex is "constructed" as a paradigm in the male imagination: "By thrusting into her, he takes her over. His thrusting into her is taken to be her capitulation to him as conqueror; it is a physical surrender of herself to him; he occupies and rules her, expresses his elemental dominance over her, by his possession of her in the f___ [expletive deleted]."

[38] Paul Evdokimov, *Sacrament of Love: The Nuptial Mystery in the Light of the Orthodox Tradition* (Crestwood, NY: St. Vladimir's, 1985), 116.

[39] For the full text of the Orthodox marriage rite in English, see Meyendorff, *Marriage: An Orthodox Perspective*, op. cit.

Chapter 15

Iconography: Windows of Life

MARIA TRUCHAN-TATARYN

Maria Truchan-Tataryn is a doctoral student in English at the University of Saskatchewan.

I make an image of the God whom I see. I do not worship matter; I worship the Creator of matter who became matter for my sake, who willed to take His abode in matter; who worked out my salvation through matter. Never will I cease honouring the matter which wrought my salvation! ... Because of this, I salute all remaining matter with reverence, because God has filled it with His grace and power. Through it my salvation has come to me.

St. John of Damascus, On the Divine Images. *I, 16.*

Iconography has enjoyed tremendous popularity in the last few decades. It is not uncommon to see iconographic images adorning book jackets, greeting cards and living spaces. Although its ubiquitous presence in the Western world attests to the icon's broad appeal as an art form, for the Eastern Christian, the icon's value extends far beyond its aesthetic merit. In fact, in our faith tradition, iconography is not a style of painting; it is rather a language that speaks to us on a multiplicity of levels – some conscious, others not. This iconographic language is rich in history, ritual and symbol. Like all languages, it compels interpretation. It speaks to us individually as well as collectively.

It conveys information of past events and figures, but its communication is dynamic, current and personal.

It may strike one as odd for such eloquence to be attributed to stylized forms inscribed on slabs of wood; however, it is precisely in this paradox of possibilities that the wonder of iconography lies. The iconographic image strives to represent the foundational truth of our Christian faith: God's incarnation – God becoming human – God as one of us. Hence, the icon emerges from the blending of natural elements of creation: vegetable, animal, mineral and human. The first three elements comprise the necessary materials. Wood provides the structure; a base is prepared by mixing crushed stone, glue and water; egg tempera is made with yolks, vinegar and vegetable dyes; oil and gelatin are used at various stages as sealants; and gold is applied for its natural and symbolic richness. The fourth, human element applies traditional rules and procedures rooted in ritual and theology, faith and prayer, to the former elements in order to create images that at once express material reality and sacred presence. Polarities of divine and carnal dissolve in iconography as they do in Christ. In the icon, rather than mundane photographic portrayals of life, we encounter recognizable events and familiar environments transformed by the incarnation. The icon reminds us that not only the human form but also the earth, animals and vegetation can no longer be perceived as they were before we knew Christ. Through Christ humanity participates in a cosmic transfiguration. This is the message that underpins the iconographic form. For this reason the iconographer's initial foray is commonly a representation of the Transfiguration, the biblical event that for Christ's disciples manifested their friend and rabbi's divinity.

Traditionally an iconographer acquired the requisite skill and knowledge by apprenticing with a master. Not surprisingly, the vocation of iconographer frequently, albeit not exclusively, came to those in monasteries. Since the icons teach theology, the writer of icons becomes a theologian who labours to bring the Word of God to the community of faithful. Iconographic images are understood as written, not painted, and their text is informed by the Church's Tradition. Icons are, therefore, not signed by the iconographer and consequently many classic icons remain anonymous.

Over the centuries, iconography has developed a strict framework of method, procedure and symbolic code. Although time and place have influenced iconographic formulae, the similarity of contemporary icons to the most ancient extant examples indicates the endurance of original practice. Iconography developed over time as a distinctly religious practice. The style derives from the catacomb symbols and drawings of first and second century Christians, bearing influences of the art of Egyptian burial masks, Greco-Roman mythology and Middle Eastern art.

Much of the history of the development of iconography has been erased, however, as a result of the Iconoclastic Controversies of the eighth and ninth centuries. In 726 the Byzantine, or Eastern, Roman Emperor Leo III the Isaurian issued his first of a series of edicts banning the use of icons. Gradually this policy became one of destruction of all icons. Effectively, the result of this policy was a civil war pitting the Iconoclasts (opponents of icons) against the Iconophiles (supporters of icons). A temporary peace was reached in 787 with the Second Council of Nicaea, called through the efforts of the Empress Irene. However, new Iconoclast Emperors came to power and it was not until 843 that the final victory of the "orthodox" was achieved. Perhaps the event of public riots defending iconographic images best illustrates the depth and intensity of meaning icons can potentially generate. Few icons survived the violence of this period; yet, despite irrevocable loss, with its legitimacy established, iconography flourished as an integral tenet of the Eastern Christian Church. Iconography became the touchstone by which Eastern Christians asserted their belief in the divine-human union in the person of Jesus Christ and today icons continue to be produced throughout the world.

In the West, Eastern Christianity often holds exotic appeal. Ancient ritual and symbolic imagery evoke mystery and mysticism. In iconography we do perceive mystery. We see the incommensurable paradoxes of incarnation and resurrection and recognize them in the daily occurring mysteries of birth and death. The miraculous wonder that encircles iconography in our Tradition is not mystifying. It rather reflects a perception of the world grounded in material reality that encompasses more than can be either apprehended or comprehended. Therefore, the symbolic structure of the icon depicts familiar scenes that evoke more than can be grasped. Although the trained iconographer becomes versed in complex symbolic patterns, we can recognize a few of the typical elements of iconographic symbolism. Appreciating its symbolic quality may not only deepen the icon's meaning but may also help to relate it to our own personal context.

Icons present images of Christ, the Mother of God, the saints, and significant events in their lives. Icons are written with a reverse perspective: that which is farthest from us (the observer) is largest, signalling that we are not the subjects of the icon. The perspective presented is not ours, but that of heaven. Icons are often called windows; as windows, they look both into heaven and from heaven. Consequently time in the icons is always *now*. In the icon of the Incarnation, various events, which happened at different times, all appear in the present because in heaven there is only *now*, not past or future. The images themselves are stylized because they speak to us about humanity transfigured by the divine presence and the divine light. We see everyone, not as we perceive them in our temporal world, but rather, as they are (divinized) in the presence of God. Thus physical qualities are minimized; bodies are draped in flowing robes. The lines of the robes as well as the lines of the natural environment flow towards the central image of Christ. We are invited into a relationship with God, through Christ. The eyes of the human figure are piercing, calling us to stand before the icon and be in the presence of the divine. Icons of Christ are remarkable in that wherever we stand in front of them, the eyes always appear to be looking at us: Christ is always calling us. This call is unceasing, inviting union with God, declaring that being fully human is being united with the divine.

This insight of unity is also reinforced symbolically with the use of colours. The earth colours – blue, brown, green – represent humanity. The royal colours – purple and red – represent divinity. All the major figures in icons wear clothing of these colours. Christ has royal-coloured garments with earth colours draped over top; he is divine and has assumed humanity. Mary and the saints have garments of earth colours with outer garments of imperials colours; they are humans who have been divinized. The gold colour signifies divine energy. All the figures and events invite us to enter into this "other" world of the divine.

Although a product of prayer and meditation, the icon serves to inspire prayer and meditation in others. The significance and symbolic power of the icon must be understood in the context of the faith community. As a visual image the icon participates in the sensual involvement of the people gathered to celebrate liturgy. When we enter an Eastern Church our vision is immediately engaged with an abundance of iconographic depictions that collectively express the continued presence of the Kingdom of Heaven. The angels, saints and those departed from our lives celebrate the liturgy with us. We may not, however, simply gaze at the spectacle; we involve our whole selves in the communal prayer. We approach the icons and demonstrate our reverence by kissing the icon, bowing, crossing ourselves, lighting candles. The scent of incense, the sound of our voices and the taste of the eucharistic bread and wine or the antidoron bread activate and fill all our senses in the liturgical event.

In the Eastern Christian Tradition, liturgy is inextricably bound with the rhythm and experience of daily life which, in turn, is enmeshed with the cyclical dance of the seasons. Just as flowers, foods and objects are brought into the Church, so too candles, incense and icons share space in the homes of the faithful. The icon corner provides a sanctuary of prayer and veneration amidst quotidian bustle. An embroidered cloth draped on the central icon denotes reverence while reinforcing the notion of icon as window – a window which opens towards God and brings God into our daily life. Although we may keep incense and candles in our home icon corner, the icon itself resonates with the experience of the liturgy, bearing with it generations of theology and faith. Since iconography is an integral part of our understanding, each Eastern Christian is called to be a theologian: to live the Gospel and thus to teach through the example of our lives. Through a celebration of our humanity, we approach divinity. In keeping with the spirit of paradox embraced by iconography, we recognize an obligation to become icons ourselves – windows that reveal the transforming power of Christ to the world.

> Praise the Lord from the earth,
> ...
> You mountains and all you hills,
> you fruit trees and all you cedars;

You wild beasts and all tame animals,
you creeping things and you winged fowl.
...
Praise the name of the Lord,
for his name alone is exalted.

Psalm 148

For Further Reading

St. John of Damascus. *On the Divine Images.* Crestwood, NY: St. Vladimir's Seminary Press, 1980.

Ouspensky, Leonid and Vladimir Lossky. *The Meaning of Icons.* Crestwood, NY: St. Vladimir's Seminary Press, 1982.

Pelikan, Jaroslav. Imago Dei: *The Byzantine Apologia for Icons.* Princeton: Princeton University Press, 1990.

Tataryn, Myroslaw. *How to Pray with Icons.* Ottawa: Novalis, 1998.

Epilogue

Opening Windows to a Dialogue of Charity

JAROSLAV Z. SKIRA

Dr. Skira is Assistant Professor of Historical Theology at Regis College (University of Toronto). He held previous appointments at the University of St. Michael's College and Andrey Sheptytsky Institute of Eastern Christian Studies (St. Paul University). He has lectured throughout Canada and in Ukraine. He is also a member of the Roman Catholic Archdiocese of Toronto's Ecumenical and Inter-Faith Commission. He is co-editor of this volume.

Looking Through the Window

When speaking about "windows to the East" there is the implicit recognition that one is not in the East, but looking to another seemingly mythical, inaccessible and far off place. The "window" can be like a portal in some science-fiction novel that transports one to a very different dimension and environment. In many respects, this "window" image is used to explain the role and function of icons within a Church. As we have heard often in these essays, the icon is a "window to eternity," which means that the icon is not the fullness of heaven, but rather it points to a fullness of meaning and life beyond itself. The East contemplates these icons, and "reads" within them a "theology in colour." One can also see through windows, open them and sense what is on the other side, which reveals to us that there is a real proximity to what lies through the window. Some may even be tempted to crawl through the window, and actually enter this Eastern world.

So what is this "window" metaphor really trying to convey to us? Mainly two things. The first is that we should realize that this window has others looking through it from the other side, and seeing in it a "window to the West." A real and vibrant community is experiencing and celebrating the Good News of salvation wrought by Christ and communicated by his Spirit. Thus, unlike a typical house, there is no exterior side of this window. Both sides of the window are "in" the house, or even better, both sides are "in" the Church, for both sides have been called to live in this house. That is exactly the meaning of the Greek word *ekklesia* or Church, where the Greek root of the word *ekklesia* means "those that are called."

The other thing that the window conveys to us is that there is diversity, but not an essential difference, between these two worlds. This window image conveys to us that both East and West need to see each other as members of this same house. Another image of the unity and complementarity that should exist in East and West was first noted by Yves Congar, and has been frequently cited ever since. It is the image of the Church needing to breathe with the "two lungs" of both East and West.[1] There is thus unity yet diversity between these two worlds. Where these metaphors have their limit is that the two sides of the window or the two lungs are not simply "parts" of the Church, but in fact are fully Churches.

In teaching courses to western students on the theology and spirituality of icons, one often needs to explain the meaning of the Greek or Slavonic inscriptions, or the liturgical tradition that inspired the "writing" (it is generally not called "painting"), and ultimately the veneration, of such holy images. There is a religious ethos that one needs to acquire, or rather, be immersed in. Being in the East (or being in the West for that matter) requires one to "live" in that tradition to fully understand and express the riches of its theology, worship and spirituality. One of the places where this is manifested in the fullest way is within the monastic setting, where one participates in the daily life and prayer cycles of the monks. For the above reasons the title of this collection of essays is so appropriate: one can only see into this Tradition through many "windows." However, a fuller understanding of the Eastern Tradition can only be achieved by actually crossing this threshold and becoming Eastern, whether that be in the Byzantine or Oriental Orthodox Traditions. It would be a grave mistake to only see in these churches a traditional theology as an alternative to perceived deficiencies in one's own church Tradition. Similarly, the East's rootedness in Holy Tradition does not make the Church simply an archaic institution that has no relevance for the contemporary world. Such churches have been culturally creative in addressing or inculturating themselves, from the earliest experiences and expressions of the faith among the ancient Greeks, to the Eastern missions and churches in North America.[2] These Eastern churches are called to inculturate the Gospel in whichever culture they find themselves. This includes worshipping in a language that the community understands, and being existentially relevant to the spiritual and material needs (e.g. the crisis in ecology, social justice issues) of their respective communities. Consequently, the Eastern Tradition is the matrix through which these churches can preach and witness to the Gospel. Today, many of these communities are rediscovering their ancient Eastern heritage, a heritage which was either partially lost or marred by "westernization." What all this means is that one can be an "Easterner" living in the so-called "western" world.

Coming Together Once Again

With new waves of immigration to western countries in these last few centuries, the West has increasingly been coming into contact with Eastern Christian communities. In fact, a number of such communities have made significant contributions in the spheres of politics, religion and culture. Not uncommon is discovering in North American cities more than one Eastern Orthodox or Eastern Catholic Tradition co-existing alongside traditional Western churches. Unfortunately, even among the Eastern Christians, some of these "sister" churches, despite recognizing in each other valid orders and sacraments, are not in full communion with each other.

In terms of the study of Eastern Christianity, many centres of study have arisen in the "Western" world, that is, in countries that have not been traditionally part of the ancient Orthodox lands. Among such places, one can name the following in Europe: the Institute of St. Sergius (Paris), the Orthodox Centre of the Ecumenical Patriarchate (Chambésy), the Pontifical Oriental Institute (Rome), and the recently formed Oriental College of the Catholic University of Eichstät (Germany) and Institute for Eastern Christian Studies (Cambridge). In the United States, there is Holy Cross Greek Orthodox Theological School (Brookline, MA), St. Vladimir's Orthodox Theological Seminary (Crestwood, NY), Dumbarton Oaks research centre (Washington, DC) and the University of Scranton's Centre for Eastern Christian Studies. Canada is also seeing a growth in centres dedicated to the study of the Christian East, like the Sheptytsky Institute of Eastern Christian Studies (Ottawa), St. Andrew's College (Winnipeg), to the institution co-publishing this edition, the Prairie Centre for the Study of Ukrainian Heritage (Saskatoon). These various schools and institutions are witnesses to a modern day renaissance in Eastern Christian theology.

We are now in a period when mass communication has made our world a seemingly smaller place to live. The fall of the Berlin Wall and the demise of the Soviet Union have opened up frontiers to cultures and peoples which had previously been cut off from the western world. All of these events have enabled the East and West to begin once again to see and become aware of each other. These events represent a monumental change, for no longer do political empires separate East and West, nor does their communication suffer because of differences in languages. This kind of direct contact has not been seen since the early formation of the Roman or Byzantine empires. Over the past century, Eastern and Western theologians have even begun to again learn from each other, with their theologies being enriched by the theology of each other's tradition. Why do I think that this is so significant? The East and West are once again re-discovering their lost intimacy and communion.

Yves Congar, in his work on the historical relationships between the Catholic Church and the Eastern Orthodox churches, very clearly showed that the East and West never formally broke off communion with each other.[3] Even the so-called schism of 1054, for various reasons, should not be regarded as the formal break between East and West.[4] Congar asserted that the lack of full communion between these two churches was not the result of schism, but the result of a mutual and gradual estrangement.

For various political, cultural and theological reasons, East and West began to drift apart. He wrote: "The 'schism' lies primarily in the acceptance [by both East and West] of the mutual estrangement...hardened by mistrust and ignorance."[5] Each of the two traditions withdrew into themselves and judged the other Church based on its own tradition, each setting its tradition up as an absolute. He concluded:

> Actually and historically, the schism is the result of a gradual and general estrangement. Not that the schism is of itself the estrangement. The sin of schism is already committed in the heart when we behave as though we were not an integral part of the whole with others.[6]

Today one can see part of this "re-integration" with the other in the modern ecumenical movement.

The Dialogue of Charity

In 1951, the Orthodox Church in Constantinople celebrated the 1900th anniversary of Paul's arrival in Greece. The Roman Catholic Church respectfully declined the invitation by the Church of Greece to attend these celebrations. Nowhere in the letter of response, written by the then Substitute for the Secretary of State, Giovanni Battista Montini, is any mention made of the Orthodox Church by name, but only references are made to the "celebrations in that illustrious country" or "in that nation."[7] However, in July of 1967, Montini, by now Pope Paul VI, broke all rules of protocol and visited the Ecumenical Patriarch Athenagoras I in Constantinople (Istanbul), a visit that was reciprocated by the Ecumenical Patriarch's visit to Rome in December of the same year. Then in 1972, after the death of Athenagoras, Pope Paul VI, referring to the wish of the late Patriarch to concelebrate the Eucharist with the pope, stated that this "unfulfilled desire remains as his heritage and as our commitment."[8] All of this came as a result of the historic act by Paul VI and Athenagoras I on December 7, 1965 – the mutual cancellation of the anathemas of 1054.

The beginnings of this change in attitude by both churches eventually paved the way for the announcement by the Vatican and the Phanar (Constantinople) that both churches were establishing preparatory commissions for theological dialogue. On December 14, 1975, while celebrations were being held in Rome and Constantinople commemorating the tenth anniversary of the removal of the excommunications between the Roman Catholic Church and the Orthodox Church, Metropolitan Meliton, representing the Ecumenical Patriarch, announced that by unanimous decision all the Orthodox churches were commencing inter-Orthodox theological dialogue with the Roman Catholic Church. The Catholic Church simultaneously announced its participation. It was at this time that Paul VI, as a sign of humility and respect for the Orthodox, spontaneously knelt and kissed the feet of Metropolitan Meliton, leader of the delegation from the Patriarch of Constantinople.

Two separate preparatory commissions consequently met from 1976–1978, and established a Joint Coordinating Committee, which drew up a Joint Preparatory Document entitled "A plan for initiating a theological dialogue between the Roman Catholic Church and the Orthodox Church." The Document outlined the purpose, method and agenda of the "dialogue of charity." The purpose of the dialogue was the re-establishment of full communion between the two churches, finding its expression in the common celebration of the Holy Eucharist. On the feast of St. Andrew, the two hierarchs formally announced that both churches were creating a Joint Commission for Theological Dialogue Between the Roman Catholic Church and the Orthodox Church.

The first plenary session (May 28–June 4, 1980) of the Joint Commission began with a pilgrimage first to Patmos and then to Rhodes in Greece. At this first meeting, the Orthodox presented a draft declaration concerning the presence of Eastern Catholics (or sometimes pejoratively called "Uniates") on the mixed Commission. The delegates of the Church of Greece had specific instructions from their synod to ensure that this matter was addressed. The Orthodox courteously stated that the membership of Eastern Catholics on the commission created a problem for the Orthodox, and that the Orthodox tolerance of the Eastern Catholic's presence did not signify recognition by the Orthodox of Eastern Catholic churches nor of the principles of "uniatism." Both sides eventually agreed that the Roman Catholic Church had a right to send those representatives it judged fit to attend the sessions.

To date, there have been four agreed statements: "The Mystery of the Church and of the Eucharist in the Light of the Mystery of the Holy Trinity" (Munich, 1982), "Faith, Sacraments and the Unity of the Church" (Bari, 1987), "The Sacrament of Order in the Sacramental Structure of the Church with Particular Reference to the Importance of Apostolic Succession for the Sanctification and Unity of the People of God" (Valamo, 1988), and "Uniatism, Method of Union of the Past and the Present Search for Full Communion" (Balamand, 1993).[9] The next proposed topic was to be on the "Ecclesiological and Canonical Consequences of the Sacramental Structure of the Church: Conciliarity and Authority," which was to begin to approach the question of the primacy of the bishop of Rome. However, there still have continued to be some problems associated with the reception of the Balamand document, and there continue to be misunderstandings about "uniatism."

At this point in the dialogue, there seems to be a need to overcome some of the issues surrounding the notion of uniatism and the existence of those Eastern Catholic churches in communion with Rome.[10] Reconciliation will be required in order to heal the past wounds of history. Perhaps it would be appropriate for the Eastern Orthodox to begin official dialogues with Eastern Catholics directly, without any other intermediaries like the Roman Church.[11] The problem on the Orthodox side is that of the question of the "recognition" of such churches, for dialoguing with them would imply a recognition of their right to existence, something Orthodoxy as a whole is officially not yet prepared to do. Interestingly, the Orthodox churches have shown a willingness to dialogue with various Protestant and Anglican churches through the World Council of Churches. The Orthodox are also dialoguing amongst themselves, that is, among the Eastern Orthodox, Oriental Orthodox and Assyrian Orthodox Traditions in order to achieve inter-Orthodox unity. However, absent from such official bilateral dialogues are the Eastern Catholic churches. On the other hand, the Eastern Catholic churches who emerged from their Orthodox "mother" churches must also admit that despite it not being their intention, their entering into communion with Rome has caused pain and hurt among the Orthodox churches. This issue of "uniatism'" will require much healing and prayer. On these relations between Eastern Orthodox and Eastern Catholics, quoting Kallistos Ware, one can state that "there can only be one way forward; mutual forgiveness."[12]

Conclusion

In light of the question of the official relations among the Eastern Catholics and Orthodox churches, one can see why these "Windows to the East" lectures are such remarkable events. It would be hard to imagine holding such events in some non-North American countries, where Eastern Christians of many different ecclesial traditions could not come together as readily in a spirit and "dialogue of charity." And yet, here in Saskatoon at the level of the local church, or at the grassroots level, Eastern Christians of many traditions, after many years of living apart, are in fact coming together to discover one another. The sense of these Christians – the sense of the faithful – is that there is a profound unity amongst them that needs to be further developed and nurtured. One can only encourage and pray for such communion to grow so that all may truly be witnesses to the Good News of salvation in Christ.

As I stated at the beginning of this epilogue, this collection of essays should reveal to its readers that a living and vibrant community exists in the Eastern churches. Moreover, just as a house has many windows, one can sense that there are many more such "windows to the East" which one may open and peek through. These windows are an invitation to those in the West to look "to the East," while also being invitations to those in the East, whether Orthodox or Catholic, to more fully experience their own traditions. In the meantime, we will patiently wait once again for the chance to open and peer through these "windows to the East."

For Further Reading

Fahey, Michael. "Orthodox and Catholic Sister Churches: East is West and West is East." *Pere Marquette Lecture in Theology, 1996.* Milwaukee: Marquette, 1996.

Limouris, Gennadios, ed. *Orthodox Visions of Ecumenism: Statements, Messages and Reports on the Ecumenical Movement, 1902-1992.* Geneva: WCC Publications, 1994.

Roberson, Ronald G. *The Eastern Christian Churches: A Brief Survey.* 6th ed. Rome: Orientalia Christiana, 1999.

Suttner, Ernst C. *Church Unity: Union or Uniatism?* Rome: Centre for Indian and Inter-Religious Studies; Bangalore: Dharmaram Publications, 1991.

---

[1] Sometimes the Roman Catholic and Eastern Orthodox churches are also called "sister churches."

[2] For examples, see Jaroslav Pelikan, *Christianity and Classical Culture: The Metamorphosis of Natural Theology in the Christian Encounter with Hellenism* (New Haven: Yale University, 1993); Thomas FitzGerald, *The Orthodox Church,* Denominations in North America 7 (Westport, Conn: Greenwood, 1995); David Goa, ed., *The Ukrainian Religious Experience: Tradition and the Canadian Cultural Context* (Edmonton: Canadian Institute of Ukrainian Studies, 1989).

[3] See his *After Nine Hundred Years: The Background of the Schism Between the Eastern and Western Churches* (New York: Fordham, 1959).

[4] One should note that the mutual anathemas of 1054 were "cast into forgetfulness" in 1965 at the end of the Second Vatican Council by Pope Paul VI and the Ecumenical Patriarch Athenagoras.

[5] Congar, *After Nine Hundred Years,* 75.

[6] Ibid., 89.

[7] Eleuterio Fortino, "The Catholic-Orthodox Dialogue," *One in Christ* 18 (1982), 194. See also Paul McPartlan, "Regaining our Lost Unity," *One in 2000? Towards Catholic-Orthodox Unity,* Paul McPartlan, ed., (Middlegreen, Slough: St. Pauls, 1993), 117-119.

[8] Cited in Fortino, "The Catholic-Orthodox Dialogue," 194.

[9] In *The Quest for Unity: Orthodox and Catholics in Dialogue: Documents of the Joint International Commission and Official Dialogues in the United States, 1965–1995,* ed. John Borelli and John H. Erickson (Crestwood, NY: St. Vladimir's, 1996).

[10] For example, see Elias Zoghby, *We Are All Schismatics* (Newton, MA: 1996) and M. Pelishka, "From Easternization to Inculturation: Re-Interpreting the Mission of the Eastern Catholic Churches," *Worship* 71 (1997), 317-35.

[11] Such a dialogue has already been begun between some members of the Ukrainian Catholic Church and the Orthodox Church (Ecumenical Patriarchate) through the unofficial ecumenical group called the Kievan Church Study Group. See their published essays in *Logos: A Journal of Eastern Christian Studies* 34–36 (1993–1995).

[12] Bishop Kallistos (Ware) of Diokleia, "The Church of God: One Shared Vision," *Logos: A Journal of Eastern Christian Studies* 34/1-2 (1993), 16.

Glossary

akribeia: strict application of the law.

anamnesis: memory, commemoration; the understanding that in a given action one can unite the past, future, and present content/meaning; in Eucharist, Christ's salvific action of the death and Resurrection, the fullness of the Second Coming, and the present experience as Christ within the community of believers are all united anamnetically.

anaphora: literally to raise up above the ordinary; comes to designate the central part of the Eucharistic celebration, also called the Eucharistic Prayer or Canon.

antinomy: the state of maintaining in balance two apparently contradictory positions.

arche: the beginning or origin.

askesis: physically and spiritually taxing practices; the root for ascetic – one who practices *askesis*.

autocephalous: literally, self-ruling; Orthodox Churches are usually autocephalous; the Church in a given country runs its own affairs, albeit in unity with other Orthodox and under the jurisdiction of a Mother Church (from whence the autocephalous Church received its Christian Tradition).

canons: the laws of the Church.

catholic: literally meaning throughout the world; throughout the whole; fullness.

cenobitic: living a common life in a monastic community.

chotki: cloth prayer beads tied on a rope; used to pray the Jesus Prayer.

chronos: routine time; the time which we use to organize our daily activities (as in chronology); contrasted with *kairos.*

deification: see theosis.

diakonia: service or ministry; the root of the diaconate – those who serve or minister in the Church.

diaphora: distinction or difference; according to Maximus the Confessor, at the core of all existence is a relationship between distinctions.

didache: the apostolic Church's teachings about Christian faith.

divinization: see *theosis.*

docetism: an early Christian heresy which regarded the humanity of Jesus as a mere phantasm or apparition.

doxology: the closing of a traditional Christian prayer which offers praise or glory (Greek *doxa*) to the Holy Trinity.

ecclesiology: the teaching about the nature and meaning of the Church.

ekklesia (sometimes in Latin as *ecclesia*): the church; those who are called.

ekstasis: the state of going out of one's self; going beyond.

epiklesis: the prayer during the Eucharistic Prayer which calls upon the Holy Spirit to descend upon the eucharistic gifts and the community.

epiphany: an event which manifests a fundamental truth; in the Western Church the coming of the Magi to the Bethlehem is often called the Epiphany, but in the East it refers more generally to an event which reveals the truth of who Jesus is.

episkopos: the order of bishops; originally the term meant overseer of the community and gradually came to designate the ordained leader of the local church.

eremos: desert; the root for hermit – a solitary living in a physical or spiritual desert.

eucharistia: initially meaning thanksgiving; came to designate the central Christian meal and experience expressing thankfulness to God for all that was done in the person of Jesus Christ.

euchelaion: the blessing or offering of thanks over oil in order to anoint the sick.

filioque: an addition made to the Niceno-Constantinopolitan Creed meaning "and the Son"; it was added to the section on the Holy Spirit and suggested that the Holy Spirit "proceeds from the Father" *and the Son.*

florilegia: compilations or anthologies of important historic ecclesiastical texts; they could pertain to doctrine, to worship, or to any other subject of significance.

hagiologia: stories about the saints (related to hagiographies).

Hellenism/Hellenization: Greek culture/the process which affected Christianity from the late first to the fourth centuries by which its Jewish roots were subsumed under the influence of Greco-Roman culture and philosophy.

heresiarch: a Church leader who preaches heresy (false teachings).

hermeneutics: the study of how we go about interpreting a text.

hesychia **(hesychasm):** the stillness of heart achieved through true contemplation; the Jesus Prayer or Prayer of the Heart was practised for the purpose of attaining this stillness which would allow one to dwell in God.

hierotonia: the granting of orders to a bishop; episcopal ordination.

higoumenia/hegoumen: the office of the elder or leader of the monastic community.

homoousios: the definition of the Council of Nicaea, 325, establishing a formal understanding of the relationship of the Father and the Son – they are of the same essence or nature (consubstantial).

horos: the formal declaration of a council on the matter being debated; it literally established the "border" of faith beyond which one could not be orthodox *(synodicon).*

hypostasis: originally a term synonymous with *ousia* or essence, but gradually it came to mean the unique existence of an essence or person (see *prosopon*).

icon (sometimes spelled as ikon): a formal and stylized Christian image which through the medium of colour and art "writes" theology.

isorropon: the right balance; a state of propriety or harmony.

kairos: that time which manifests the action of God; for example, the Descent of the Holy Spirit is an experience of *kairos,* not *chronos.*

kenosis: the act of self-emptying; Paul describes the coming of Christ into the world as an expression of self-emptying or kenotic love: "he emptied himself, taking the form of a servant" (Phil. 2:7).

kerygma: the apostolic Church's proclamation of their faith in Christ.

koinonia: communion, fellowship, a community of people; came to be used by the early Church to describe the Church.

kondak: a piece of liturgical poetry used during liturgical services to explain the day, season or feast day of the celebration.

kosmos (in English as cosmos): the entire created order; all that is created by God.

kyriake: the day of the Lord (Greek *Kyrios*); the original term for Sunday – the day on which the Lord (Christ) rose from the dead.

latreia: offering worship to God.

leitourgia: the common work of the people; Christian worship or liturgy.

Logos: literally meaning "word" or "communication"; in Platonic philosophy designating the One who proceeds the ultimate reality and from which all reality flows; taken over by the author of the Gospel of John to designate the person of Jesus Christ who was with God in the beginning, but came into the world (John 1:1f.).

Manicheaism: a dualistic philosophy which greatly affected early Christianity, including the thought of Augustine of Hippo in the fourth century; it condemned the material world as evil.

martyria: witness; martyrs witnessed to the truth of Christian faith.

Melkite: those Arab Christians in the ancient Church who maintained their unity with the Emperor (or melek), that is to say, those who accepted the Chalcedonian formula.

metabole: a trans-portation of the contents or a transformation in the state of the thing under consideration.

metania: an action or bow whereby one falls to the floor in reverence before God.

metanoia: transformation or repentance.

monarchia: one source or origin; the Father is the *monarchos* in that the Son is begotten of the Father and the Son proceeds from the Father as from a unique source.

nous: the ancient Greek term for mind.

oikonomia: literally the ordering of the household; how God acts in order to save the world; also designates the compassion of God.

omophorion: shroud which in certain icons is placed by the Mother of God over the people she is protecting; the shroud which is placed over the bishop's garb and is symbolic of the solicitude of Christ for the Church.

orarion: a long cloth worn by the deacon as a sign of office and which is raised to designate the deacon is leading the community in prayer.

orthodox: those who are standing upright in the true faith and so proclaiming that true faith gloriously.

ousia: the essence of something or its nature.

panagia: the title given to Mary, the Mother of God as "All-Holy"; it also designates the icon-medallion *(encolpion)* worn by Eastern Christian Bishops as a sign of their episcopal office.

Pantokrator (Pantocrator): the all-ruler; the name of the icon of Christ placed in the central dome of an Orthodox Church.

patriarch: literally the senior male in the family; designating the ecclesiastical elder.

pelagianism: the teachings of Pelagius and his followers condemned in the West by Augustine of Hippo because they were seen as denying the necessity of divine grace for salvation.

perichoresis: mutual indwelling; usually referring to the relationships of the Holy Trinity.

prelest': spiritual delusion; passion as a seeking after that which is unimportant.

proskomidia: the introductory, non-public part of the eucharistic liturgy when the gifts are prepared on a side altar (the proskomidijnyk).

prosopon: the human person created in the image and likeness of God (see the related definition of *hypostasis*).

prosphora: the loaves specially baked for use in the eucharistic celebration.

sacerdotium: the orders of ordained persons within the Church.

Shekinah: the abiding holy presence of God.

starets': literally elder; a Slavic term designating the wise and holy elders of a monastic community.

synodical: an action expressing the community's coming together (in synod) or unity.

synergeia: a common action or common energy.

synod: an assembly of the bishops of a church which is expressive of the Church's unity.

synodicon: the formal declaration of a synod (related to *horos*).

theophany: an event which reveals a profound truth about God *(Theos);* the Theophany is the feast celebrating the Baptism of Jesus in the Jordan, when the Holy Trinity was revealed.

theosis: the state of becoming like God and sharing in the divine life; the transformative process which in Eastern Christianity is seen to be the true destiny of all human beings (synonyms: deification, divinization).

Theotokos: literally the God-bearer; the title given to Mary, the Mother of God.

tropar: a verse or proper used during liturgies which commemorate the saint of the day, the season or the feast day being celebrated.

typicon (sometimes typika): the book outlining the order of services of a monastic or parish community.

ustav: the regulations governing liturgical services and the order of those services.

Index